C000219080

THE ESSAYS

OF

"GEORGE ELIOT."

COMPLETE.

COLLECTED AND ARRANGED, WITH AN INTRODUCTION ON HER "ANALYSIS OF MOTIVES,"

BY

NATHAN SHEPPARD,

EDITOR OF "CHARACTER READINGS FROM GEORGE ELIOT," AND "THE DICKENS READER;" AND AUTHOR OF "SHUT UP IN PARIS."

NEW YORK:

FUNK & WAGNALLS, PUBLISHERS,

10 AND 12 DEY STREET.

This important reprint was made from an old and scarce book.

Therefore, it may have defects such as missing pages, erroneous pagination, blurred pages, missing text, poor pictures, markings, marginalia and other issues beyond our control.

Because this is such an important and rare work, we believe it is best to reproduce this book regardless of its original condition.

Thank you for your understanding and enjoy this unique book!

CONTENTS.

PREFACE.

Since the death of George Eliot much public curiosity has been excited by the repeated allusions to, and quotations from, her contributions to periodical literature, and a leading newspaper gives expression to a general wish when it says that "this series of striking essays ought to be collected and reprinted, both because of substantive worth and because of the light they throw on the author's literary canons and predilections." In fact, the articles which were published anonymously in *The Westminster Review* have been so pointedly designated by the editor, and the biographical sketch in the "Famous Women" series is so emphatic in its praise of them, and so copious in its extracts from one and the least important one of them, that the publication of all the Review and magazine articles of the renowned novelist, without abridgment or alteration, would seem but an act of fair play to her fame, while at the same time a compliance with a reasonable public demand.

Nor are these first steps in her wonderful intellectual progress any the less, but are all the more noteworthy, for being first steps. "To ignore this stage," says the author of the valuable little volume to which we have just referred—"to ignore this stage in George Eliot's mental development would be to lose one of the connecting links in her history." Furthermore, "nothing in her fictions excels the style of these papers." Here is all her "epigrammatic felicity," and an irony not surpassed by Heine himself, while her paper on the poet Young is one of her wittiest bits of critical analysis.

Her translation of Strauss's "Life of Jesus" was published in 1846, and her translation of Feuerbach's "Essence of Christianity" in 1854. Her translation of Spinoza's "Ethics" was finished the same year, but remains unpublished. She was associate editor of *The Westminster Review* from 1851 to 1853. She was about twenty-seven years of age when her first translation appeared, thirty-three when the first of these magazine articles appeared, thirty-eight at the publication of her first story, and fifty-nine when she finished "Theophrastus Such." Two years after she died, at the age of sixty-one. So that George Eliot's literary life covered a period of about thirty-two years.

The introductory chapter on her "Analysis of Motives" first appeared as a magazine article, and appears here at the request of the publishers, after having been carefully revised, indeed almost entirely rewritten by its author.

"GEORGE ELIOT'S" ANALYSIS OF MOTIVES.

George Eliot is the greatest of the novelists in the delineation of feeling and the analysis of motives. In " uncovering certain human lots, and seeing how they are woven and interwoven," some marvellous work has been done by this master in the two arts of rhetoric and fiction.

If you say the telling of a story is her forte, you put her below Wilkie Collins or Mrs. Oliphant ; if you say her object is to give a picture of English society, she is surpassed by Bulwer and Trollope ; if she be called a satirist of society, Thackeray is her superior ; if she intends to illustrate the absurdity of behavior, she is eclipsed by Dickens ; but if the analysis of human motives be her forte and art, she stands first, and it is very doubtful whether any artist in fiction is entitled to stand second. She reaches clear in and touches the most secret and the most delicate spring of human action. She has done this so well, so apart from the doing of everything else, and so, in spite of doing some other things indifferently, that she works on a line quite her own, and quite alone, as a creative artist in fiction. Others have done this incidentally and occasionally, as Charlotte Brontë and Walter Scott, but George Eliot does it elaborately, with laborious painstaking, with purpose aforethought. Scott said of Richardson : " In his survey of the heart he left neither head, bay, nor inlet behind him until he had traced its soundings, and laid it down in his chart with all its minute sinuosities, its depths and its shallows."

This is too much to say of Richardson, but it is not too much to say of George Eliot. She has sounded depths and explored sinuosities of the human heart which were utterly unknown to the author of "Clarissa Harlowe." It is like looking into the translucent brook—you see the wriggling tad, the darting minnow, the leisurely trout, the motionless pike, while in the bays and inlets you see the infusoria and animalculæ as well.

George Eliot belongs to and is the greatest of the school of artists in fiction who write fiction as a means to an end, instead of as an end. And, while she certainly is not a story-teller of the first order, considered simply as a story-teller, her novels are a striking illustration of the power of fiction as a means to an end. They remind us, as few other stories do, of the fact that however inferior the story may be considered simply as a story, it is indispensable to the delineation of character. No other form of composition, no discourse, or essay, or series of independent sketches, however successful, could succeed in bringing out character equal to the novel. Herein is at once the justification of the power of fiction. "He spake a parable," with an "end" in view which could not be so expeditiously attained by any other form of address.

A story of the first-class, with the story as end in itself, and a story of the first class told as a means to an end, has never been, and it is not likely ever will be, found together. The novel with a purpose is fatal to the novel written simply to excite by a plot, or divert by pictures of scenery, or entertain as a mere panorama of social life. So intense is George Eliot's desire to dissect the human heart and discover its motives, that plot, diction, situations, and even consistency in the vocabulary of the characters, are all made subservient to it. With her it is not so much that the characters do thus and so, but why they do thus and so. Dickens portrays the behavior, George Eliot dissects the motive of the behavior. Here comes the human creature, says Dickens, now let us see how he will behave. Here comes the human creature, says George Eliot, now let us see why he behaves.

"Suppose," she says, "suppose we turn from outside estimates of a man, to wonder with keener interest what is the report of his own consciousness about his doings, with what hindrances he is carrying on his daily labors, and with what spirit he wrestles against universal pressure, which may one day be too heavy for him and bring his heart to a final pause." The outside estimate is the work of Dickens and Thackeray, the inside estimate is the work of George Eliot.

Observe in the opening pages of the great novel of "Middlemarch" how soon we pass from the outside dress to the inside reasons for it, from the costume to the motives which control it and color it. It was "only to close observers that Celia's dress differed from her sister's," and had "a shade of coquetry in its arrangements." Dorothea's "plain dressing was due to mixed conditions, in most of which her sister shared." They were both influenced by "the pride of being ladies," of belonging to a stock not exactly aristocratic, but unquestionably "good." The very quotation of the word good is significant and suggestive. There were "no parcel-tying forefathers" in the Brooke pedigree. A Puritan forefather, "who served under Cromwell, but afterward conformed and managed to come out of all political troubles as the proprietor of a respectable family estate," had a hand in Dorothea's "plain" wardrobe. "She could not reconcile the anxieties of a spiritual life involving eternal consequences with a keen interest in gimp and artificial protrusions of drapery," but Celia "had that common-sense which is able to accept momentous doctrines without any eccentric agitation." Both were examples of "reversion." Then, as an instance of heredity working itself out in character "in Mr. Brooke, the hereditary strain of Puritan energy was clearly in abeyance, but in his niece Dorothea it glowed alike through faults and virtues."

Could anything be more natural than for a woman with this passion for, and skill in, "unravelling certain human lots," to lay herself out upon the human lot of woman, with all her "passionate patience of genius?" One would say this was inevitable. And, for a delineation of what that lot of woman really is, as made for her, there is nothing in all literature equal to what we find in "Middlemarch," "Romola," "Daniel Deronda," and "Janet's Repentance." "She was a woman, and could not make her own lot." Never before, indeed, was so much got out of the word "lot." Never was that little word so hard worked, or well worked. "We women," says Gwendolen Harleth, "must stay where we grow, or where the gardeners like to transplant us. We are brought up like the flowers, to look as pretty as we can, and be dull without complaining. That is my notion about the plants, and that is the reason why some of them have got poisonous." To appreciate the work that George Eliot has done you must read her with the determination of finding out the reason why Gwendolen Harleth "became poisonous," and Dorothea, with all her brains and "plans," a failure; why "the many Theresas find for themselves no epic life, only a life of mistakes, the offspring of a certain spiritual grandeur ill-matched with the meanness of opportunity." You must search these marvellous studies in motives for the key to the blunders of "the blundering lives" of woman which "some have felt are due to the inconvenient indefiniteness with which the Supreme power has fashioned the natures of women." But as there is not "one level of feminine incompetence as strict as the ability to count three and no more, the social lot of woman cannot be treated with scientific certitude." It is treated with a dissective delineation in the women of George Eliot unequalled in the pages of fiction.

And then woman's lot, as respects her "social promotion" in matrimony, so much sought, and so necessary for her to seek, even in spite of her conscience, and at the expense of her happiness—the unravelling of that lot would also come very natural to this expert unraveller. And never have we had the causes of woman's "blunders" in match-making, and man's blunders in love-making, told with such analytic acumen, or with such pathetic and sarcastic eloquence. It is not far from the question of woman's social lot to the question of questions of human life, the question which has so tremendous an influence upon the fortunes of mankind and womankind, the question which it is so easy for one party to "pop" and so difficult for the other party to answer intelligently or sagaciously.

Why does the young man fall in love with the young woman who is most unfit for him of all the young women of his acquaintance, and why does the young woman accept the young man, or the old man, who is better adapted to making her life unendurable than any other man of her circle of acquaintances? Why does the stalwart Adam Bede fall in love with Hetty Sorrel, "who had nothing more than her beauty to recommend her?" The delineator of his motives "respects him none the less." She thinks that "the deep love he had for that sweet, rounded, dark-eyed Hetty, of whose inward self he was really very ignorant, came out of the very strength of his nature, and not out of any inconsistent weakness. Is it any weakness, pray, to be wrought upon by exquisite music? To feel its wondrous harmonies searching the subtlest windings of your soul, the delicate fibres of life which no memory can penetrate, and binding together your whole being, past and present, in one unspeakable vibration? If not, then neither is it a weakness to be so wrought upon by the exquisite curves of a woman's cheek, and neck, and arms; by the liquid depth of her beseeching eyes, or the sweet girlish pout of her lips. For the beauty of a lovely woman is like music—what can one say more?" And so "the noblest nature is often blinded to the character of the woman's soul that beauty clothes." Hence "the tragedy of human life is likely to continue for a long time to come, in spite of mental philosophers who are ready with the best receipts for avoiding all mistakes of the kind."

How simple the motive of the Rev. Edward Casaubon in popping the question to Dorothea Brooke, how complex her motives in answering the question! He wanted an amanuensis to "love, honor, and obey" him. She wanted a husband who would be "a sort of father, and could teach you even Hebrew if you wished it." The matrimonial motives are worked to draw out the character of Dorothea, and nowhere does the method of George Eliot show to greater advantage than in probing the motives of this fine, strong, conscientious, blundering young woman, whose voice "was like the voice of a soul that once lived in an Æolian harp." She had a theoretic cast of mind. She was "enamored of intensity and greatness, and rash in embracing what seemed to her to have those aspects." The awful divine had those aspects, and she embraced him. "Certainly such elements in the character of a marriageable girl tended to interfere with her lot, and hinder it from being decided, according to custom, by good looks, vanity, and merely canine affection." That's a George Eliot stroke. If the reader does not see from that what she is driving at he may as well abandon all hope of ever appreciating her great forte and art. Dorothea's goodness and sincerity did not save her from the worst blunder that a woman can make, while her conscientiousness only made it inevitable. "With all her eagerness to know the truths of life she retained very childlike ideas about marriage." A little of the goose as well as the child in her conscientious simplicity, perhaps. She "felt sure she would have accepted the judicious Hooker if she had been born in time to save him from that wretched mistake he made in matrimony, or John Milton, when his blindness had come on, or any other great man whose odd habits it would be glorious piety to endure.

True to life, our author furnishes the "great man," and the "odd habits," and the miserable years of "glorious" endurance. "Dorothea looked deep into the ungauged reservoir of Mr. Casaubon's mind, seeing reflected there every quality she herself brought." They exchanged experiences—he his desire to have an amanuensis, and she hers, to be one. He told her in the billy-cooing of their courtship that "his notes made a formidable range of volumes, but the crowning task would be to condense these voluminous, still accumulating results, and bring them, like the earlier vintage of Hippocratic books, to fit a little shelf." Dorothea was altogether captivated by the wide embrace of this conception. Here was something beyond the shallows of ladies' school literature. Here was a modern Augustine who united the glories of doctor and saint. Dorothea said to herself: "His feeling, his experience, what a lake compared to my little pool!" The little pool runs into the great reservoir.

Will you take this reservoir to be your husband, and will you promise to be unto him a fetcher of slippers, a dotter of I's and crosser of T's and a copier and condenser of manuscripts until death doth you part? I will.

They spend their honeymoon in Rome, and on page 211 of Vol. I. we find poor Dorothea "alone in her apartments, sobbing bitterly, with such an abandonment to this relief of an oppressed heart as a woman habitually controlled by pride will sometimes allow herself when she feels securely alone." What was she crying about? "She thought her feeling of desolation was the fault of her own spiritual poverty." A characteristic George Eliot probe. Why does not Dorothea give the real reason for her desolateness? Because she does not know what the real reason is—conscience makes blunderers of us all. "How was it that in the weeks since their marriage Dorothea had not distinctly observed, but felt, with a stifling depression, that the large vistas and wide fresh air which she had dreamed of finding in her husband's mind were replaced by anterooms and winding passages which seemed to lead no whither? I suppose it was because in courtship everything is regarded as provisional and preliminary, and the smallest sample of virtue or accomplishment is taken to guarantee delightful stores which the broad leisure of marriage will reveal. But, the door-sill of marriage once crossed, expectation is concentrated on the present. Having once embarked on your marital voyage, you may become aware that you make no way, and that the sea is not within sight—that in fact you are exploring an inclosed basin." So the ungauged reservoir turns out to be an inclosed basin, but Dorothea was prevented by her social lot, and perverse goodness, and puritanical "reversion," from foreseeing that. She might have been saved from her gloomy marital voyage "if she could have fed her affection with those childlike caresses which are the bent of every sweet woman who has begun by showering kisses on the hard pate of her bald doll, creating a happy soul within that woodenness from the wealth of her own love." Then, perhaps, Ladislaw would have been her first husband instead of her second, as he certainly was her first and only love. Such are the chances and mischances in the lottery of matrimony.

Equally admirable is the diagnosis of Gwendolen Harleth's motives in "drifting toward the tremendous decision," and finally landing in it. "We became poor, and I was tempted." Marriage came to her as it comes to many, as a temptation, and like the deadening drug or the maddening bowl, to keep off the demon of remorse or the cloud of sorrow, like the forgery or the robbery to save from want. "The brilliant position she had longed for, the imagined freedom she would create for herself in marriage"—these "had come to her hunger like food, with the taint of sacrilege upon it," which she "snatched with terror." Grandcourt "fulfilled his side of the bargain by giving her the rank and luxuries she coveted." Matrimony as a bargain never had and never will have but one result. "She had a root of conscience in her, and the process of purgatory had begun for her on earth." Without the root of conscience it would have been purgatory all the same. So much for resorting to marriage for deliverance from poverty or old-maidhood. Better be an old maid than an old fool. But how are we to be guaranteed against "one of those convulsive motiveless actions by which wretched men and women leap from a temporary sorrow into a lifelong misery"? Rosamond Lydgate says, "Marriage stays with us like a murder." Yes, if she could only have found that out before instead of after her own marriage!

But "what greater thing," exclaims our novelist, "is there for two human souls than to feel that they are joined for life, to strengthen each other in all labor, to minister to each other in all pain, to be one with each other in silent, unspeakable memories at the last parting?"

While a large proportion of her work in the analysis of motives is confined to woman, she has done nothing more skilful or memorable than the "unravelling" of Bulstrode's mental processes by which he "explained the gratification of his desires into satisfactory agreement with his beliefs." If there were no Dorothea in "Middlemarch" the character of Bulstrode would give that novel a place by itself among the masterpieces of fiction. The Bulstrode wound was never probed in fiction with more scientific precision. The pious villain finally finds himself so near discovery that he becomes conscientious. "His equivocation now turns venomously upon him with the full-grown fang of a discovered lie." The past came back to make the present unendurable. "The terror of being judged sharpens the memory." Once more "he saw himself the banker's clerk, as clever in figures as he was fluent in speech, and fond of theological definition. He had striking experience in conviction and sense of pardon; spoke in prayer-meeting and on religious platforms. That was the time he would have chosen now to awake in and find the rest of dream. He remembered his first moments of shrinking. They were private and were filled with arguments—some of these taking the form of prayer.

Private prayer—but "is private prayer necessarily candid? Does it necessarily go to the roots of action? Private prayer is inaudible speech, and speech is representative. Who can represent himself just as he is, even in his own reflections?"

Bulstrode's course up to the time of his being suspected "had, he thought, been sanctioned by remarkable providences, appearing to point the way for him to be the agent in making the best use of a large property." Providence would have him use for the glory of God the money he had stolen. "Could it be for God's service that this fortune should go to" its rightful owners, when its rightful owners were "a young woman and her husband who were given up to the lightest pursuits, and might scatter it abroad in triviality—people who seemed to lie outside the path of remarkable providences?"

Bulstrode felt at times "that his action was unrighteous, but how could he go back? He had mental exercises calling himself naught, laid hold on redemption and went on in his course of instrumentality. He was "carrying on two distinct lives" —a religious one and a wicked one. "His religious activity could not be incompatible with his wicked business as soon as he had argued himself into not feeling it incompatible."

"The spiritual kind of rescue was a genuine need with him. There may be coarse hypocrites, who consciously affect beliefs and emotions for the sake of gulling the world, but Bulstrode was not one of them. He was simply a man whose desires had been stronger than his theoretic beliefs, and who had gradually explained the gratification of his desires into satisfactory agreement with those beliefs."

And now Providence seemed to be taking sides against him. "A threatening Providence—in other words, a public exposure —urged him to a kind of propitiation which was not a doctrinal transaction. The divine tribunal had changed its aspect to him. Self-prostration was no longer enough. He must bring restitution in his hand. By what sacrifice could he stay the rod? He believed that if he did something right God would stay the rod, and save him from the consequences of his wrong-doing." His religion was "the religion of personal fear," which "remains nearly at the level of the savage." The exposure comes, and the explosion. Society shudders with hypocritical horror, especially in the presence of poor Mrs. Bulstrode, who "should have some hint given her, that if she knew the truth she would have less complacency in her bonnet." Society when it is very candid, and very conscientious, and very scrupulous, cannot "allow a wife to remain ignorant long that the town holds a bad opinion of her husband." The photograph of the Middlemarch gossips sitting upon the case of Mrs. Bulstrode is taken accurately. Equally accurate, and far more impressive, is the narrative of circumstantial evidence gathering against the innocent Lydgate and the guilty Bulstrode—circumstances that will sometimes weave into one tableau of public odium the purest and the blackest characters. From this tableau you may turn to that one in "Adam Bede," and see how circumstances are made to crush the weak woman and clear the wicked man. And then you can go to "Romola," or indeed to almost any of these novels, and see how wrong-doing may come of an indulged infirmity of purpose, that unconscious weakness and conscious wickedness may bring about the same disastrous results, and that repentance has no more effect in averting or altering the consequences in one case than the other. Tito's ruin comes of a feeble, Felix Holt's victory of an unconquerable, will. Nothing is more characteristic of George Eliot than her tracking of Tito through all the motives and counter motives from which he acted. "Because he tried to slip away from everything that was unpleasant, and cared for nothing so much as his own safety, he came at last to commit such deeds as make a man infamous." So poor Romola tells her son, as a warning, and adds: "If you make it the rule of your life to escape from what is disagreeable, calamity may come just the same, and it would be calamity falling on a base mind, which is the one form of sorrow that has no balm in it."

Out of this passion for the analysis of motives comes the strong character, slightly gnarled and knotted by natural circumstances, as trees that are twisted and misshapen by storms and floods—or characters gnarled by some interior force working in conjunction with or in opposition to outward circumstances. She draws no monstrosities, or monsters, thus avoiding on the one side romance and on the other burlesque. She keeps to life—the life that fails from "the meanness of opportunity," or is "dispersed among hindrances," or "wrestles" unavailingly "with universal pressure."

Why had Mr. Gilfil in those late years of his beneficent life "more of the knots and ruggedness of poor human nature than there lay any clear hint of it in the open-eyed, loving" young

Maynard? Because "it is with men as with trees: if you lop off their finest branches into which they were pouring their young life-juice, the wounds will be healed over with some rough boss, some odd excrescence, and what might have been a grand tree, expanding into liberal shade, is but a whimsical, misshapen trunk. Many an irritating fault, many an unlovely oddity, has come of a hard sorrow which has crushed and maimed the nature just when it was expanding into plenteous beauty; and the trivial, erring life, which we visit with our harsh blame, may be but as the unsteady motion of a man whose best limb is withered. The dear old Vicar had been sketched out by nature as a noble tree. The heart of him was sound, the grain was of the finest, and in the gray-haired man, with his slipshod talk and caustic tongue, there was the main trunk of the same brave, faithful, tender nature that had poured out the finest, freshest forces of its life-current in a first and only love."

Her style is influenced by her purpose—may be said, indeed, to be created by it. The excellences and the blemishes of the diction come of the end sought to be attained by it. Its subtleties and obscurities were equally inevitable. Analytical thinking takes on an analytical phraseology. It is a striking instance of a mental habit creating a vocabulary. The method of thought produces the form of rhetoric. Some of the sentences are mental landscapes. The meaning seems to be in motion on the page. It is elusive from its very subtlety. It is more our analyst than her character of Rufus Lyon, who "would fain find language subtle enough to follow the utmost intricacies of the soul's pathways." Mrs. Transome's "lancet-edged epigrams" are dull in comparison with her own. She uses them with startling success in dissecting motive and analyzing feeling. They deserve as great renown as "Nélaton's probe."

For example: "Examine your words well, and you will find that even when you have no motive to be false, it is a very hard thing to say the exact truth, especially about your own feelings

—much harder than to say something fine about them which is not the exact truth." That ought to make such a revelation of the religious diary-keeper to himself as to make him ashamed of himself. And this will fit in here: "Our consciences are not of the same pattern, an inner deliverance of fixed laws—they are the voice of sensibilities as various as our memories;" and this: "Every strong feeling makes to itself a conscience of its own—has its own piety."

Who can say that the joints of his armor are not open to this thrust? "The lapse of time during which a given event has not happened is in the logic of habit, constantly alleged as a reason why the event should never happen, even when the lapse of time is precisely the added condition which makes the event imminent. A man will tell you that he worked in a mine for forty years unhurt by an accident as a reason why he should apprehend no danger, though the roof is beginning to sink." Silas Marner lost his money through his "sense of security," which "more frequently springs from habit than conviction." He went unrobbed for fifteen years, which supplied the only needed condition for his being robbed now. A compensation for stupidity: "If we had a keen vision and feeling of all ordinary human life, it would be like hearing the grass grow and the squirrel's heart beat, and we should die of that roar that lies on the other side of silence. As it is, the quickest of us walk about well wadded with stupidity." Who does not at once recognize "that mixture of pushing forward and being pushed forward" as "the brief history of most human beings?" Who has not seen "advancement hindered by impetuous candor?" or "private grudges christened by the name of public zeal?" or "a church built with an exuberance of faith and a deficiency of funds?" or a man "who would march determinedly along the road he thought best, but who was easily convinced which was best?" or a preacher "whose oratory was like a Belgian railway horn, which shows praiseworthy intentions inadequately fulfilled?"

There is something chemical about such an analysis as this

of Rosamond: "Every nerve and muscle was adjusted to the consciousness that she was being looked at. She was by nature an actress of parts that entered into her physique. She even acted her own character, and so well that she did not know it to be precisely her own!" Nor is the exactness of this any less cruel: "We may handle extreme opinions with impunity, while our furniture and our dinner-giving link us to the established order." Why not own that "the emptiness of all things is never so striking to us as when we fail in them?" Is it not better to avoid "following great reformers beyond the threshold of their own homes?" Does not "our moral sense learn the manners of good society?"

The lancet works impartially, because the hand that holds it is the hand of a conscientious artist. She will endure the severest test you can apply to an artist in fiction. She does not betray any religious bias in her novels, which is all the more remarkable now that we find it in these essays. Nor is it at all remarkable that this bias is so very easily discovered in the novels by those who have found it in her essays! Whatever opinions she may have expressed in her critical reviews, she is not the Evangelical, or the Puritan, or the Jew, or the Methodist, or the Dissenting Minister, or the Churchman, any more than she is the Radical, the Liberal, or the Tory, who talks in the pages of her fiction.

Every side has its say, every prejudice its voice, and every prejudice and side and vagary even has the philosophical reason given for it, and the charitable explanation applied to it. She analyzes the religious motives without obtrusive criticism or acrid cynicism or nauseous cant—whether of the orthodox or heretical form.

The art of fiction has nothing more elevated, or more touching, or fairer to every variety of religious experience, than the delineation of the motives that actuated Dinah Morris the Methodist preacher, Deronda the Jew, Dorothea the Puritan, Adam and Seth Bede, and Janet Dempster.

Who can object to this? "Religious ideas have the fate of

melodies, which, once set afloat in the world, are taken up by all sorts of instruments, some of them woefully coarse, feeble, or out of tune, until people are in danger of crying out that the melody itself is detestable." Is it not one of the "mixed results of revivals" that "some gain a religious vocabulary rather than a religious experience?" Is there a descendant of the Puritans who will not relish the fair play of this? "They might give the name of piety to much that was only Puritanic egoism; they might call many things sin that were not sin, but they had at least the feeling that sin was to be avoided and resisted, and color-blindness, which may mistake drab for scarlet, is better than total blindness, which sees no distinction of color at all." Is not Adam Bede justified in saying that "to hear some preachers you'd think a man must be doing nothing all his life but shutting his eyes and looking at what's going on in the inside of him," or that "the doctrines are like finding names for your feelings so that you can talk of them when you've never known them?" Read all she has said before you object to anything she has said. Then see whether you will find fault with her for delineating the motives of those with whom "great illusions" are mistaken for "great faith;" of those "whose celestial intimacies do not improve their domestic manners," however "holy" they may claim to be; of those who "contrive to conciliate the consciousness of filthy rags with the best damask;" of those "whose imitative piety and native worldliness is equally sincere;" of those who "think the invisible powers will be soothed by a bland parenthesis here and there, coming from a man of property"—parenthetical recognition of the Almighty! May not "religious scruples be like spilled needles, making one afraid of treading or sitting down, or even eating?"

But if this is a great mind fascinated with the insoluble enigma of human motives, it is a mind profoundly in sympathy with those who are puzzling hopelessly over the riddle or are struggling hopelessly in its toils. She is "on a level and in the press with them as they struggle their way along the stony road through the crowd of unloving fellow-men. She says "the only true knowledge of our fellows is that which enables us to feel with them, which gives us a finer ear for the heart-pulses that are beating under the mere clothes of circumstance and opinion." No artist in fiction ever had a finer ear or a more human sympathy for the struggler who "pushes manfully on" and "falls at last," leaving "the crowd to close over the space he has left." Her extraordinary skill in disclosing "the peculiar combination of outward with inward facts which constitute a man's critical actions," only makes her the more charitable in judging them. "Until we know what this combination has been, or will be, it will be better not to think ourselves wise about" the character that results. "There is a terrible coercion in our deeds which may first turn the honest man into a deceiver, and then reconcile him to the change. And for this reason the second wrong presents itself to him in the guise of the only practicable right." There is nothing of the spirit of "served him right," or "just what she deserved," or "they ought to have known better," in George Eliot. That is not in her line. The opposite of that is exactly in her line. This is characteristic of her: "In this world there are so many of these common, coarse people, who have no picturesque or sentimental wretchedness! And it is so needful we should remember their existence, else we may happen to leave them quite out of our religion and philosophy, and frame lofty theories which only fit a world of extremes." She does not leave them out. Her books are full of them, and of a Christly charity and plea for them. Who can ever forget little Tiny, "hidden and uncared for as the pulse of anguish in the breast of the bird that has fluttered down to its nest with the long-sought food, and has found the nest torn and empty?" There is nothing in fiction to surpass in pathos the picture of the death of Mrs. Amos Barton. George Eliot's fellow-feeling comes of the habit she ascribes to Daniel Deronda, "the habit of thinking herself imaginatively into the experience of others." That is the reason why her novels come home so pitilessly to those who have had a deep experience of human life. These are the men and women whom she fascinates and alienates. I know strong men and brave women who are afraid of her books, and say so. It is because of her realness, her unrelenting fidelity to human nature and human life. It is because the analysis is so delicate, subtle, and far-in. Hence the atmosphere of sadness that pervades her pages. It was unavoidable. To see only the behavior, as Dickens did, amuses us ; to study only the motive at the root of the behavior, as George Eliot does, saddens us. The humor of Mrs. Poyser and the wit of Mrs. Transome only deepen the pathos by relieving it. There is hardly a sarcasm in these books but has its pensive undertone.

It is all in the key of "Ye Banks and Braes o' Bonnie Doon," and that would be an appropriate key for a requiem over the grave of George Eliot.

All her writings are now before the world, and are accessible to all. They have taken their place, and will keep their place, high among the writings of those of our age who have made that age illustrious in the history of the English tongue.

THE ESSAYS OF "GEORGE ELIOT."

I.

CARLYLE'S LIFE OF STERLING.

As soon as the closing of the Great Exhibition afforded a reasonable hope that there would once more be a reading public, "The Life of Sterling" appeared. A new work by Carlyle must always be among the literary births eagerly chronicled by the journals and greeted by the public. In a book of such parentage we care less about the subject than about its treatment, just as we think the "Portrait of a Lord" worth studying if it come from the pencil of a Vandyck. The life of John Sterling, however, has intrinsic interest, even if it be viewed simply as the struggle of a restless aspiring soul, yearning to leave a distinct impress of itself on the spiritual development of humanity, with that fell disease which, with a refinement of torture, heightens the susceptibility and activity of the faculties, while it undermines their creative force. Sterling, moreover, was a man thoroughly in earnest, to whom poetry and philosophy were not merely another form of paper currency or a ladder to fame, but an end in themselves—one of those finer spirits with whom, amid the jar and hubbub of our daily life,

> "The melodies abide
> Of the everlasting chime."

But his intellect was active and rapid, rather than powerful, and in all his writings we feel the want of a stronger electric current to give that vigor of conception and felicity of expression, by which we distinguish the undefinable something called genius; while his moral nature, though refined and elevated, seems to have been subordinate to his intellectual tendencies and social qualities, and to have had itself little determining influence on his life. His career was less exceptional than his charactor: a youth marked by delicate health and studious tastes, a short-lived and not very successful share in the management of the *Athenæum*, a fever of sympathy with Spanish patriots, arrested before it reached a dangerous crisis by an early love affair ending in marriage, a fifteen months' residence in the West Indies, eight months of curate's duty at Herstmonceux, relinquished on the ground of failing health, and through his remaining years a succession of migrations to the South in search of a friendly climate, with the occasional publication of an "article," a tale, or a poem in *Blackwood* or elsewhere—this, on the prosaic background of an easy competence, was what made up the outer tissue of Sterling's existence. The impression of his intellectual power on his personal friends seems to have been produced chiefly by the eloquence and brilliancy of his conversation; but the mere reader of his works and letters would augur from them neither the wit nor the *curiosa felicitas* of epithet and imagery, which would rank him with the men whose sayings are thought worthy of perpetuation in books of table-talk and "ana." The public, then, since it is content to do without biographies of much more remarkable men, cannot be supposed to have felt any pressing demand even for a single life of Sterling; still less, it might be thought, when so distinguished a writer as Archdeacon Hare had furnished this, could there be any need for another. But, in opposition to the majority of Mr. Carlyle's critics, we agree with him that the first life is properly the justification of the second. Even among the readers personally unacquainted with Sterling, those who sympathized with his ultimate alienation from the Church, rather than with his transient conformity, were likely to be dissatisfied with the entirely apologetic tone of Hare's life, which, indeed, is confessedly an incomplete presentation of Sterling's mental course after his opinions diverged from those of his clerical biographer ; while those attached friends (and Sterling possessed the happy magic that secures many such) who knew him best during this latter part of his career, would naturally be pained to have it represented, though only by implication, as a sort of deepening declension ending in a virtual retraction. Of such friends Carlyle was the most eminent, and perhaps the most highly valued, and, as co-trustee with Archdeacon Hare of Sterling's literary character and writings, he felt a kind of responsibility that no mistaken idea of his departed friend should remain before the world without correction. Evidently, however, his "Life of Sterling" was not so much the conscientious discharge of a trust as a labor of love, and to this is owing its strong charm. Carlyle here shows us his "sunny side." We no longer see him breathing out threatenings and slaughter as in the Latter-Day Pamphlets, but moving among the charities and amenities of life, loving and beloved—a Teufelsdröckh still, but humanized by a Blumine worthy of him. We have often wished that genius would incline itself more frequently to the task of the biographer—that when some great or good personage dies, instead of the dreary three or five volumed compilations of letter, and diary, and detail, little to the purpose, which two thirds of the reading public have not the chance, nor the other third the inclination, to read, we could have a real "Life," setting forth briefly and vividly the man's inward and outward struggles, aims, and achievements, so as to make clear the meaning which his experience has for his fellows. A few such lives (chiefly, indeed, autobiographies) the world possesses, and they have, perhaps, been more influential on the formation of character than any other kind of reading. But the conditions required for the perfection of life writing—personal intimacy, a loving and poetic nature which sees the beauty and the depth of familiar things, and the artistic power which seizes characteristic points and renders them with life-like effect—are seldom found in combination. "The Life of Sterling" is an instance of this rare conjunction. Its comparatively tame scenes and incidents gather picturesqueness and interest under the rich lights of Carlyle's mind. We are told neither too little nor too much; the facts noted, the letters selected, are all such as serve to give the liveliest conception of what Sterling was and what he did; and though the book speaks much of other persons, this collateral matter is all a kind of scene-painting, and is accessory to the main purpose. The portrait of Coleridge, for example, is precisely adapted to bring before us the intellectual region in which Sterling lived for some time before entering the Church. Almost every review has extracted this admirable description, in which genial veneration and compassion struggle with irresistible satire; but the emphasis of quotation cannot be too often given to the following pregnant paragraph:

> "The truth is, I now see Coleridge's talk and speculation was the emblem of himself. In it, as in him, a ray of heavenly inspiration struggled, in a tragically ineffectual degree, with the weakness of flesh and blood. He says once, he 'had skirted the howling deserts of infidelity.' This was evident enough; but he had not had the courage, in defiance of pain and terror, to press resolutely across said deserts to the new firm lands of faith beyond; he preferred to create logical *fata-morganas* for himself on this hither side, and laboriously solace himself with these."

The above mentioned step of Sterling—his entering the Church—is the point on which Carlyle is most decidedly at issue with Archdeacon Hare. The latter holds that had Sterling's health permitted him to remain in the Church, he would have escaped those aberrations from orthodoxy, which, in the clerical view, are to be regarded as the failure and shipwreck of his career, appparently thinking, like that friend of Arnold's who recommended a curacy as the best means of clearing up Trinitarian difficulties, that "orders" are a sort of spiritual backboard, which, by dint of obliging a man to look as if he were strait, end by making him so. According to Carlyle, on the contrary, the real "aberration" of Sterling was his choice of the clerical profession, which was simply a mistake as to his true vocation :

"Sterling," he says, "was not intrinsically, nor had ever been in the highest or chief degree, a devotional mind. Of course all excellence in man, and worship as the supreme excellence, was part of the inheritance of this gifted man ; but if called to define him, I should say artist, not saint, was the real bent of his being."

Again :

"No man of Sterling's veracity, had he clearly consulted his own heart, or had his own heart been capable of clearly responding, and not been bewildered by transient fantasies and theosophic moonshine, could have undertaken this function. His heart would have answered, 'No, thou canst not. What is incredible to thee, thou shalt not, at thy soul's peril, attempt to believe ! Elsewhither for a refuge, or die here. Go to perdition if thou must, but not with a lie in thy mouth ; by the eternal Maker, no !'"

From the period when Carlyle's own acquaintance with Sterling commenced, the Life has a double interest, from the glimpses it gives us of the writer, as well as of his hero. We are made present at their first introduction to each other ; we get a lively idea of their colloquies and walks together, and in this easy way, without any heavy disquisition or narrative, we obtain a clear insight into Sterling's character and mental progress. Above all, we are gladdened with a perception of the affinity that exists between noble souls, in spite of diversity in ideas—in what Carlyle calls "the logical outcome" of the faculties. This "Life of Sterling" is a touching monument of the capability human nature possesses of the highest love, the love of the good and beautiful in character, which is, after all, the essence of piety. The style of the work, too, is for the most part at once pure and rich ; there are passages of deep pathos which come upon the reader like a strain of solemn music, and others which show that aptness of epithet, that masterly power of close delineation, in which, perhaps, no writer has excelled Carlyle.

We have said that we think this second "Life of Sterling" justified by the first; but were it not so, the book would justify itself.

II.

WOMAN IN FRANCE: MADAME DE SABLÉ.*

In 1847, a certain Count Leopold Ferri died at Padua, leaving a library entirely composed of works written by women, in various languages, and this library amounted to nearly 32,000 volumes. We will not hazard any conjecture as to the proportion of these volumes which a severe judge, like the priest in Don Quixote, would deliver to the flames, but for our own part, most of these we should care to rescue would be the works of French women. With a few remarkable exceptions, our own feminine literature is made up of books which could have been better written by men—books which have the same relation to literature is general, as academic prize poems have to poetry: when not a feeble imitation, they are usually an absurd exaggeration of the masculine style, like the swaggering gait of a bad actress in male attire. Few English women have written so much like a woman as Richardson's Lady G. Now we think it an immense mistake to maintain that there is no sex in literature. Science has no sex: the mere knowing and reasoning faculties, if they act correctly, must go through the same process, and arrive at the same result. But in art and literature, which imply the action of the entire being, in which every fibre of the nature is engaged, in which every peculiar modification of the individual makes itself felt, woman has something specific to contribute. Under every imaginable

* 1. "Madame de Sablé. Etudes sur les Femmes illustres et la Société du XVIIe siècle." Par M. Victor Cousin. Paris: Didier. 2. "Portraits de Femmes." Par C. A. Sainte-Beuve. Paris: Didier. 3. "Les Femmes de la Révolutions." Par J. Michelet.

social condition, she will necessarily have a class of sensations and emotions—the maternal ones—which must remain unknown to man ; and the fact of her comparative physical weakness, which, however it may have been exaggerated by a vicious civilization, can never be cancelled, introduces a distinctively feminine condition into the wondrous chemistry of the affections and sentiments, which inevitably gives rise to distinctive forms and combinations. A certain amount of psychological difference between man and woman necessarily arises out of the difference of sex, and instead of being destined to vanish before a complete development of woman's intellectual and moral nature, will be a permanent source of variety and beauty as long as the tender light and dewy freshness of morning affect us differently from the strength and brilliancy of the midday sun. And those delightful women of France, who from the beginning of the seventeenth to the close of the eighteenth century, formed some of the brightest threads in the web of political and literary history, wrote under circumstances which left the feminine character of their minds uncramped by timidity, and unstrained by mistaken effort. They were not trying to make a career for themselves ; they thought little, in many cases not at all, of the public ; they wrote letters to their lovers and friends, memoirs of their every-day lives, romances in which they gave portraits of their familiar acquaintances, and described the tragedy or comedy which was going on before their eyes. Always refined and graceful, often witty, sometimes judicious, they wrote what they saw, thought, and felt in their habitual language, without proposing any model to themselves, without any intention to prove that women could write as well as men, without affecting manly views or suppressing womanly ones. One may say, at least with regard to the women of the seventeenth century, that their writings were but a charming accident of their more charming lives, like the petals which the wind shakes from the rose in its bloom. And it is but a twin fact with this, that in France alone woman has had a vital influence on the development of literature; in France alone the mind of woman has passed like an electric current through the language, making crisp and definite what is elsewhere heavy and blurred; in France alone, if the writings of women were swept away, a serious gap would be made in the national history.

Patriotic gallantry may perhaps contend that English women could, if they had liked, have written as well as their neighbors; but we will leave the consideration of that question to the reviewers of the literature that might have been. In the literature that actually is, we must turn to France for the highest examples of womanly achievement in almost every department. We confess ourselves unacquainted with the productions of those awful women of Italy, who held professorial chairs, and were great in civil and canon law; we have made no researches into the catacombs of female literature, but we think we may safely conclude that they would yield no rivals to that which is still unburied; and here, we suppose, the question of pre-eminence can only lie between England and France. And to this day, Madame de Sévigné remains the single instance of a woman who is supreme in a class of literature which has engaged the ambition of men; Madame Dacier still reigns the queen of blue stockings, though women have long studied Greek without shame;* Madame de Staël's name still rises first to the lips when we are asked to mention a woman of great intellectual power; Madame Roland is still the unrivalled type of the sagacious and sternly heroic, yet lovable woman; George Sand is the unapproached artist who, to Jean Jacques' eloquence and deep sense of external nature, unites the clear delineation of character and the tragic depth of passion. These great names, which mark different epochs, soar like tall pines amidst a forest of less conspicuous, but not less fascinating, female writers; and beneath these, again, are

* Queen Christina, when Mme. Dacier (then Mlle. Le Fèvre) sent her a copy of her edition of "Callimachus," wrote in reply: "Mais vous, de qui on m'assure que vous êtes une belle et agréable fille, n'avez vous pas honte d'être si savante?"

spread, like a thicket of hawthorns, eglantines, and honeysuckles, the women who are known rather by what they stimulated men to write, than by what they wrote themselves—the women whose tact, wit, and personal radiance created the atmosphere of the *Salon*, where literature, philosophy, and science, emancipated from the trammels of pedantry and technicality, entered on a brighter stage of existence.

What were the causes of this earlier development and more abundant manifestation of womanly intellect in France? The primary one, perhaps, lies in the physiological characteristics of the Gallic race—the small brain and vivacious temperament which permit the fragile system of woman to sustain the superlative activity requisite for intellectual creativeness; while, on the other hand, the larger brain and slower temperament of the English and Germans are, in the womanly organization, generally dreamy and passive. The type of humanity in the latter may be grander, but it requires a larger sum of conditions to produce a perfect specimen. Throughout the animal world, the higher the organization, the more frequent is the departure from the normal form; we do not often see imperfectly developed or ill-made insects, but we rarely see a perfectly developed, well-made man. And thus the *physique* of a woman may suffice as the substratum for a superior Gallic mind, but is too thin a soil for a superior Teutonic one. Our theory is borne out by the fact that among our own countrywomen those who distinguish themselves by literary production more frequently approach the Gallic than the Teutonic type; they are intense and rapid rather than comprehensive. The woman of large capacity can seldom rise beyond the absorption of ideas; her physical conditions refuse to support the energy required for spontaneous activity; the voltaic-pile is not strong enough to produce crystallizations; phantasms of great ideas float through her mind, but she has not the spell which will arrest them, and give them fixity. This, more than unfavorable external circumstances, is, we think, the reason why woman has not yet contributed any new form to art, any discovery in science, any deep-searching inquiry in philosophy. The necessary physiological conditions are not present in her. That under more favorable circumstances in the future, these conditions may prove compatible with the feminine organization, it would be rash to deny. For the present, we are only concerned with our theory so far as it presents a physiological basis for the intellectual effectiveness of French women.

A secondary cause was probably the laxity of opinion and practice with regard to the marriage-tie. Heaven forbid that we should enter on a defence of French morals, most of all in relation to marriage! But it is undeniable that unions formed in the maturity of thought and feeling, and grounded only on inherent fitness and mutual attraction, tended to bring women into more intelligent sympathy with men, and to heighten and complicate their share in the political drama. The quiescence and security of the conjugal relation are doubtless favorable to the manifestation of the highest qualities by persons who have already attained a high standard of culture, but rarely foster a passion sufficient to rouse all the faculties to aid in winning or retaining its beloved object—to convert indolence into activity, indifference into ardent partisanship, dulness into perspicuity. Gallantry and intrigue are sorry enough things in themselves, but they certainly serve better to arouse the dormant faculties of woman than embroidery and domestic drudgery, especially when, as in the high society of France in the seventeenth century, they are refined by the influence of Spanish chivalry, and controlled by the spirit of Italian causticity. The dreamy and fantastic girl was awakened to reality by the experience of wifehood and maternity, and became capable of loving, not a mere phantom of her own imagination, but a living man, struggling with the hatreds and rivalries of the political arena; she espoused his quarrels, she made herself, her fortune, and her influence, the stepping-stones of his ambition; and the languid beauty, who had formerly seemed ready to "die of a rose," was seen to become the heroine of an insurrection. The vivid interest in affairs which was thus excited in woman must obviously have tended to quicken her intellect, and give it a practical application; and the very sorrows—the heart-pangs and regrets which are inseparable from a life of passion—deepened her nature by the questioning of self and destiny which they occasioned, and by the energy demanded to surmount them and live on. No wise person, we imagine, wishes to restore the social condition of France in the seventeenth century, or considers the ideal programme of woman's life to be a *mariage de convenance* at fifteen, a career of gallantry from twenty to eight-and-thirty, and penitence and piety for the rest of her days. Nevertheless, that social condition has its good results, as much as the madly superstitious Crusades had theirs.

But the most indisputable source of feminine culture and development in France was the influence of the *salons*, which, as all the world knows, were *réunions* of both sexes, where conversation ran along the whole gamut of subjects, from the frothiest *vers de société* to the philosophy of Descartes. Richelieu had set the fashion of uniting a taste for letters with the habits of polite society and the pursuits of ambition; and in the first quarter of the seventeenth century there were already several hôtels in Paris, varying in social position from the closest proximity of the Court to the debatable ground of the aristocracy and the bourgeoisie, which served as a rendezvous for different circles of people, bent on entertaining themselves either by showing talent or admiring it. The most celebrated of these rendezvous was the Hôtel de Rambouillet, which was at the culmination of its glory in 1630, and did not become quite extinct until 1648, when the troubles of the Fronde commencing, its *habitués* were dispersed or absorbed by political interests. The presiding genius of this *salon*, the Marquise de Rambouillet, was the very model of the woman who can act as anamalgam to the most incongruous elements; beautiful, but not preoccupied by coquetry or passion; an enthusiastic admirer of talent, but with no pretensions to talent on her own part; exquisitely refined in language and manners, but warm and generous withal; not given to entertain her guests with her own compositions, or to paralyze them by her universal knowledge. She had once *meant* to learn Latin, but had been prevented by an illness; perhaps she was all the better acquainted with Italian and Spanish productions, which, in default of a national literature, were then the intellectual pabulum of all cultivated persons in France who are unable to read the classics. In her mild, agreeable presence was accomplished that blending of the high-toned chivalry of Spain with the caustic wit and refined irony of Italy, which issued in the creation of a new standard of taste—the combination of the utmost exaltation in sentiment with the utmost simplicity of language. Women are peculiarly fitted to further such a combination—first, from their greater tendency to mingle affection and imagination with passion, and thus subtilize it into sentiment; and next, from that dread of what overtaxes their intellectual energies, either by difficulty or monotony, which gives them an instinctive fondness for lightness of treatment and airiness of expression, thus making them cut short all prolixity and reject all heaviness. When these womanly characteristics were brought into conversational contact with the materials furnished by such minds as those of Richelieu, Corneille, the Great Condé, Balzac, and Bossuet, it is no wonder that the result was something piquant and charming. Those famous *habitués* of the Hôtel de Rambouillet did not, apparently, first lay themselves out to entertain the ladies with grimacing "small-talk," and then take each other by the sword-knot to discuss matters of real interest in a corner; they rather sought to present their best ideas in the guise most acceptable to intelligent and accomplished women. And the conversation was not of literature only: war, politics, religion, the lightest details of daily news—everything was admissible, if only it were treated with refinement and intelligence. The Hôtel de Rambouillet was no mere literary *réunion*; it included *hommes d'affaires* and soldiers as well as authors, and in such a circle women would not become *bas bleus* or dreamy moralizers, ignorant of the world and of human nature, but intelligent observers of character and events. It is easy to understand, however, that with the herd of imitators who, in Paris and the provinces, aped the style of this famous *salon*, simplicity degenerated into affectation, and nobility of sentiment was replaced by an inflated effort to outstrip nature, so that the *genre précieux* drew down the satire, which reached its climax in the *Précieuses Ridicules* and *Les Femmes Savantes*, the former of which appeared in 1660, and the latter in 1673. But Madelon and Caltros are the lineal descendants of Mademoiselle Scudery and her satellites, quite as much as of the Hôtel de Rambouillet. The society which assembled every Saturday in her *salon* was exclusively literary, and although occasionally visited by a few persons of high birth, bourgeois in its tone, and enamored of madrigals, sonnets, stanzas, and *bouts rimés*. The affectation that decks trivial things in fine language belongs essentially to a class which sees another above it, and is uneasy in the sense of its inferiority; and this affectation is precisely the opposite of the original *genre précieux*.

Another centre from which feminine influence radiated into the national literature was the Palais du Luxembourg, where Mademoiselle d'Orleans, in disgrace at court on account of her share in the Fronde, held a little court of her own, and for want of anything else to employ her active spirit busied herself with literature. One fine morning it occurred to this princess to ask all the persons who frequented her court, among whom were Madame de Sévigné, Madame de la Fayette, and La Rochefoucauld, to write their own portraits, and she at once set the example. It was understood that defects and virtues were to be spoken of with like candor. The idea was carried out; those who were not clever or bold enough to write for themselves employing the pen of a friend.

"Such," says M. Cousin, "was the pastime of Mademoiselle and her friends during the years 1657 and 1658: from this pastime proceeded a complete literature. In 1659 Ségrais revised these portraits, added a considerable number in prose and even in verse, and published the whole in a handsome quarto volume, admirably printed, and now become very rare, under the title, 'Divers Portraits.' Only thirty copies were printed, not for sale, but to be given as presents by Mademoiselle. The work had a prodigious success. That which had made the fortune of Mademoiselle de Scudéry's romances—the pleasure of seeing one's portrait a little flattered, curiosity to see that of others, the passion which the middle class always have had and will have for knowing what goes on in the aristocratic world (at that time not very easy of access), the names of the illustrious persons who were here for the first time described physically and morally with the utmost detail, great ladies transformed all at once into writers, and unconsciously inventing a new manner of writing, of which no book gave the slightest idea, and which was the ordinary manner of speaking of the aristocracy; this undefinable mixture of the natural, the easy, and at the same time of the agreeable, and supremely distinguished—all this charmed the court and the town, and very early in the year 1659 permission was asked of Mademoiselle to give a new edition of the privileged book for the use of the public in general."

The fashion thus set, portraits multiplied throughout France, until in 1688 La Bruyère adopted the form in his "Characters," and ennobled it by divesting it of personality. We shall presently see that a still greater work than La Bruyère's also owed its suggestion to a woman, whose salon was hardly a less fascinating resort than the Hôtel de Rambouillet itself.

In proportion as the literature of a country is enriched and culture becomes more generally diffused, personal influence is less effective in the formation of taste and in the furtherance of social advancement. It is no longer the coterie which acts on literature, but literature which acts on the coterie; the circle represented by the word *public* is ever widening, and ambition, poising itself in order to hit a more distant mark, neglects the successes of the salon. What was once lavished prodigally in conversation is reserved for the volume or the "article," and the effort is not to betray originality rather than to communicate it. As the old coach-roads have sunk into disuse through the creation of railways, so journalism tends more and more to divert information from the channel of conversation into the channel of the Press; no one is satisfied with a more circumscribed audience than that very indeterminate abstraction "the public," and men find a vent for their opinions not in talk, but in "copy." We read the *Athenæum* askance at the tea-table, and take notes from the *Philosophical Journal* at a soirée; we invite our friends that we may thrust a book into their hands, and presuppose an exclusive desire in the "ladies" to discuss their own matters, "that we may crackle the *Times*" at our ease. In fact, the evident tendency of things to contract personal communication within the narrowest limits makes us tremble lest some further development of the electric telegraph should reduce us to a society of mutes, or to a sort of insects communicating by ingenious antennæ of our own invention. Things were far from having reached this pass in the last century; but even then literature and society had outgrown the nursing of coteries, and although many *salons* of that period were worthy successors of the Hôtel de Rambouillet, they were simply a recreation, not an influence. Enviable evenings, no doubt, were passed in them; and if we could be carried back to any of them at will, we should hardly know whether to choose the Wednesday dinner at Madame Geoffrin's, with d'Alembert, Mademoiselle de l'Espinasse, Grimm, and the rest; or the graver society which, thirty years later, gathered round Condorcet and his lovely young wife. The *salon* retained its attractions, but its power was gone: the stream of life had become too broad and deep for such small rills to affect it.

A fair comparison between the French women of the seventeenth century and those of the eighteenth would, perhaps, have a balanced result, though it is common to be a partisan on this subject. The former have more exaltation, perhaps more nobility of sentiment, and less consciousness in their intellectual activity—less of the *femme auteur*, which was Rousseau's horror in Madame d'Epinay; but the latter have a richer fund of ideas—not more ingenuity, but the materials of an additional century for their ingenuity to work upon. The women of the seventeenth century, when love was on the wane, took to devotion, at first mildly and by halves, as English women take to caps, and finally without compromise; with the women of the eighteenth century, Bossuet and Massillon had given way to Voltaire and Rousseau; and when youth and beauty failed, then they were thrown on their own moral strength.

M. Cousin is especially enamored of the women of the seventeenth century, and relieves himself from his labors in philosophy by making researches into the original documents which throw light upon their lives. Last year he gave us some results of these researches in a volume on the youth of the Duchess de Longueville; and he has just followed it up with a second volume, in which he further illustrates her career by tracing it in connection with that of her friend, Madame de Sablé. The materials to which he has had recourse for this purpose are chiefly two celebrated collections of manuscript: that of Conrart, the first secretary to the French Academy, one of those universally curious people who seem made for the annoyance of contemporaries and the benefit of posterity; and that of Valant, who was at once the physician, the secretary, and general steward of Madame de Sablé, and who, with or without her permission, possessed himself of the letters addressed to her by her numerous correspondents during the latter part of her life, and of various papers having some personal or literary interest attached to them. From these stores M. Cousin has selected many documents previously unedited; and though he often leaves us something to desire in the arrangement of his materials, this volume of his on Madame de Sablé is very acceptable to us, for she interests us quite enough to carry us through more than three hundred pages of rather scattered narrative, and through an appendix of correspondence in small type. M. Cousin justly appreciates her character as "un heureux mélange de raison, d'esprit, d'agrément, et de bonté;" and perhaps there are few better specimens of the woman who is extreme in nothing but sympathetic in all things; who affects us by no special quality, but by her entire being; whose nature has no *tons criards*, but is like those textures which, from their harmonious blending of all colors, give repose to the eye, and do not weary us though we see them every day. Madame de Sablé is also a striking example of the one order of influence which woman has exercised over literature in France; and on this ground, as well as intrinsically, she is worth studying. If the reader agrees with us he will perhaps be inclined, as we are, to dwell a little on the chief points in her life and character.

Madeline de Souvré, daughter of the Marquis of Courtenvaux, a nobleman distinguished enough to be chosen as governor of Louis XIII., was born in 1599, on the threshold of that seventeenth century, the brilliant genius of which is mildly reflected in her mind and history. Thus, when in 1635 her more celebrated friend, Mademoiselle de Bourbon, afterward the Duchess de Longueville, made her appearance at the Hôtel de Rambouillet, Madame de Sable had nearly crossed that table-land of maturity which precedes a woman's descent toward old age. She had been married in 1614, to Philippe Emanuel de Laval-Montmorency, Seigneur de Bois-Dauphin, and Marquis de Sablé, of whom nothing further is known than that he died in 1640, leaving her the richer by four children, but with a fortune considerably embarrassed. With beauty and high rank added to the mental attractions of which we have abundant evidence, we may well believe that Madame de Sablé's youth was brilliant. For her beauty, we have the testimony of sober Madame de Motteville, who also speaks of her as having "beaucoup de lumière et de sincérité;" and in the following passage very graphically indicates one phase of Madame de Sablé's character:

"The Marquise de Sablé was one of those whose beauty made the most noise when the Queen came into France. But if she was amiable, she was still more desirous of appearing so; this lady's self-love rendered her too sensitive to the regard which men exhibited toward her. There yet existed in France some remains of the politeness which Catherine de Medici had introduced from Italy, and the new dramas, with all the other works in prose and verse, which came from Madrid, were thought to have such great delicacy, that she (Madame de Sablé) had conceived a high idea of the gallantry which the Spaniards had learned from the Moors.

"She was persuaded that men can, without crime, have tender sentiments for women—that the desire of pleasing them led men to the greatest and finest actions—roused their intelligence, and inspired them with liberality, and all sorts of virtues; but, on the other hand, women, who were the ornament of the world, and made to be served and adored, ought not to admit anything from them but their respectful attentions. As this lady supported her views with much talent and great beauty, she had given them authority in her time, and the number and consideration of those who continued to associate with her have caused to subsist in our day what the Spaniards call *finezas*."

Here is the grand element of the original *femme précieuse*, and it appears further, in a detail also reported by Madame de Motteville, that Madame de Sablé had a passionate admirer in the accomplished Duc de Montmorency, and apparently reciprocated his regard; but discovering (at what period of their attachment is unknown) that he was raising a lover's eyes toward the queen, she broke with him at once. "I have heard her say," tells Madame de Motteville, "that her pride was such with regard to the Duc de Montmorency, that at the first demonstrations which he gave of his change, she refused to see him any more, being unable to receive with satisfaction attentions which she had to share with the greatest princess in the world." There is no evidence except the untrustworthy assertion of Tallement de Réaux, that Madame de Sablé had any other *liaison* than this; and the probability of the negative is increased by the ardor of her friendships. The strongest of these was formed early in life with Mademoiselle Dona d'Attichy, afterward Comtesse de Maure; it survived the effervescence of youth, and the closest intimacy of middle age, and was only terminated by the death of the latter in 1663. A little incident in this friendship is so characteristic in the transcendentalism which was then carried into all the affections, that it is worth relating at length. Mademoiselle d'Attichy, in her grief and indignation at Richelieu's treatment of her relative, quitted Paris, and was about to join her friend at Sablé, when she suddenly discovered that Madame de Sablé, in a letter to Madame de Rambouillet, had said that her greatest happiness would be to pass her life with Julie de Rambouillet, afterward Madame de Montausier. To Anne d'Attichy this appears nothing less than the crime of *lèse-amitié*. No explanations will appease her: she refuses to accept the assurance that the offensive expression was used simply out of unreflecting conformity to the style of the Hôtel de Rambouillet—that it was mere "*galimatias.*" She gives up her journey, and writes a letter, which is the only one Madame de Sable chose to preserve, when, in her period of devotion, she sacrificed the records of her youth. Here it is:

"I have seen this letter in which you tell me there is so much *galimatias*, and I assure you that I have not found any at all. On the contrary, I find everything very plainly expressed, and among others, one which is too explicit for my satisfaction—namely, what you have said to Madame de Rambouillet, that if you tried to imagine a perfectly happy life for yourself, it would be to pass it all alone with Mademoiselle de Rambouillet. You know whether any one can be more persuaded than I am of her merit; but I confess to you that that has not prevented me from being surprised that you could entertain a thought which did so great an injury to our friendship. As to believing that you said this to one, and wrote it to the other, simply for the sake of paying them an agreeable compliment, I have too high an esteem for your courage to be able to imagine that complaisance would cause you thus to betray the sentiments of your heart, especially on a subject in which, as they were unfavorable to me, I think you would have the more reason for concealing them, the affection which I have for you being so well known to every one, and especially to Mademoiselle de Rambouillet, so that I doubt whether she will not have been more sensible of the wrong you have done me, than of the advantage you have given her. The circumstance of this letter falling into my hands has forcibly reminded me of these lines of Bertaut:

"'Malheureuse est l'ignorance
Et plus malheureux le savoir."

"Having through this lost a confidence which alone rendered life supportable to me, it is impossible for me to take the journey so much thought of. For would there be any propriety in travelling sixty miles in this season, in order to burden you with a person so little suited to you, that after years of a passion without parallel, you cannot help thinking that the greatest pleasure of your life would be to pass it without her? I return, then, into my solitude, to examine the defects which cause me so much unhappiness, and unless I can correct them, I should have less joy than confusion in seeing you."

It speaks strongly for the charm of Madame de Sablé's nature that she was able to retain so susceptible a friend as Mademoiselle d'Attichy in spite of numerous other friendships, some of which, especially that with Madame de Longueville, were far from lukewarm—in spite too of a tendency in herself to distrust the affection of others toward her, and to wait for advances rather than to make them. We find many traces of this tendency in the affectionate remonstrances addressed to her by Madame de Longueville, now for shutting herself up from her friends, now for doubting that her letters are acceptable. Here is a little passage from one of these remonstrances which indicates a trait of Madame de Sablé, and is in itself a bit of excellent sense, worthy the consideration of lovers and friends in general: "I am very much afraid that if I leave to you the care of letting me know when I can see you, I shall be a long time without having that pleasure, and that nothing will incline you to procure it me, for I have always observed a certain lukewarmness in your friendship after our *explanations*, from which I have never seen you thoroughly recover; and that is why I dread explanations, for however good they may be in themselves, since they serve to reconcile people, it must always be admitted, to their shame, that they are at least the effect of a bad cause, and that if they remove it for a time they *sometimes leave a certain facility in getting angry again*, which, without diminishing friendship, renders its intercourse less agreeable. It seems to me that I find all this in your behavior to me; so I am not wrong in sending to know if you wish to have me to-day." It is clear that Madame de Sablé was far from having what Sainte-Beuve calls the one fault of Madame Necker—absolute perfection. A certain exquisiteness in her physical and moral nature was, as we shall see, the source of more than one weakness, but the perception of these weaknesses, which is indicated in Madame de Longueville's letters, heightens our idea of the attractive qualities which notwithstanding drew from her, at the sober age of forty, such expressions as these: "I assure you that you are the person in all the world whom it would be most agreeable to me to see, and there is no one whose intercourse is a ground of truer satisfaction to me. It is admirable that at all times, and amidst all changes, the taste for your society remains in me; and, *if one ought to thank God for the joys which do not tend to salvation*, I should thank him with all my heart for having preserved that to me at a time in which he has taken away from me all others."

Since we have entered on the chapter of Madame de Sablé's weaknesses, this is the place to mention what was the subject of endless raillery from her friends—her elaborate precaution about her health, and her dread of infection, even from diseases the least communicable. Perhaps this anxiety was founded as much on æsthetic as on physical grounds, on disgust at the details of illness as much as on dread of suffering: with a cold in the head or a bilious complaint, the exquisite *précieuse* must have been considerably less conscious of being "the ornament of the world," and "made to be adored." Even her friendship, strong as it was, was not strong enough to overcome her horror of contagion; for when Mademoiselle de Bourbon, recently become Madame de Longueville, was attacked by small-pox, Madame de Sablé for some time had not courage to visit her, or even to see Mademoiselle de Rambouillet, who was assiduous in her attendance on the patient. A little correspondence *à propos* of these circumstances so well exhibits the graceful badinage in which the great ladies of that day were adepts, that we are attempted to quote one short letter.

"*Mlle. de Rambouillet to the Marquise de Sablé.*

"Mlle. de Chalais (*dame de compagnie* to the Marquise) will please to read this letter to Mme. la Marquise, *out of* a draught.

"Madame, I do not think it possible to begin my treaty with you too early, for I am convinced that between the first proposition made to me that I should see you, and the conclusion, you will have so many reflections to make, so many physicians to consult, and so many fears to surmount, that I shall have full leisure to air myself. The conditions which I offer to fulfil for this purpose are, not to visit you until I have been three days absent from the Hôtel de Condé (where Mme. de Longueville was ill), to choose a frosty day, not to approach you within four paces, not to sit down on more than one seat. You may also have a great fire in your room, burn juniper in the four corners, surround yourself with imperial vinegar, with rue and wormwood. If you can feel yourself safe under these conditions, without my cutting off my hair, I swear to you to execute them religiously; and if you want examples to fortify you, I can tell you that the Queen consented to see M. Chaudebonne, when he had come directly from Mlle. de Bourbon's room, and that Mme. d'Aiguillon, who has good taste in such matters, and is free from reproach on these points, has just sent me word that if I did not go to see her she would come to me."

Madame de Sablé betrays in her reply that she winces under this raillery, and thus provokes a rather severe though polite rejoinder, which, added to the fact that Madame de Longueville is convalescent, rouses her courage to the pitch of paying the formidable visit. Mademoiselle de Rambouillet, made aware through their mutual friend Voiture, that her sarcasm has cut rather too deep, winds up the matter by writing that very difficult production a perfectly conciliatory yet dignified apology. Peculiarities like this always deepen with age, and accordingly, fifteen years later, we find Madame D'Orleans in her "Princesse de Paphlagonia"—a romance in which she describes her court, with the little quarrels and other affairs that agitated it—giving the following amusing picture, or rather caricature, of the extent to which Madame de Sablé carried her pathological mania, which seems to have been shared by her friend the Countess de Maure (Mademoiselle d'Attichy). In the romance, these two ladies appear under the names of Princesse Parthénie and the Reine de Mionie.

"There was not an hour in the day in which they did not confer together on the means of avoiding death, and on the art of rendering themselves immortal. Their conferences did not take place like those of other people; the fear of breathing an air which was too cold or too warm, the dread lest the wind should be too dry or too moist—in short, the imagination that the weather might not be as temperate as they thought necessary for the preservation of their health, caused them to write letters from one room to the other. It would be extremely fortunate if these notes could be found, and formed into a collection. I am convinced that they would contain rules for the regimen of life, precautions even as to the proper time for applying remedies, and also remedies which Hippocrates and Galen, with all their science, never heard of. Such a collection would be very useful to the public, and would be highly profitable to the faculties of Paris and Montpellier. If these letters were discovered, great advantages of all kinds might be derived from them, for they were princesses who had nothing mortal about them but the *knowledge* that they were mortal. In their writings might be learned all politeness in style, and the most delicate manner of speaking on all subjects. There is nothing with which they were not acquainted; they knew the affairs of all the States in the world, through the share they had in all the intrigues of its private members, either in matters of gallantry, as in other things, on which their advice was necessary; either to adjust embroilments and quarrels, or to excite them, for the sake of the advantages which their friends could derive from them;—in a word, they were persons through whose hands the secrets of the whole world had to pass. The Princess Parthénie (Mme. de Sablé) had a palate as delicate as her mind; nothing could equal the magnificence of the entertainments she gave; all the dishes were exquisite, and her cleanliness was beyond all that could be imagined. It was in their time that writing came into use; previously nothing was written but marriage contracts, and letters were never heard of; thus it is to them that we owe a practice so convenient in intercourse."

Still later in 1669, when the most uncompromising of the Port Royalists seemed to tax Madame de Sablé with lukewarmness that she did not join them at Port-Royal-des-Champs, we find her writing to the stern M. de Sévigny: "En vérité, je crois que je ne pourrois mieux faire que de tout quitter et de m'en aller là. Mais que deviendroient ces frayeurs de n'avoir pas de médicines à choisir, ni de chirurgien pour me saigner?"

Mademoiselle, as we have seen, hints at the love of delicate eating, which many of Madame de Sablé's friends numbered among her foibles, especially after her religious career had commenced. She had a genius in *friandise*, and knew how to gratify the palate without offending the highest sense of refinement. Her sympathetic nature showed itself in this as in other things; she was always sending *bonnes bouches* to her friends, and trying to communicate to them her science and taste in the affairs of the table. Madame de Longueville, who had not the luxurious tendencies of her friend, writes: "Je vous demande au nom de Dieu, que vous ne me prépariez aucun ragoût. Surtout ne me donnez point de festin. Au nom de Dieu, qu'il n'y ait rien que ce qu'on peut manger, car vous savez que c'est inutile pour moi; de plus j'en ai scrupule." But other friends had more appreciation of her niceties. Voiture thanks her for her melons, and assures her that they are better than those of yesterday; Madame de Choisy hopes that her ridicule of Jansenism will not provoke Madame de Sablé to refuse her the receipt for salad; and La Rochefoucauld writes: "You cannot do me a greater charity than to permit the bearer of this letter to enter into the mysteries of your marmalade and your genuine preserves, and I humbly entreat you to do everything you can in his favor. If I could hope for two dishes of those preserves, which I did not deserve to eat before, I should be indebted to you all my life." For our own part, being as far as possible from fraternizing with those spiritual people who convert a deficiency into a principle, and pique themselves on an obtuse palate as a point of superiority, we are not inclined to number Madame de Sablé's *friandise* among her defects. M. Cousin, too, is apologetic on this point. He says:

"It was only the excess of a delicacy which can be really understood, and a sort of fidelity to the character of *précieuse*. As the *précieuse* did nothing according to common usage, she could not dine like another. We have cited a passage from Mme. de Motteville, where Mme. de Sablé is represented in her first youth at the Hôtel de Rambouillet, maintaining that woman is born to be an ornament to the world, and to receive the adoration of men. The woman worthy of the name ought always to appear above material wants, and retain, even in the most vulgar details of life, something distinguished and purified. Eating is a very necessary operation, but one which is not agreeable to the eye. Mme. de Sablé insisted on its being conducted with a peculiar cleanliness. According to her it was not every woman who could with impunity be at table in the presence of a lover; the first distortion of the face, she said, would be enough to spoil all. Gross meals made for the body merely ought to be abandoned to *bourgeoises*, and the refined woman should appear to take a little nourishment merely to sustain her, and even to divert her, as one takes refreshments and ices. Wealth did not suffice for this: a particular talent was required. Mme. de Sablé was a mistress in this art. She had transported the aristocratic spirit, and the *genre précieux*, good breeding and good taste, even into cookery. Her dinners, without any opulence, were celebrated and sought after."

It is quite in accordance with all this that Madame de Sablé should delight in fine scents, and we find that she did; for being threatened, in her Port Royal days, when she was at an advanced age, with the loss of smell, and writing for sympathy and information to Mère Agnès, who had lost that sense early in life, she receives this admonition from the stern saint: "You would gain by this loss, my very dear sister, if you made use of it as a satisfaction to God, for having had too much pleasure in delicious scents." Scarron describes her as

> "La non pareille Bois-Dauphine,
> *Entre dames perle très fine*,"

and the superlative delicacy implied by this epithet seems to have belonged equally to her personal habits, her affections, and her intellect.

Madame de Sablé's life, for anything we know, flowed on evenly enough until 1640, when the death of her husband threw upon her the care of an embarrassed fortune. She found a friend in Réné de Longueil, Seigneur de Maisons, of whom we are content to know no more than that he helped

Madame de Sablé to arrange her affairs, though only by means of alienating from her family the estate of Sablé, that his house was her refuge during the blockade of Paris in 1649, and that she was not unmindful of her obligations to him, when, subsequently, her credit could be serviceable to him at court. In the midst of these pecuniary troubles came a more terrible trial —the loss of her favorite son, the brave and handsome Guy de Laval, who, after a brilliant career in the campaigns of Condé, was killed at the siege of Dunkirk, in 1646, when scarcely four-and-twenty. The fine qualities of this young man had endeared him to the whole army, and especially to Condé, had won him the hand of the Chancellor Séguire's daughter, and had thus opened to him the prospect of the highest honors. His loss seems to have been the most real sorrow of Madame de Sablé's life. Soon after followed the commotions of the Fronde, which put a stop to social intercourse, and threw the closest friends into opposite ranks. According to Lenet, who relies on the authority of Gourville, Madame de Sablé was under strong obligations to the court, being in the receipt of a pension of 2000 crowns; at all events, she adhered throughout to the Queen and Mazarin, but being as far as possible from a fierce partisan, and given both by disposition and judgment to hear both sides of the question, she acted as a conciliator, and retained her friends of both parties. The Countess de Maure, whose husband was the most obstinate of *frondeurs*, remained throughout her most cherished friend, and she kept up a constant correspondence with the lovely and intrepid heroine of the Fronde, Madame de Longueville. Her activity was directed to the extinction of animosities, by bringing about marriages between the Montagues and Capulets of the Fronde—between the Prince de Condé, or his brother, and the niece of Mazarin, or between the three nieces of Mazarin and the sons of three noblemen who were distinguished leaders of the Fronde. Though her projects were not realized, her conciliatory position enabled her to preserve all her friendships intact, and when the political tempest was over, she could assemble around her in her residence, in the Place Royal, the same society as before. Madame de Sablé was now approaching her twelfth lustrum, and though the charms of her mind and character made her more sought after than most younger women, it is not surprising that, sharing as she did in the religious ideas of her time, the concerns of "salvation" seemed to become pressing. A religious retirement, which did not exclude the reception of literary friends or the care for personal comforts, made the most becoming frame for age and diminished fortune. Jansenism was then to ordinary Catholicism what Puseyism is to ordinary Church of Englandism in these days—it was a *rècherchè* form of piety unshared by the vulgar; and one sees at once that it must have special attractions for the *précieuse*. Madame de Sablé, then, probably about 1655 or '56, determined to retire to Port Royal, not because she was already devout, but because she hoped to become so; as, however, she wished to retain the pleasure of intercourse with friends who were still worldly, she built for herself a set of apartments at once distinct from the monastery and attached to it. Here, with a comfortable establishment, consisting of her secretary, Dr. Valant, Mademoiselle de Chalais, formerly her *dame de compagnie*, and now become her friend; an excellent cook; a few other servants, and for a considerable time a carriage and coachman; with her best friends within a moderate distance, she could, as M. Cousin says, be out of the noise of the world without altogether forsaking it, preserve her dearest friendships, and have before her eyes edifying examples—"vaquer enfin à son aise aux soins de son salut et à ceux de sa santé."

We have hitherto looked only at one phase of Madame de Sablé's character and influence—that of the *précieuse*. But she was much more than this: she was the valuable, trusted friend of noble women and distinguished men; she was the animating spirit of a society, whence issued a new form of French literature; she was the woman of large capacity and large heart, whom Pascal sought to please, to whom Arnauld submitted the Discourse prefixed to his "Logic," and to whom La Rochefoucauld writes: "Vous savez que je ne crois que vous êtes sur de certains chapitres, et surtout sur les replis du cœur." The papers preserved by her secretary, Valant, show that she maintained an extensive correspondence with persons of various rank and character; that her pen was untiring in the interest of others; that men made her the depositary of their thoughts, women of their sorrows; that her friends were as impatient, when she secluded herself, as if they had been rival lovers and she a youthful beauty. It is into her ear that Madame de Longueville pours her troubles and difficulties, and that Madame de la Fayette communicates her little alarms, lest young Count de St. Paul should have detected her intimacy with La Rochefoucauld.* The few of Madame de Sablé's letters which survive show that she excelled in that epistolary style which was the specialty of the Hôtel de Rambouillet: one to Madame de Montausier, in favor of M. Périer, the brother-in-law of Pascal, is a happy mixture of good taste and good sense; but among them all we prefer quoting one to the Duchess de la Tremouille. It is light and pretty, and made out of almost nothing, like soap-bubbles.

"Je croix qu'il n'y a que moi qui face si bien tout le contraire de ce que je veux faire, car il est vrai qu'il n'y a personne que j'honore plus que vous, et j'ai si bien fait qu'il est quasi impossible que vous le puissiez croire. Ce n'estoit pas assez pour vous persuader que je suis indigne de vos bonnes grâces et de votre souvenir que d'avoir manqué fort longtemps à vous écrire; il falloit encore retarder quinze jours à me donner l'honneur de répondre à votre lettre. En vérité, Madame, cela me fait paroître si coupable, que vers tout autre que vous j'aimeroix mieux l'être en effet que d'entreprendre une chose si difficile qu' est celle de me justifier. Mais je me sens si innocente

* The letter to which we allude has this charming little touch: "Je hais comme la mort que les gens de son age puissent croire que j'ai des galanteries. Il semble qu'on leur parait cent ans des qu'on est plus vieille qu'eux, et ils sont tout propre à s'étonner qu'il y ait encore question des gens."

dans mon âme, et j'ai tant d'estime, de respect et d'affection pour vous, qu'il me semble que vous devez le connôitre à cent lieues de distance d'ici, encore que je ne vous dise pas un mot. C'est ce que me donne le courage de vous écrire à cette heure, mais non pas ce qui m'en a empêché si longtemps. J'ai commencé a faillir par force, ayant eu beaucoup de maux, et depuis je l'ai faite par honte, et je vous avoue que si je n'avois à cette heure la confiance que vous m'avez donnée en me rassurant, et celle que je tire de mes propres sentimens pour vous, je n'oserois jamais entreprendre de vous faire souvenir de moi ; mais je m'assure que vous oublierez tout, sur la protestation que je vous fais de ne me laisser plus endurcir en mes fautes et de demeurer inviolablement, Madame, votre, etc."

Was not the woman, who could unite the ease and grace indicated by this letter, with an intellect that men thought worth consulting on matters of reasoning and philosophy, with warm affections, untiring activity for others, no ambition as an authoress, and an insight into *confitures* and *ragoûts*, a rare combination? No wonder that her *salon* at Port Royal was the favorite resort of such women as Madame de la Fayette, Madame de Montausier, Madame de Longueville, and Madame de Hautefort ; and of such men as Pascal, La Rochefoucauld, Nicole, and Domat. The collections of Valant contain papers which show what were the habitual subjects of conversation in this salon. Theology, of course, was a chief topic ; but physics and metaphysics had their turn, and still more frequently morals, taken in their widest sense. There were "Conferences on Calvinism," of which an abstract is preserved. When Rohault invented his glass tubes to serve for the barometrical experiments in which Pascal had roused a strong interest, the Marquis de Sourdis entertained the society with a paper entitled "Why Water Mounts in a Glass Tube." Cartesianism was an exciting topic here, as well as everywhere else in France ; it had its partisans and opponents, and papers were read containing "Thoughts on the Opinions of M. Descartes." These lofty matters were varied by discussions on love and friendship, on the drama, and on most of the things in heaven and earth which the philosophy of that day dreamt of. Morals—generalizations on human affections, sentiments, and conduct — seem to have been the favorite theme; and the aim was to reduce these generalizations to their briefest form of expression, to give them the epigrammatic turn which made them portable in the memory. This was the specialty of Madame de Sablé's circle, and was, probably, due to her own tendency. As the Hôtel de Rambouillet was the nursery of graceful letter-writing, and the Luxembourg of "portraits" and "characters," so Madame de Sablé's *salon* fostered that taste for the sententious style, to which we owe, probably, some of the best *Pensées* of Pascal, and certainly, the "Maxims" of La Rochefoucauld. Madame de Sablé herself wrote maxims, which were circulated among her friends; and, after her death, were published by the Abbé d'Ailly. They have the excellent sense and nobility of feeling which we should expect in everything of hers; but they have no stamp of genius or individual character: they are, to the "Maxims" of La Rochefoucauld, what the vase moulded in dull, heavy clay is to the vase which the action of fire has made light, brittle, and transparent. She also wrote a treatise on Education, which is much praised by La Rochefoucauld and M. d'Andilly; but which seems no longer to be found: probably it was not much more elaborate than her so-called "Treatise on Friendship," which is but a short string of maxims. Madame de Sablé's forte was evidently not to write herself, but to stimulate others to write; to show that sympathy and appreciation which are as genial and encouraging as the morning sunbeams. She seconded a man's wit with understanding —one of the best offices which womanly intellect has rendered to the advancement of culture; and the absence of originality made her all the more receptive toward the originality of others.

The manuscripts of Pascal show that many of the *Pensées*, which are commonly supposed to be raw materials for a great work on religion, were remodelled again and again, in order to bring them to the highest degree of terseness and finish, which would hardly have been the case if they had only been part of a quarry for a greater production. Thoughts, which are merely collected as materials, as stones out of which a building is to be erected, are not cut into facets, and polished like amethysts or emeralds. Since Pascal was from the first in the habit of visiting Madame de Sablé, at Port Royal, with his sister, Madame Périer (who was one of Madame de Sablé's dearest friends), we may well suppose that he would throw some of his jewels among the large and small coin of maxims, which were a sort of subscription-money there. Many of them have an epigrammatical piquancy, which was just the thing to charm a circle of vivacious and intelligent women: they seem to come from a La Rochefoucauld who has been dipped over again in philosophy and wit, and received a new layer. But whether or not Madame de Sablé's influence served to enrich the *Pensées* of Pascal, it is clear that but for her influence the "Maxims" of La Rochefoucauld would never have existed. Just as in some circles the effort is, who shall make the best puns (*horibile dictu!*), or the best charades, in the *salon* of Port Royal the amusement was to fabricate maxims. La Rochefoucauld said, "L'envie de faire des maximes se gagne comme le rhume." So far from claiming for himself the initiation of this form of writing, he accuses Jacques Esprit, another *habitué* of Madame de Sablé's *salon*, of having excited in him the taste for maxims, in order to trouble his repose. The said Esprit was an academician, and had been a frequenter of the Hôtel de Rambouillet. He had already published "Maxims in Verse," and he subsequently produced a book called "La Fausseto des Vertus Humaines," which seems to consist of Rochefoucauldism become flat with an infusion of sour Calvinism. Nevertheless, La Rochefoucauld seems to have prized him, to have appealed to his judgment, and to have concocted maxims with him, which he afterward begs him to submit to Madame Sablé. He sends a little batch of maxims to her himself, and asks for an equivalent in the shape of good eatables: "Voilà tout ce que j'ai de maximes; mais comme je ne donne rien pour rien, je vous demande un potage aux carottes, un ragoût de mouton," etc. The taste and the talent enhanced each other; until, at last, La Rochefoucauld began to be conscious of his pre-eminence in the circle of maxim-mongers, and thought of a wider audience. Thus grew up the famous "Maxims," about which little need be said. Every at once is now convinced, or professes to be convinced, that, as to form, they are perfect, and that as to matter, they are at once undeniably true and miserably false; true as applied to that condition of human nature in which the selfish instincts are still dominant, false if taken as a representation of all the elements and possibilities of human nature. We think La Rochefoucauld himself wavered as to their universality, and that this wavering is indicated in the qualified form of some of the maxims; it occasionally struck him that the shadow of virtue must have a substance, but he had never grasped that substance—it had never been present to his consciousness.

It is curious to see La Rochefoucauld's nervous anxiety about presenting himself before the public as an author; far from rushing into print, he stole into it, and felt his way by asking private opinions. Through Madame de Sablé he sent manuscript copies to various persons of taste and talent, both men and women, and many of the written opinions which he received in reply are still in existence. The women generally find the maxims distasteful, but the men write approvingly. These men, however, are for the most part ecclesiastics, who decry human nature that they may exalt divine grace. The coincidence between Augustinianism or Calvinism, with its doctrine of human corruption, and the hard cynicism of the maxims, presents itself in quite a piquant form in some of the laudatory opinions on La Rochefoucauld. One writer says: "On ne pourroit faire une instruction plus propre à un catechumène pour convertir à Dieu son esprit et sa volonté . . . Quand il n'y auroit que cet escrit au monde et l'Evangile je voudrois etre chretien. L'un m'apprendroit à connoistre mes misères, et l'autre à implorer mon libérateur." Madame de Maintenon sends word to La Rochefoucauld, after the publication of his work, that the "Book of Job" and the "Maxims" are her only reading.

That Madame de Sablé herself had a tolerably just idea of La Rochefoucauld's character, as well as of his maxims, may be gathered not only from the fact that her own maxims are as full of the confidence in human goodness which La Rochefoucauld wants, as they are empty of the style which he possesses, but also from a letter in which she replies to the criticisms of Madame de Schomberg. "The author," she says, "derived the maxim on indolence from his own disposition, for never was there so great an indolence as his, and I think that his heart, inert as it is, owes this defect as much to his idleness as his will. It has never permitted him to do the least action for others; and I think that, amid all his great desires and great hopes, he is sometimes indolent even on his own behalf." Still she must have felt a hearty interest in the "Maxims," as in some degree her foster-child, and she must also have had considerable affection for the author, who was lovable enough to those who observed the rule of Helvetius, and expected nothing from him. She not only assisted him, as we have seen, in getting criticisms, and carrying out the improvements suggested by them, but when the book was actually published she prepared a notice of it for the only journal then existing—the *Journal des Savants.* This notice was originally a brief statement of the nature of the work, and the opinions which had been formed for and against it, with a moderate eulogy, in conclusion, on its good sense, wit, and insight into human nature. But when she submitted it to La Rochefoucauld he objected to the paragraph which stated the adverse opinion, and requested her to alter it. She, however, was either unable or unwilling to modify her notice, and returned it with the following note:

"Je vous envoie ce que j'ai pu tirer de ma teste pour mettre dans le *Journal des Savants.* J'y ai mis cet endroit qui vous est le plus sensible, afin que cela vous fasse surmonter la mauvaise honte qui vous fit mettre la préface sans y rien retrancher, et je n'ai pas craint dele mettre, parce que je suis assurée que vous ne le ferez pas imprimer, quand même le reste vous plairoit. Je vous assure aussi que je vous serai plus obligée, si vous en usez comme d'une chose qui servit à vous pour le corriger ou pour le jeter au feu. Nous autres grands auteurs, nous sommes trop riches pour craindre de rien perdre de nos productions. Mandez-moi ce qu'il vous semble de ce dictum."

La Rochefoucauld availed himself of this permission, and "edited" the notice, touching up the style, and leaving out the blame. In this revised form it appeared in the *Journal des Savants*. In some points, we see, the youth of journalism was not without promise of its future.

While Madame de Sablé was thus playing the literary confidante to La Rochefoucauld, and was the soul of a society whose chief interest was the *belles-lettres*, she was equally active in graver matters. She was in constant intercourse or correspondence with the devout women of Port Royal, and of the neighboring convent of the Carmelites, many of whom had once been the ornaments of the court; and there is a proof that she was conscious of being highly valued by them in the fact that when the Princess Marie-Madeline, of the Carmelites, was dangerously ill, not being able or not daring to visit her, she sent her youthful portrait to be hung up in the sick-room, and received from the same Mère Agnès, whose grave admonition we have quoted above, a charming note, describing the pleasure which the picture had given in the infirmary of "Notre bonne Mère. She was interesting herself deeply in the translation of the New Testament, which was the work of Sacy, Arnauld, Nicole, Le Maître, and the Duc de Luynes conjointly, Sacy having the principal share. We have mentioned that Arnauld asked her opinion on the "Discourse" prefixed to his "Logic," and we may conclude from this that he had found her judgment valuable in many other cases. Moreover, the persecution of the Port Royalists had commenced, and she was uniting with Madame de Longueville in aiding and protecting her pious friends. Moderate in her Jansenism, as in everything else, she held that the famous formulary denouncing the Augustinian doctrine, and declaring it to have been originated by Jansenius, should be signed without reserve, and, as usual, she had faith in conciliatory measures ; but her moderation was no excuse for inaction. She was at one time herself threatened with the necessity of abandoning her residence at Port Royal, and had thought of retiring to a religious house at Auteuil, a village near Paris. She did, in fact, pass some summers there, and she sometimes took refuge with her brother, the Commandeur de Souvré, with Madame de Montausier, or Madame de Longueville. The last was much bolder in her partisanship than her friend, and her superior wealth and position enabled her to give the Port Royalists more efficient aid. Arnauld and Nicole resided five years in her house ; it was under her protection that the translation of the New Testament was carried on and completed, and it was chiefly through her efforts that, in 1669, the persecution was brought to an end. Madame de Sablé co-operated with all her talent and interest in the same direction ; but here, as elsewhere, her influence was chiefly valuable in what she stimulated others to do, rather than in what she did herself. It was by her that Madame de Longueville was first won to the cause of Port Royal ; and we find this ardent brave woman constantly seeking the advice and sympathy of her more timid and self-indulgent, but sincere and judicious friend.

In 1669, when Madame de Sablé had at length rest from these anxieties, she was at the good old age of seventy, but she lived nine years longer — years, we may suppose, chiefly dedicated to her spiritual concerns. This gradual, calm decay allayed the fear of death, which had tormented her more vigorous days ; and she died with tranquillity and trust. It is a beautiful trait of these last moments that she desired not to be buried with her family, or even at Port Royal, among her saintly and noble companions—but in the cemetery of her parish, like one of the people, without pomp or ceremony.

It is worth while to notice, that with Madame de Sablé, as

with some other remarkable French women, the part of her life which is richest in interest and results is that which is looked forward to by most of her sex with melancholy as the period of decline. When between fifty and sixty, she had philosophers, wits, beauties, and saints clustering around her; and one naturally cares to know what was the elixir which gave her this enduring and general attraction. We think it was, in a great degree, that well-balanced development of mental powers which gave her a comprehension of varied intellectual processes, and a tolerance for varied forms of character, which is still rarer in women than in men. Here was one point of distinction between her and Madame de Longueville; and an amusing passage, which Sainte-Beuve has disinterred from the writings of the Abbé St. Pierre, so well serves to indicate, by contrast, what we regard as the great charm of Madame de Sablé's mind, that we shall not be wandering from our subject in quoting it.

"I one day asked M. Nicole what was the character of Mme. de Longueville's intellect; he told me it was very subtle and delicate in the penetration of character; but very small, very feeble, and that her comprehension was extremely narrow in matters of science and reasoning, and on all speculations that did not concern matters of sentiment. For example, he added, I one day said to her that I could wager and demonstrate that there were in Paris at least two inhabitants who had the same number of hairs, although I could not point out who these two men were. She told me I could never be sure of it until I had counted the hairs of these two men. Here is my demonstration, I said: I take it for granted that the head which is most amply supplied with hairs has not more than 200,000, and the head which is least so has but one hair. Now, if you suppose that 200,000 heads have each a different number of hairs, it necessarily follows that they have each one of the numbers of hairs which form the series from one to 200,000; for if it were supposed that there were two among these 200,000 who had the same number of hairs, I should have gained my wager. Supposing, then, that these 200,000 inhabitants have all a different number of hairs, if I add a single inhabitant who has hairs, and who has not more than 200,000, it necessarily follows that this number of hairs, whatever it may be, will be contained in the series from one to 200,000, and consequently will be equal to the number of hairs on one of the previous 200,000 inhabitants. Now as, instead of one inhabitant more than 200,000, there are nearly 800,000 inhabitants in Paris, you see clearly that there must be many heads which have an equal number of hairs, though I have not counted them. Still Mme. de Longueville could never comprehend that this equality of hairs could be demonstrated, and always maintained that the only way of proving it was to count them."

Surely, the most ardent admirer of feminine shallowness must have felt some irritation when he found himself arrested by this dead wall of stupidity, and have turned with relief to the larger intelligence of Madame de Sablé, who was not the less graceful, delicate, and feminine because she could follow a train of reasoning, or interest herself in a question of science. In this combination consisted her pre-eminent charm : she was not a genius, not a heroine, but a woman whom men could more than love—whom they could make their friend, confidante, and counsellor ; the sharer, not of their joys and sorrows only, but of their ideas and aims.

Such was Madame de Sablé, whose name is, perhaps, new to some of our readers, so far does it lie from the surface of literature and history. We have seen, too, that she was only one among a crowd—one in a firmament of feminine stars which, when once the biographical telescope is turned upon them, appear scarcely less remarkable and interesting. Now, if the reader recollects what was the position and average intellectual character of women in the high society of England during the reigns of James the First and the two Charleses—the period through which Madame de Sablé's career extends—we think he will admit our position as to the early superiority of womanly development in France, and this fact, with its causes, has not merely an historical interest : it has an important bearing on the culture of women in the present day. Women become superior in France by being admitted to a common fund of ideas, to common objects of interest with men ; and this must ever be the essential condition at once of true womanly culture and of true social well-being. We have no faith in feminine conversazioni, where ladies are eloquent on Apollo and Mars; though we sympathize with the yearning activity of faculties which, deprived of their proper material, waste themselves in weaving fabrics out of cobwebs. Let the whole field of reality be laid open to woman as well as to man, and then that which is peculiar in her mental modification, instead of being, as it is now, a source of discord and repulsion between the sexes, will be found to be a necessary complement to the truth and beauty of life. Then we shall have that marriage of minds which alone can blend all the hues of thought and feeling in one lovely rainbow of promise for the harvest of human happiness.

III.

EVANGELICAL TEACHING: DR. CUMMING.*

GIVEN, a man with moderate intellect, a moral standard not higher than the average, some rhetorical affluence and great glibness of speech, what is the career in which, without the aid of birth or money, he may most easily attain power and reputation in English society? Where is that Goshen of mediocrity in which a smattering of science and learning will pass for profound instruction, where platitudes will be accepted as wisdom, bigoted narrowness as holy zeal, unctuous egoism as God-given piety? Let such a man become an evangelical preacher; he will then find it possible to reconcile small ability with great ambition, superficial knowledge with the prestige of erudition, a middling morale with a high reputation for sanctity. Let him shun practical extremes and be ultra only in what is purely theoretic; let him be stringent on predestination, but latitudinarian on fasting; unflinching in insisting on the Eternity of punishment, but diffident of curtailing the substantial comforts

* 1. "The Church before the Flood." By the Rev. John Cumming, D.D. 2. "Occasional Discourses." By the Rev. John Cumming, D.D. In two vols. 3. "Signs of the Times; or, Present, Past, and Future." By the Rev. John Cumming, D.D. 4. "The Finger of God." By the Rev. John Cumming, D.D. 5. "Is Christianity from God? or, a Manual of Christian Evidence, for Scripture-Readers, City Missionaries, Sunday-School Teachers, etc." By the Rev. John Cumming, D.D. 6. Apocalyptic Sketches; or, Lectures on the Book of Revelation." First Series. By the Rev. John Cumming, D.D. 7. "Apocalyptic Sketches." Second Series. By the Rev. John Cumming, D.D. 8 "Prophetic Studies; or, Lectures on the Book of Daniel." By the Rev. John Cumming, D.D.

of Time; ardent and imaginative on the pre-millennial advent of Christ, but cold and cautious toward every other infringement of the *status quo*. Let him fish for souls not with the bait of inconvenient singularity, but with the drag-net of comfortable conformity. Let him be hard and literal in his interpretation only when he wants to hurl texts at the heads of unbelievers and adversaries, but when the letter of the Scriptures presses too closely on the genteel Christianity of the nineteenth century, let him use his spiritualizing alembic and disperse it into impalpable ether. Let him preach less of Christ than of Antichrist; let him be less definite in showing what sin is than in showing who is the Man of Sin, less expansive on the blessedness of faith than on the accursedness of infidelity. Above all, let him set up as an interpreter of prophecy, and rival Moore's Almanack in the prediction of political events, tickling the interest of hearers who are but moderately spiritual by showing how the Holy Spirit has dictated problems and charades for their benefit, and how, if they are ingenious enough to solve these, they may have their Christian graces nourished by learning precisely to whom they may point as the "horn that had eyes," "the lying prophet," and the "unclean spirits." In this way he will draw men to him by the strong cords of their passions, made reason-proof by being baptized with the name of piety. In this way he may gain a metropolitan pulpit; the avenues to his church will be as crowded as the passages to the opera; he has but to print his prophetic sermons and bind them in lilac and gold, and they will adorn the drawing-room table of all evangelical ladies, who will regard as a sort of pious "light reading" the demonstration that the prophecy of the locusts whose sting is in their tail, is fulfilled in the fact of the Turkish commander's having taken a horse's tail for his standard, and that the French are the very frogs predicted in the Revelations.

Pleasant to the clerical flesh under such circumstances is the arrival of Sunday! Somewhat at a disadvantage during the week, in the presence of working-day interests and lay splendors, on Sunday the preacher becomes the cynosure of a thousand eyes, and predominates at once over the Amphitryon with whom he dines, and the most captious member of his church or vestry. He has an immense advantage over all other public speakers. The platform orator is subject to the criticism of hisses and groans. Counsel for the plaintiff expects the retort of counsel for the defendant. The honorable gentleman on one side of the House is liable to have his facts and figures shown up by his honorable friend on the opposite side. Even the scientific or literary lecturer, if he is dull or incompetent, may see the best part of his audience quietly slip out one by one. But the preacher is completely master of the situation: no one may hiss, no one may depart. Like the writer of imaginary conversations, he may put what imbecilities he pleases into the mouths of his antagonists, and swell with triumph when he has refuted them. He may riot in gratuitous assertions, confident that no man will contradict him; he may exercise perfect free-will in logic, and invent illustrative experience; he may give an evangelical edition of history with the inconvenient facts omitted:—all this he may do with impunity, certain that those of his hearers who are not sympathizing are not listening. For the Press has no band of critics who go the round of the churches and chapels, and are on the watch for a slip or defect in the preacher, to make a "feature" in their article: the clergy are, practically, the most irresponsible of all talkers. For this reason, at least, it is well that they do not always allow their discourses to be merely fugitive, but are often induced to fix them in that black and white in which they are open to the criticism of any man who has the courage and patience to treat them with thorough freedom of speech and pen.

It is because we think this criticism of clerical teaching desirable for the public good that we devote some pages to Dr. Cumming. He is, as every one knows, a preacher of immense popularity, and of the numerous publications in which he perpetuates his pulpit labors, all circulate widely, and some, according to their title-page, have reached the sixteenth thousand. Now our opinion of these publications is the very opposite of that given by a newspaper eulogist : we do *not* "believe that the repeated issues of Dr. Cumming's thoughts are having a beneficial effect on society," but the reverse ; and hence, little inclined as we are to dwell on his pages, we think it worth while to do so, for the sake of pointing out in them what we believe to be profoundly mistaken and pernicious. Of Dr. Cumming personally we know absolutely nothing : our acquaintance with him is confined to a perusal of his works, our judgment of him is founded solely on the manner in which he has written himself down on his pages. We know neither how he looks nor how he lives. We are ignorant whether, like St. Paul, he has a bodily presence that is weak and contemptible, or whether his person is as florid and as prone to amplification as his style. For aught we know, he may not only have the gift of prophecy, but may bestow the profits of all his works to feed the poor, and be ready to give his own body to be burned with as much alacrity as he infers the everlasting burning of Roman Catholics and Puseyites. Out of the pulpit he may be a model of justice, truthfulness, and the love that thinketh no evil ; but we are obliged to judge of his charity by the spirit we find in his sermons, and shall only be glad to learn that his practice is, in many respects, an amiable *non sequitur* from his teaching.

Dr. Cumming's mind is evidently not of the pietistic order. There is not the slightest leaning toward mysticism in his Christianity—no indication of religious raptures, of delight in God, of spiritual communion with the Father. He is most at home in the forensic view of Justification, and dwells on salvation as a scheme rather than as an experience. He insists on good works as the sign of justifying faith, as labors to be achieved to the glory of God, but he rarely represents them as the spontaneous, necessary outflow of a soul filled with Divine love. He is at home in the external, the polemical, the historical, the circumstantial, and is only episodically devout and practical. The great majority of his published sermons are occupied with argument or philippic against Romanists and unbelievers, with "vindications" of the Bible, with the political interpretation of prophecy, or the criticism of public events; and the devout aspiration, or the spiritual and practical exhortation, is tacked to them as a sort of fringe in a hurried sentence or two at the end. He revels in the demonstration that the Pope is the Man of Sin; he is copious on the downfall of the Ottoman empire; he appears to glow with satisfaction in turning a story which tends to show how he abashed an "infidel;" it is a favorite exercise with him to form conjectures of the process by which the earth is to be burned up, and to picture Dr. Chalmers and Mr. Wilberforce being caught up to meet Christ in the air, while Romanists, Puseyites, and infidels are given over to gnashing of teeth. But of really spiritual joys and sorrows, of the life and death of Christ as a manifestation of love that constrains the soul, of sympathy with that yearning over the lost and erring which made Jesus weep over Jerusalem, and prompted the sublime prayer, "Father, forgive them," of the gentler fruits of the Spirit, and the peace of God which passeth understanding —of all this, we find little trace in Dr. Cumming's discourses.

His style is in perfect correspondence with this habit of mind. Though diffuse, as that of all preachers must be, it has rapidity of movement, perfect clearness, and some aptness of illustration. He has much of that literary talent which makes a good journalist—the power of beating out an idea over a large space, and of introducing far-fetched *à propos*. His writings have, indeed, no high merit: they have no originality or force of thought, no striking felicity of presentation, no depth of emotion. Throughout nine volumes we have alighted on no passage which impressed us as worth extracting, and placing among the "beauties" of evangelical writers, such as Robert Hall, Foster the Essayist, or Isaac Taylor. Everywhere there is commonplace cleverness, nowhere a spark of rare thought, of lofty sentiment, or pathetic tenderness. We feel ourselves in company with a voluble retail talker, whose language is exuberant but not exact, and to whom we should never think of referring for precise information or for well-digested thought and experience. His argument continually slides into wholesale assertion and vague declamation, and in his love of ornament he frequently becomes tawdry. For example, he tells us ("Apoc. Sketches," p. 265) that "Botany weaves around the cross her amaranthine garlands; and Newton comes from his starry home—Linnæus from his flowery resting-place—and Werner and Hutton from their subterranean graves at the voice of Chalmers, to acknowledge that all they learned and elicited in their respective provinces has only served to show more clearly that Jesus of Nazareth is enthroned on the riches of the universe:"—and so prosaic an injunction to his hearers as that they should choose a residence within an easy distance of church, is magnificently draped by him as an exhortation to prefer a house "that basks in the sunshine of the countenance of God." Like all preachers of his class, he is more fertile in imaginative paraphrase than in close exposition, and in this way he gives us some remarkable fragments of what we may call the romance of Scripture, filling up the outline of the record with an elaborate coloring quite undreamed of by more literal minds. The serpent, he informs us, said to Eve, "Can it be so? Surely you are mistaken, that God hath said you shall die, a creature so fair, so lovely, so beautiful. It is impossible. *The laws of nature and physical science tell you that my interpretation is correct;* you shall not die. I can tell you by my own experience as an angel that you shall be as gods, knowing good and evil." ("Apoc. Sketches," p. 294.) Again, according to Dr. Cumming, Abel had so clear an idea of the Incarnation and Atonement, that when he offered his sacrifice "he must have said, 'I feel myself a guilty sinner, and that in myself I cannot meet thee alive; I lay on thine altar this victim, and I shed its blood as my testimony that mine should be shed; and I look for forgiveness and undeserved mercy through him who is to bruise the serpent's head, and whose atonement this typifies.' " ("Occas. Disc." vol. i. p. 23.) Indeed, his productions are essentially ephemeral; he is essentially a journalist, who writes sermons instead of leading articles, who, instead of venting diatribes against her Majesty's Ministers, directs his power of invective against Cardinal Wiseman and the Puseyites; instead of declaiming on public spirit, perorates on the "glory of God." We fancy he is called, in the more refined evangelical circles, an "intellectual preacher;" by the plainer sort of Christians, a "flowery preacher;" and we are inclined to think that the more spiritually minded class of believers, who look with greater anxiety for the kingdom of God within them than for the visible advent of Christ in 1864, will be likely to find Dr. Cumming's declamatory flights and historico-prophetical exercitations as little better than "clouts o' cauld parritch."

Such is our general impression from his writings after an attentive perusal. There are some particular characteristics which we shall consider more closely, but in doing so we must be understood as altogether declining any doctrinal discussion. We have no intention to consider the grounds of Dr. Cumming's dogmatic system, to examine the principles of his prophetic exegesis, or to question his opinion concerning the little horn, the river Euphrates, or the seven vials. We identify ourselves with no one of the bodies whom he regards it as his special mission to attack: we give our adhesion neither to Romanism, Puseyism, nor to that anomalous combination of opinions which he introduces to us under the name of infidelity. It is simply as spectators that we criticise Dr. Cumming's mode of warfare, and we concern ourselves less with what he holds to be Christian truth than with his manner of enforcing that truth, less with the doctrines he teaches than with the moral spirit and tendencies of his teaching.

One of the most striking characteristics of Dr. Cumming's writings is *unscrupulosity of statement*. His motto apparently is, *Christiahitatem, quocunque modo, Christianitatem;* and the only system he includes under the term Christianity is Calvinistic Protestantism. Experience has so long shown that the human brain is a congenial nidus for inconsistent beliefs that we do not pause to inquire how Dr. Cumming, who attributes the conversion of the unbelieving to the Divine Spirit, can think it necessary to co-operate with that Spirit by argumentative white lies. Nor do we for a moment impugn the genuineness of his zeal for Christianity, or the sincerity of his conviction that the doctrines he preaches are necessary to salvation; on the contrary, we regard the flagrant unveracity that we find on his pages as an indirect result of that conviction—as a result, namely, of the intellectual and moral distortion of view which is inevitably produced by assigning to dogmas, based on a very complex structure of evidence, the place and authority of first truths. A distinct appreciation of the value of evidence—in other words, the intellectual perception of truth—is more closely allied to truthfulness of statement, or the moral quality of veracity, than is generally admitted. There is not a more pernicious fallacy afloat, in common parlance, than the wide distinction made between intellect and morality. Amiable impulses without intellect, man may have in common with dogs and horses; but morality, which is specifically human, is dependent on the regulation of feeling by intellect. All human beings who can be said to be in any degree moral have their impulses guided, not indeed always by their own intellect, but by the intellect of human beings who have gone before them, and created traditions and associations which have taken the rank of laws. Now that highest moral habit, the constant preference of truth, both theoretically and practically, pre-eminently demands the co-operation of the intellect with the impulses, as is indicated by the fact that it is only found in anything like completeness in the highest class of minds. In accordance with this we think it is found that, in proportion as religious sects exalt feeling above intellect, and believe themselves to be guided by direct inspiration rather than by a spontaneous exertion of their faculties—that is, in proportion as they are removed from rationalism—their sense of truthfulness is misty and confused. No one can have talked to the more enthusiastic Methodists and listened to their stories of miracles without perceiving that they require no other passport to a statement than that it accords with their wishes and their general conception of God's dealings; nay, they regard as a symptom of sinful scepticism an inquiry into the evidence for a story which they think unquestionably tends to the glory of God, and in retailing such stories, new particulars, further tending to his glory, are "borne in" upon their minds. Now, Dr. Cumming, as we have said, is no enthusiastic pietist: within a certain circle—within the mill of evangelical orthodoxy—his intellect is perpetually at work; but that principle of sophistication which our friends the Methodists derive from the predominance of their pietistic feelings, is involved for him in the doctrine of verbal inspiration; what is for them a state of emotion submerging the intellect, is with him a formula imprisoning the intellect, depriving it of its proper function—the free search for truth—and making it the mere servant-of-all-work to a foregone conclusion. Minds fettered by this doctrine no longer inquire concerning a proposition whether it is attested by sufficient evidence, but whether it accords with Scripture; they do not search for facts, as such, but for facts that will bear out their doctrine. They become accustomed to reject the more direct evidence in favor of the less direct, and where adverse evidence reaches demonstration they must resort to devices and expedients in order to explain away contradiction. It is easy to see that this mental habit blunts not only the perception of truth, but the sense of truthfulness, and that the man whose faith drives him into fallacies treads close upon the precipice of falsehood.

We have entered into this digression for the sake of mitigating the inference that is likely to be drawn from that characteristic of Dr. Cumming's works to which we have pointed. He is much in the same intellectual condition as that professor of Padua, who, in order to disprove Galileo's discovery of

Jupiter's satellites, urged that as there were only seven metals there could not be more than seven planets—a mental condition scarcely compatible with candor. And we may well suppose that if the professor had held the belief in seven planets, and no more, to be a necessary condition of salvation, his mental condition would have been so dazed that even if he had consented to look through Galileo's telescope, his eyes would have reported in accordance with his inward alarms rather than with the external fact. So long as a belief in propositions is regarded as indispensable to salvation, the pursuit of truth *as such* is not possible, any more than it is possible for a man who is swimming for his life to make meteorological observations on the storm which threatens to overwhelm him. The sense of alarm and haste, the anxiety for personal safety, which Dr. Cumming insists upon as the proper religious attitude, unmans the nature, and allows no thorough, calm thinking no truly noble, disinterested feeling. Hence, we by no means suspect that the unscrupulosity of statement with which we charge Dr. Cumming, extends beyond the sphere of his theological prejudices; we do not doubt that, religion apart, he appreciates and practices veracity.

A grave general accusation must be supported by details, and in adducing those we purposely select the most obvious cases of misrepresentation—such as require no argument to expose them, but can be perceived at a glance. Among Dr. Cumming's numerous books, one of the most notable for unscrupulosity of statement is the "Manual of Christian Evidences," written, as he tells us in his Preface, not to give the deepest solutions of the difficulties in question, but to furnish Scripture Readers, City Missionaries, and Sunday School Teachers, with a "ready reply" to sceptical arguments. This announcement that *readiness* was the chief quality sought for in the solutions here given, modifies our inference from the other qualities which those solutions present; and it is but fair to presume that when the Christian disputant is not in a hurry Dr. Cumming would recommend replies less ready and more veracious. Here is an example of what in another place* he tells his readers is "change in their pocket . . . a little ready argument which they can employ, and therewith answer a fool according to his folly." From the nature of this argumentative small coin, we are inclined to think Dr. Cumming understands answering a fool according to his folly to mean, giving him a foolish answer. We quote from the "Manual of Christian Evidences," p. 62.

"Some of the gods which the heathen worshipped were among the greatest monsters that ever walked the earth. Mercury was a thief; and because he was an expert thief he was enrolled among the gods. Bacchus was a mere sensualist and drunkard, and therefore he was enrolled among the gods. Venus was a dissipated and abandoned courtesan, and therefore she was enrolled among the goddesses. Mars was a savage, that gloried in battle and in blood, and therefore he was deified and enrolled among the gods."

Does Dr. Cumming believe the purport of these sentences? If so, this passage is worth handing down as his theory of the Greek myth—as a specimen of the astounding ignorance which was possible in a metropolitan preacher, A.D. 1854. And if he does not believe them . . . The inference must then be, that he thinks delicate veracity about the ancient Greeks is not a Christian virtue, but only a "splendid sin" of the unregenerate. This inference is rendered the more probable by our finding, a little further on, that he is not more scrupulous about the moderns, if they come under his definition of "Infidels." But the passage we are about to quote in proof of this has a worse quality than its discrepancy with fact. Who that has a spark of generous feeling, that rejoices in the presence of good in a fellow-being, has not dwelt with pleasure on the thought that Lord Byron's unhappy career was ennobled and purified toward its close by a high and sympathetic purpose, by honest and energetic efforts for his fellow-men? Who has not read with deep emotion those last pathetic lines, beau-

* "Lect. on Daniel," p. 6.

tiful as the after-glow of sunset, in which love and resignation are mingled with something of a melancholy heroism? Who has not lingered with compassion over the dying scene at Missolonghi—the sufferer's inability to make his farewell messages of love intelligible, and the last long hours of silent pain? Yet for the sake of furnishing his disciples with a "ready reply," Dr. Cumming can prevail on himself to inoculate them with a bad-spirited falsity like the following:

"We have one striking exhibition of *an infidel's brightest thoughts*, in some lines *written in his dying moments* by a man, gifted with great genius, capable of prodigious intellectual prowess, but of worthless principle, and yet more worthless practices—I mean the celebrated Lord Byron. He says:

"'Though gay companions o'er the bowl
Dispel awhile the sense of ill,
Though pleasure fills the maddening soul,
The heart—*the heart* is lonely still.

"'Ay, but to die, and go, alas!
Where all have gone and all must go;
To be the *Nothing* that I was,
Ere born to life and living woe!

"'Count o'er the joys thine hours have seen,
Count o'er thy days from anguish free,
And know, whatever thou hast been,
'Tis *something better* not to be.

"'Nay, for myself, so dark my fate
Through every turn of life hath been,
Man and the *world* so much *I hate*,
I care not when I quit the scene.'"

It is difficult to suppose that Dr. Cumming can have been so grossly imposed upon—that he can be so ill-informed as really to believe that these lines were "written" by Lord Byron in his dying moments; but, allowing him the full benefit of that possibility, how shall we explain his introduction of this feebly rabid doggrel as "an infidel's brightest thoughts?"

In marshalling the evidences of Christianity, Dr. Cumming directs most of his arguments against opinions that are either totally imaginary, or that belong to the past rather than to the present, while he entirely fails to meet the difficulties actually felt and urged by those who are unable to accept Revelation. There can hardly be a stronger proof of misconception as to the character of free-thinking in the present day, than the recommendation of Leland's "Short and Easy Method with the Deists"—a method which is unquestionably short and easy for preachers disinclined to reconsider their stereotyped modes of thinking and arguing, but which has quite ceased to realize those epithets in the conversion of Deists. Yet Dr. Cumming not only recommends this book, but takes the trouble himself to write a feebler version of its arguments. For example, on the question of the genuineness and authenticity of the New Testament writing's, he says: "If, therefore, at a period long subsequent to the death of Christ, a number of men had appeared in the world, drawn up a book which they christened by the name of the Holy Scripture, and recorded these things which appear in it as facts when they were only the fancies of their own imagination, surely the *Jews* would have instantly reclaimed that no such events transpired, that no such person as Jesus Christ appeared in their capital, and that *their* crucifixion of Him, and their alleged evil treatment of his apostles, were mere fictions."* It is scarcely necessary to say that, in such argument as this, Dr. Cumming is beating the air. He is meeting a hypothesis which no one holds, and totally missing the real question. The only type of "infidel" whose existence Dr. Cumming recognizes is that fossil personage who "calls the Bible a lie and a forgery." He seems to be ignorant—or he chooses to ignore the fact—that there is a large body of eminently instructed and earnest men who regard the Hebrew and Christian Scriptures as a series of historical documents, to be dealt with according to the rules of historical criticism, and that an equally large number of men, who are not historical critics, find

* "Man of Ev." p. 81.

the dogmatic scheme built on the letter of the Scriptures opposed to their profoundest moral convictions. Dr. Cumming's infidel is a man who, because his life is vicious, tries to convince himself that there is no God, and that Christianity is an imposture, but who is all the while secretly conscious that he is opposing the truth, and cannot help "letting out" admissions "that the Bible is the Book of God." We are favored with the following "Creed of the Infidel:"

"I believe that there is no God, but that matter is God, and God is matter; and that it is no matter whether there is any God or not. I believe also that the world was not made, but that the world made itself, or that it had no beginning, and that it will last forever. I believe that man is a beast; that the soul is the body, and that the body is the soul; and that after death there is neither body nor soul. I believe there is no religion, that *natural religion is the only religion, and all religion unnatural.* I believe not in Moses; I believe in the first philosophers. I believe not in the evangelists; I believe in Chubb, Collins, Toland, Tindal, and Hobbes. I believe in Lord Bolingbroke, and I believe not in St. Paul. I believe not in revelation; *I believe in tradition; I believe in the Talmud; I believe in the Koran;* I believe not in the Bible. I believe in Socrates; I believe in Confucius; I believe in Mahomet; I believe not in Christ. And lastly, *I believe* in all unbelief."

The intellectual and moral monster whose creed is this complex web of contradictions, is, moreover, according to Dr. Cumming, a being who unites much simplicity and imbecility with his Satanic hardihood—much tenderness of conscience with his obdurate vice. Hear the "proof:"

"I once met with an acute and enlightened infidel, with whom I reasoned day after day, and for hours together; I submitted to him the internal, the external, and the experimental evidences, but made no impression on his scorn and unbelief. At length I entertained a suspicion that there was something morally, rather than intellectually wrong, and that the bias was not in the intellect, but in the heart; one day therefore I said to him, 'I must now state my conviction, and you may call me uncharitable, but duty compels me; you are living in some known and gross sin.' *The man's countenance became pale; he bowed and left me.*"—"Man. of Evidences," p. 254.

Here we have the remarkable psychological phenomenon of an "acute and enlightened" man who, deliberately purposing to indulge in a favorite sin, and regarding the Gospel with scorn and unbelief, is, nevertheless, so much more scrupulous than the majority of Christians, that he cannot "embrace sin and the Gospel simultaneously;" who is so alarmed at the Gospel in which he does not believe, that he cannot be easy without trying to crush it; whose acuteness and enlightenment suggest to him, as a means of crushing the Gospel, to argue from day to day with Dr. Cumming; and who is withal so naïve that he is taken by surprise when Dr. Cumming, failing in argument, resorts to accusation, and so tender in conscience that, at the mention of his sin, he turns pale and leaves the spot. If there be any human mind in existence capable of holding Dr. Cumming's "Creed of the Infidel," of at the same time believing in tradition and "believing in all unbelief," it must be the mind of the infidel just described, for whose existence we have Dr. Cumming's *ex officio* word as a theologian; and to theologians we may apply what Sancho Panza says of the bachelors of Salamanca, that they never tell lies—except when it suits their purpose.

The total absence from Dr. Cumming's theological mind of any demarcation between fact and rhetoric is exhibited in another passage, where he adopts the dramatic form:

"Ask the peasant on the hills—*and I have asked amid the mountains of Braemar and Deeside*—"How do you know that this book is divine, and that the religion you profess is true? You never read Paley?' 'No, I never heard of him.'—'You have never read Butler?' 'No, I have never heard of him.'—'Nor Chalmers?' 'No, I do not know him.'—'You have never read any books on evidence?' 'No, I have read no such books.'—'Then, how do you know this book is true?' 'Know it! Tell me that the Dee, the Clunie, and the Garrawalt, the streams at my feet, do not run; that the winds do not sigh amid the gorges of these blue hills; that the sun does not kindle the peaks of Loch-na-Gar; tell me my heart does not beat, and I will believe you; but do not tell me the Bible is not divine. I have found its truth illuminating my footsteps; its consolations sustaining my heart. May my tongue cleave to my mouth's roof, and my right hand forget its cunning, if I every deny what is my deepest inner experience, that this blessed book is the book of God.' "—" Church Before the Flood," p. 35.

Dr. Cumming is so slippery and lax in his mode of presentation that we find it impossible to gather whether he means to assert that this is what a peasant on the mountains of Braemar *did* say, or that it is what such a peasant *would* say : in the one case, the passage may be taken as a measure of his truthfulness ; in the other, of his judgment.

His own faith, apparently, has not been altogether intuitive, like that of his rhetorical peasant, for he tells us (" Apoc. Sketches," p. 405) that he has himself experienced what it is to have religious doubts. " I was tainted while at the University by this spirit of scepticism. I thought Christianity might not be true. The very possibility of its being true was the thought I felt I must meet and settle. Conscience could give me no peace till I had settled it. I read, and I read from that day, for fourteen or fifteen years, till this, and now I am as convinced, upon the clearest evidence, that this book is the book of God as that I now address you." This experience, however, instead of impressing on him the fact that doubt may be the stamp of a truth-loving mind—that *sunt quibus non credidisse honor est, et fidei futuræ pignus*—seems to have produced precisely the contrary effect. It has not enabled him even to conceive the condition of a mind " perplext in faith but pure in deeds," craving light, yearning for a faith that will harmonize and cherish its highest powers and aspirations, but unable to find that faith in dogmatic Christianity. His own doubts apparently were of a different kind. Nowhere in his pages have we found a humble, candid, sympathetic attempt to meet the difficulties that may be felt by an ingenuous mind. Everywhere he supposes that the doubter is hardened, conceited, consciously shutting his eyes to the light —a fool who is to be answered according to his folly—that is, with ready replies made up of reckless assertions, of apocryphal anecdotes, and, where other resources fail, of vituperative imputation. As to the reading which he has prosecuted for fifteen years—*either* it has left him totally ignorant of the relation which his own religious creed bears to the criticism and philosophy of the nineteenth century, *or* he systematically blinks that criticism and that philosophy; and instead of honestly and seriously endeavoring to meet and solve what he knows to be the real difficulties, contents himself with setting up popinjays to shoot at, for the sake of confirming the ignorance and winning the heap admiration of his evangelical hearers and readers. Like the Catholic preacher who, after throwing down his cap and apostrophizing it as Luther, turned to his audience and said, "You see this heretical fellow has not a word to say for himself," Dr. Cumming, having drawn his ugly portrait of the infidel, and put arguments of a convenient quality into his mouth, finds a "short and easy method" of confounding this "croaking frog."

In his treatment of infidels, we imagine he is guided by a mental process which may be expressed in the following syllogism: Whatever tends to the glory of God is true; it is for the glory of God that infidels should be as bad as possible; therefore, whatever tends to show that infidels are as bad as possible is true. All infidels, he tells us, have been men of "gross and licentious lives." Is there not some well-known unbeliever, David Hume, for example, of whom even Dr. Cumming's readers may have heard as an exception? No matter. Some one suspected that he was *not* an exception, and as that suspicion tends to the glory of God, it is one for a Christian to entertain. (See "Man. of Ev.," p. 73.)—If we were unable to imagine this kind of self-sophistication, we should be obliged to suppose that, relying on the ignorance of his evangelical disciples, he fed them with direct and conscious falsehoods. "Voltaire," he informs them, "declares there is no God;" he was "an antitheist, that is one who deliberately and avowedly opposed and hated God; who swore in his blasphemy that he would dethrone him;" and "advocated the very depths of the lowest sensuality." With regard to many statements of a similar kind, equally at variance with truth, in Dr. Cumming's volumes, we presume that he has been misled by hearsay or by the second-hand character of his acquaintance with free-thinking literature. An evangelical preacher is not obliged to be well-read. Here, however, is a case which the extremest supposition of educated ignorance will not reach. Even books of "evidences" quote from Voltaire the line—

"Si Dieu n'existait pas, il faudrait l'inventer;"

even persons fed on the mere whey and buttermilk of literature must know that in philosophy Voltaire was nothing if not a theist—must know that he wrote not against God, but against Jehovah, the God of the Jews, whom he believed to be a false God—must know that to say Voltaire was an atheist on this ground is as absurd as to say that a Jacobite opposed hereditary monarchy because he declared the Brunswick family had no title to the throne. That Dr. Cumming should repeat the vulgar fables about Voltaire's death is merely what we might expect from the specimens we have seen of his illustrative stories. A man whose accounts of his own experience are apocryphal is not likely to put borrowed narratives to any severe test.

The alliance between intellectual and moral perversion is strikingly typified by the way in which he alternates from the unveracious to the absurd, from misrepresentation to contradiction. Side by side with the abduction of "facts" such as those we have quoted, we find him arguing on one page that the Trinity was too grand a doctrine to have been conceived by man, and was *therefore* Divine; and on another page, that the Incarnation *had* been preconceived by man, and is *therefore* to be accepted as Divine. But we are less concerned with the fallacy of his "ready replies" than with their falsity; and even of this we can only afford space for a very few specimens. Here is one: "There is a *thousand times* more proof that the gospel of John was written by him than there is that the Αναβασις was written by Xenophon, or the Ars Poetica by Horace." If Dr. Cumming had chosen Plato's Epistles or Anacreon's Poems instead of the Anabasis or the Ars Poetica, he would have reduced the extent of the falsehood, and would have furnished a ready reply which would have been equally effective with his Sunday-school teachers and their disputants. Hence we conclude this prodigality of misstatement, this exuberance of mendacity, is an effervescence of zeal *in majorem gloriam Dei.* Elsewhere he tells us that "the idea of the author of the 'Vestiges' is, that man is the development of a monkey, that the monkey is the embryo man, so that *if you keep a baboon long enough, it will develop itself into a man.*" How well Dr. Cumming has qualified himself to judge of the ideas in "that very unphilosophical book," as he pronounces it, may be inferred from the fact that he implies the author of the "Vestiges" to have *originated* the nebular hypothesis.

In the volume from which the last extract is taken, even the hardihood of assertion is surpassed by the suicidal character of the argument. It is called "The Church before the Flood," and is devoted chiefly to the adjustment of the question between the Bible and Geology. Keeping within the limits we have prescribed to ourselves, we do not enter into the matter of this discussion; we merely pause a little over the volume in order to point out Dr. Cumming's mode of treating the question. He first tells us that "the Bible has not a single scientific error in it;" that "*its slightest intimations of scientific principles or natural phenomena have in every instance been demonstrated to be exactly and strictly true,*" and he asks:

"How is it that Moses, with no greater education than the Hindoo or the ancient philosopher, has written his book, touching science at a thousand points, so accurately that scientific research has discovered no flaws in it; and yet in those investigations which have taken place in more recent centuries, it has not been shown that he has committed one single error, or made one solitary assertion which can be proved by the maturest science, or by the most eagle-eyed philosopher, to be incorrect, scientifically or historically?"

According to this the relation of the Bible to science should be one of the strong points of apologists for revelation : the scientific accuracy of Moses should stand at the head of their evidences ; and they might urge with some cogency, that since Aristotle, who devoted himself to science, and lived many ages after Moses, does little else than err ingeniously, this fact, that the Jewish Lawgiver, though touching science at a thousand points, has written nothing that has not been "demonstrated to be exactly and strictly true," is an irrefragable proof of his having derived his knowledge from a supernatural source. How does it happen, then, that Dr. Cumming forsakes this strong position? How is it that we find him, some pages further on, engaged in reconciling Genesis with the discoveries of science, by means of imaginative hypotheses and feats of "interpretation?" Surely, that which has been demonstrated to be exactly and strictly true does not require hypothesis and critical argument, in order to show that it may *possibly* agree with those very discoveries by means of which its exact and strict truth has been demonstrated. And why should Dr. Cumming suppose, as we shall presently find him supposing, that men of science hesitate to accept the Bible, because it appears to contradict their discoveries? By his own statement, that appearance of contradiction does not exist ; on the contrary, it has been demonstrated that the Bible precisely agrees with their discoveries. Perhaps, however, in saying of the Bible that its "slightest intimations of scientific principles or natural phenomena have in every instance been demonstrated to be exactly and strictly true," Dr. Cumming merely means to imply that theologians have found out a way of explaining the biblical text so that it no longer, in their opinion, appears to be in contradiction with the discoveries of science. One of two things, therefore : either he uses language without the slightest appreciation of its real meaning, or the assertions he makes on one page are directly contradicted by the arguments he urges on another.

Dr. Cumming's principles—or, we should rather say, confused notions—of biblical interpretation, as exhibited in this volume, are particularly significant of his mental calibre. He says ("Church before the Flood," p. 93): "Men of science, who are full of scientific investigation and enamored of scientific discovery, will hesitate before they accept a book which, they think, contradicts the plainest and the most unequivocal disclosures they have made in the bowels of the earth, or among the stars of the sky. To all these we answer, as we have already indicated, there is not the least dissonance between God's written book and the most mature discoveries of geological science. One thing, however, there may be: *there may be a contradiction between the discoveries of geology and our preconceived interpretations of the Bible.* But this is not because the Bible is wrong, but because our interpretation is wrong." (The italics in all cases are our own.)

Elsewhere he says: "It seems to me plainly evident that the record of Genesis, when read fairly, and not in the light of our prejudices—*and mind you, the essence of Popery is to read the Bible in the light of our opinions, instead of viewing our opinions in the light of the Bible, in its plain and obvious sense*—falls in perfectly with the assertion of geologists."

On comparing these two passages, we gather that when Dr. Cumming, under stress of geological discovery, assigns to the biblical text a meaning entirely different from that which, on his own showing, was universally ascribed to it for more than three thousand years, he regards himself as "viewing his opinions in the light of the Bible in its plain and obvious sense!" Now he is reduced to one of two alternatives: either he must hold that the "plain and obvious meaning" of the whole Bible differs from age to age, so that the criterion of its meaning lies in the sum of knowledge possessed by each successive age—the Bible being an elastic garment for the growing thought of mankind; or he must hold that some portions are amenable to this criterion, and others not so. In the former case, he accepts the principle of interpretation adopted by the early German rationalists; in the latter case he has to show a further criterion by which we can judge what parts of the Bible are elastic and what rigid. If he says that the interpretation of the text is rigid wherever it treats of doctrines necessary to salvation, we answer, that for doctrines to be necessary to salvation they must first be true; and in order to be true, according to his own principle, they must be founded on a correct interpretation of the biblical text. Thus he makes the necessity of doctrines to salvation the criterion of infallible interpretation, and infallible interpretation the criterion of doctrines being necessary to salvation. He is whirled round in a circle, having, by admitting the principle of novelty in interpretation, completely deprived himself of a basis. That he should seize the very moment in which he is most palpably betraying that he has no test of biblical truth beyond his own opinion, as an appropriate occasion for flinging the rather novel reproach against Popery that its essence is to "read the Bible in the light of our opinions," would be an almost pathetic self-exposure, if it were not disgusting. Imbecility that is not even meek, ceases to be pitiable, and becomes simply odious.

Parenthetic lashes of this kind against Popery are very frequent with Dr. Cumming, and occur even in his more devout passages, where their introduction must surely disturb the spiritual exercises of his hearers. Indeed, Roman Catholics fare worse with him even than infidels. Infidels are the small vermin—the mice to be bagged *en passant*. The main object of his chase—the rats which are to be nailed up as trophies—are the Roman Catholics. Romanism is the masterpiece of Satan; but reassure yourselves! Dr. Cumming has been created. Antichrist is enthroned in the Vatican; but he is stoutly withstood by the Boanerges of Crown-court. The personality of Satan, as might be expected, is a very prominent tenet in Dr. Cumming's discourses; those who doubt it are, he thinks, "generally specimens of the victims of Satan as a triumphant seducer;" and it is through the medium of this doctrine that he habitually contemplates Roman Catholics.

They are the puppets of which the devil holds the strings. It is only exceptionally that he speaks of them as fellow-men, acted on by the same desires, fears, and hopes as himself; his *rule* is to hold them up to his hearers as foredoomed instruments of Satan and vessels of wrath. If he is obliged to admit that they are "no shams," that they are "thoroughly in earnest"—that is because they are inspired by hell, because they are under an "infra-natural" influence. If their missionaries are found wherever Protestant missionaries go, this zeal in propagating their faith is not in them a consistent virtue, as it is in Protestants, but a "melancholy fact," affording additional evidence that they are instigated and assisted by the devil. And Dr. Cumming is inclined to think that they work miracles, because that is no more than might be expected from the known ability of Satan who inspires them.* He admits, indeed, that "there is a fragment of the Church of Christ in the very bosom of that awful apostasy,"† and that there are members of the Church of Rome in glory; but this admission is rare and episodical—is a declaration, *pro formâ*, about as influential on the general disposition and habits as an aristocrat's profession of democracy.

This leads us to mention another conspicuous characteristic of Dr. Cumming's teaching—the *absence of genuine charity*. It is true that he makes large profession of tolerance and liberality within a certain circle; he exhorts Christians to unity; he would have Churchmen fraternize with Dissenters, and exhorts these two branches of God's family to defer the settlement of their differences till the millennium. But the love thus taught is the love of the *clan*, which is the correlative of antagonism to the rest of mankind. It is not sympathy and helpfulness toward men as men, but toward men as Christians, and as Christians in the sense of a small minority. Dr. Cumming's religion may demand a tribute of love, but it gives a charter to hatred; it may enjoin charity, but it fosters

* "Signs of the Times," p. 38.
† "Apoc. Sketches," p. 243.

all uncharitableness. If I believe that God tells me to love my enemies, but at the same time hates His own enemies and requires me to have one will with Him, which has the larger scope, love or hatred? And we refer to those pages of Dr. Cumming's in which he opposes Roman Catholics, Puseyites, and infidels—pages which form the larger proportion of what he has published—for proof that the idea of God which both the logic and spirit of his discourses keep present to his hearers, is that of a God who hates his enemies, a God who teaches love by fierce denunciations of wrath—a God who encourages obedience to his precepts by elaborately revealing to us that his own government is in precise opposition to those precepts. We know the usual evasions on this subject. We know Dr. Cumming would say that even Roman Catholics are to be loved and succored as men; that he would help even that "unclean spirit," Cardinal Wiseman, out of a ditch. But who that is in the slightest degree acquainted with the action of the human mind will believe that any genuine and large charity can grow out of an exercise of love which is always to have an *arrière-pensée* of hatred? Of what quality would be the conjugal love of a husband who loved his spouse as a wife, but hated her as a woman? It is reserved for the regenerate mind, according to Dr. Cumming's conception of it, to be "wise, amazed, temperate and furious, loyal and neutral, in a moment." Precepts of charity uttered with a faint breath at the end of a sermon are perfectly futile, when all the force of the lungs has been spent in keeping the hearer's mind fixed on the conception of his fellow-men not as fellow-sinners and fellow-sufferers, but as agents of hell, as automata through whom Satan plays his game upon earth—not on objects which call forth their reverence, their love, their hope of good even in the most strayed and perverted, but on a minute identification of human things with such symbols as the scarlet whore, the beast out of the abyss, scorpions whose sting is in their tails, men who have the mark of the beast, and unclean spirits like frogs. You might as well attempt to educate the child's sense of beauty by hanging its nursery with the horrible and grotesque pictures in which the early painters represented the Last Judgment, as expect Christian graces to flourish on that prophetic interpretation which Dr. Cumming offers as the principal nutriment of his flock. Quite apart from the critical basis of that interpretation, quite apart from the degree of truth there may be in Dr. Cumming's prognostications—questions into which we do not choose to enter—his use of prophecy must be *à priori* condemned in the judgment of right-minded persons, by its results as testified in the net moral effect of his sermons. The best minds that accept Christianity as a divinely inspired system, believe that the great end of the Gospel is not merely the saving but the educating of men's souls, the creating within them of holy dispositions, the subduing of egoistical pretensions, and the perpetual enhancing of the desire that the will of God—a will synonymous with goodness and truth—may be done on earth. But what relation to all this has a system of interpretation which keeps the mind of the Christian in the position of a spectator at a gladiatorial show, of which Satan is the wild beast in the shape of the great red dragon, and two thirds of mankind the victims—the whole provided and got up by God for the edification of the saints? The demonstration that the Second Advent is at hand, if true, can have no really holy, spiritual effect; the highest state of mind inculcated by the Gospel is resignation to the disposal of God's providence—"Whether we live, we live unto the Lord; whether we die, we die unto the Lord"—not an eagerness to see a temporal manifestation which shall confound the enemies of God and give exaltation to the saints; it is to dwell in Christ by spiritual communion with his nature, not to fix the date when He shall appear in the sky. Dr. Cumming's delight in shadowing forth the downfall of the Man of Sin, in prognosticating the battle of Gog and Magog, and in advertising the pre-millennial Advent, is simply the transportation of political passions on to a so-called religious platform; it is the anticipation of the triumph of "our party," accomplished by our principal men being "sent for" into the clouds. Let us be understood to speak in all seriousness. If we were in search of amusement, we should not seek for it by examining Dr. Cumming's works in order to ridicule them. We are simply discharging a disagreeable duty in delivering our opinion that, judged by the highest standard even of orthodox Christianity, they are little calculated to produce—

"A closer walk with God,
A calm and heavenly frame;"

but are more likely to nourish egoistic complacency and pretension, a hard and condemnatory spirit toward one's fellow-men, and a busy occupation with the minutiæ of events, instead of a reverent contemplation of great facts and a wise application of great principles. It would be idle to consider Dr. Cumming's theory of prophecy in any other light; as a philosophy of history or a specimen of biblical interpretation, it bears about the same relation to the extension of genuine knowledge as the astrological "house" in the heavens bears to the true structure and relations of the universe.

The slight degree in which Dr. Cumming's faith is imbued with truly human sympathies is exhibited in the way he treats the doctrine of Eternal Punishment. *Here* a little of that readiness to strain the letter of the Scriptures which he so often manifests when his object is to prove a point against Romanism, would have been an amiable frailty if it had been applied on the side of mercy. When he is bent on proving that the prophecy concerning the Man of Sin, in the Second Epistle to the Thessalonians, refers to the Pope, he can extort from the innocent word *καθισαι* the meaning *cathedrize*, though why we are to translate "He as God cathedrizes in the temple of God," any more than we are to translate "cathedrize here, while I go and pray yonder," it is for Dr. Cumming to show more clearly than he has yet done. But when rigorous literality will favor the conclusion that the greater proportion of the human race will be eternally miserable—*then* he is rigorously literal.

He says: "The Greek words, *εἰς τους αἰῶνας των αἰώνων*, here translated 'everlasting,' signify literally 'unto the ages of ages; *αἰεὶ ὢν*, 'always being,' that is, everlasting, ceaseless existence. Plato uses the word in this sense when he says, 'The gods that live forever.' *But I must also admit* that this word is used several times in a limited extent—as for instance, 'The everlasting hills.' Of course this does not mean that there never will be a time when the hills will cease to stand; the expression here is evidently figurative, but it implies eternity. The hills shall remain as long as the earth lasts, and no hand has power to remove them but that Eternal One which first called them into being; *so the state of the soul* remains the same after death as long as the soul exists, and no one has power to alter it. The same word is often applied to denote the existence of God—'the Eternal God.' Can we limit the word when applied to him? Because occasionally used in a limited sense, we must not infer it is always so. 'Everlasting' plainly means in Scripture 'without end;' it is only to be explained figuratively when it is evident it cannot be interpreted in any other way."

We do not discuss whether Dr. Cumming's interpretation accords with the meaning of the New Testament writers: we simply point to the fact that the text becomes elastic for him when he wants freer play for his prejudices, while he makes it an adamantine barrier against the admission that mercy will ultimately triumph—that God, *i.e.*, Love, will be all in all. He assures us that he does not "delight to dwell on the misery of the lost:" and we believe him. That misery does not seem to be a question of feeling with him, either one way or the other. He does not merely resign himself to the awful mystery of eternal punishment; he contends for it. Do we object, he asks,* to everlasting happiness? then why object to everlasting misery?—reasoning which is perhaps felt to be cogent by theologians who anticipate the everlasting happiness for themselves, and the everlasting misery for their neighbors.

* "Man. of Christ. Ev." p. 184.

The compassion of some Christians has been glad to take refuge in the opinion that the Bible allows the supposition of annihilation for the impenitent ; but the rigid sequence of Dr. Cumming's reasoning will not admit of this idea. He sees that flax is made into linen, and linen into paper ; that paper, when burned, partly ascends as smoke and then again descends in rain, or in dust and carbon. "Not one particle of the original flax is lost, although there may be not one particle that has not undergone an entire change : annihilation is not, but change of form is. *It will be thus with our bodies at the resurrection.* The death of the body means not annihilation. *Not one feature of the face* will be annihilated." Having established the perpetuity of the body by this close and clear analogy, namely, that *as* there is a total change in the particles of flax in consequence of which they no longer appear as flax, *so* there will *not* be a total change in the particles of the human body, but they will reappear as the human body, he does not seem to consider that the perpetuity of the body involves the perpetuity of the soul, but requires separate evidence for this, and finds such evidence by begging the very question at issue—namely, by asserting that the text of the Scripture implies "the perpetuity of the punishment of the lost, and the consciousness of the punishment which they endure." Yet it is drivelling like this which is listened to and lauded as eloquence by hundreds, and which a Doctor of Divinity can believe that he has his "reward as a saint" for preaching and publishing !

One more characteristic of Dr. Cumming's writings, and we have done. This is the *perverted moral judgment* that everywhere reigns in them. Not that this perversion is peculiar to Dr. Cumming : it belongs to the dogmatic system which he shares with all evangelical believers. But the abstract tendencies of systems are represented in very different degrees, according to the different characters of those who embrace them ; just as the same food tells differently on different constitutions : and there are certain qualities in Dr.

Cumming that cause the perversion of which we speak to exhibit itself with peculiar prominence in his teaching. A single extract will enable us to explain what we mean:

"The 'thoughts' are evil. If it were possible for human eye to discern and to detect the thoughts that flutter around the heart of an unregenerate man—to mark their hue and their multitude, it would be found that they are indeed 'evil.' We speak not of the thief, and the murderer, and the adulterer, and such like, whose crimes draw down the cognizance of earthly tribunals, and whose unenviable character it is to take the lead in the paths of sin; but we refer to the men who are marked out by their practice of many of the seemliest moralities of life—by the exercise of the kindliest affections, and the interchange of the sweetest reciprocities—and of these men, if unrenewed and unchanged, we pronounce that their thoughts are evil. To ascertain this, we must refer to the object around which our thoughts ought continually to circulate. The Scriptures assert that this object is *the glory of God;* that for this we ought to think, to act, and to speak; and that in thus thinking, acting, and speaking, there is involved the purest and most endearing bliss. Now it will be found true of the most amiable men, that with all their good society and kindliness of heart, and all their strict and unbending integrity, they never or rarely think of the glory of God. The question never occurs to them—Will this redound to the glory of God? Will this make his name more known, his being more loved, his praise more sung? And just inasmuch as their every thought comes short of this lofty aim, in so much does it come short of good, and entitle itself to the character of evil. If the glory of God is not the absorbing and the influential aim of their thoughts, then they are evil; but God's glory never enters into their minds. They are amiable, because it chances to be one of the constitutional tendencies of their individual character, left uneffaced by the Fall; and *they are just and upright, because they have perhaps no occasion to be otherwise, or find it subservient to their interests to maintain such a character.*"—"Occ. Disc." vol. i. p. 8.

Again we read (Ibid. p. 236):

"There are traits in the Christian character which the mere worldly man cannot understand. He can understand the outward morality, but he cannot understand the inner spring of it; he can understand Dorcas' liberality to the poor, but he cannot penetrate the ground of Dorcas' liberality. *Some men give to the poor because they are ostentatious, or because they think the poor will ultimately avenge their neglect; but the Christian gives to the poor, not only because he has sensibilities like other men,* but because inasmuch as ye did it to the least of these my brethren ye did it unto me."

Before entering on the more general question involved in these quotations, we must point to the clauses we have marked with italics, where Dr. Cumming appears to express sentiments which, we are happy to think, are not shared by the majority of his brethren in the faith. Dr. Cumming, it seems, is unable to conceive that the natural man can have any other motive for being just and upright than that it is useless to be otherwise, or that a character for honesty is profitable; according to his experience, between the feelings of ostentation and selfish alarm and the feeling of love to Christ, there lie no sensibilities which can lead a man to relieve want. Granting, as we should prefer to think, that it is Dr. Cumming's exposition of his sentiments which is deficient rather than his sentiments themselves, still, the fact that the deficiency lies precisely here, and that he can overlook it not only in the haste of oral delivery but in the examination of proof-sheets, is strongly significant of his mental bias—of the faint degree in which he sympathizes with the disinterested elements of human feeling, and of the fact, which we are about to dwell upon, that those feelings are totally absent from his religious theory. Now, Dr. Cumming invariably assumes that, in fulminating against those who differ from him, he is standing on a moral elevation to which they are compelled reluctantly to look up; that his theory of motives and conduct is in its loftiness and purity a perpetual rebuke to their low and vicious desires and practice. It is time he should be told that the reverse is the fact; that there are men who do not merely cast a superficial glance at his doctrine, and fail to see its beauty or justice, but who, after a close consideration of that doctrine, pronounce it to be subversive of true moral development, and therefore positively noxious. Dr. Cumming is fond of showing up the teaching of Romanism, and accusing it of undermining true morality: it is time he should be told that there is a large body, both of thinkers and practical men, who hold precisely the same opinion of his own teaching—with this difference, that they do not regard it as the inspiration of Satan, but as the natural crop of a human mind where the soil is chiefly made up of egoistic passions and dogmatic beliefs.

Dr. Cumming's theory, as we have seen, is that actions are good or evil according as they are prompted or not prompted by an exclusive reference to the "glory of God." God, then, in Dr. Cumming's conception, is a being who has no pleasure in the exercise of love and truthfulness and justice, considered as affecting the well-being of his creatures; He has satisfaction in us only in so far as we exhaust our motives and dispositions of all relation to our fellow-beings, and replace sympathy with men by anxiety for the "glory of God." The deed of Grace Darling, when she took a boat in the storm to rescue drowning men and women, was not good if it was only compassion that nerved her arm and impelled her to brave death for the chance of saving others; it was only good if she asked herself—Will this redound to the glory of God? The man who endures tortures rather than betray a trust, the man who spends years in toil in order to discharge an obligation from which the law declares him free, must be animated not by the spirit of fidelity to his fellow-man, but by a desire to make "the name of God more known." The sweet charities of domestic life — the ready hand and the soothing word in sickness, the forbearance toward frailties, the prompt helpfulness in all efforts and sympathy in all joys, are simply evil if they result from a "constitutional tendency," or from dispositions disciplined by the experience of suffering and the perception of moral loveliness. A wife is not to devote herself to her husband out of love to him and a sense of the duties implied by a close relation—she is to be a faithful wife for the glory of God; if she feels her natural affections welling up too strongly, she is to repress them; it will not do to act from natural affection—she must think of the glory of God. A man is to guide his affairs with energy and discretion, not from an honest desire to fulfil his responsibilities as a member of society and a father, but—that "God's praise may be sung." Dr. Cumming's Christian pays his debts for the glory of God; were it not for the coercion of that supreme motive, it would be evil to pay them. A man is not to be just from a feeling of justice; he is not to help his fellow-men out of good-will to his fellow-men; he is not to be a tender husband and father out of affection: all these natural muscles and fibres are to be torn away and replaced by a patent steel-spring—anxiety for the "glory of God."

Happily, the constitution of human nature forbids the complete prevalence of such a theory. Fatally powerful as religious systems have been, human nature is stronger and wider than religious systems, and though dogmas may hamper, they cannot absolutely repress its growth: build walls round the living tree as you will, the bricks and mortar have by and by to give way before the slow and sure operation of the sap. But next to the hatred of the enemies of God which is the principle of persecution, there perhaps has been no perversion more obstructive of true moral development than this substitution of a reference to the glory of God for the direct promptings of the sympathetic feelings. Benevolence and justice are strong only in proportion as they are directly and inevitably called into activity by their proper objects; pity is strong only because we are strongly impressed by suffering; and only in proportion as it is compassion that speaks through the eyes when we soothe, and moves the arm when we succor, is a deed strictly benevolent. If the soothing or the succor be given because another being wishes or approves it, the deed ceases to be one of benevolence, and becomes one of deference, of obedience, of self-interest, or vanity. Accessory motives may aid in producing an *action*, but they presuppose the weakness of the direct motive; and conversely, when the direct motive is strong, the action of accessory motives will be excluded. If, then, as Dr. Cumming inculcates, the glory of God is to be "the absorbing and the influential aim" in our thoughts and actions, this must tend to neutralize the human sympathies ; the stream of feeling will be diverted from its natural current in order to feed an artificial canal. The idea of God is really moral in its influence—it really cherishes all that is best and loveliest in man —only when God is contemplated as sympathizing with the pure elements of human feeling, as possessing infinitely all those attributes which we recognize to be moral in humanity. In this light, the idea of God and the sense of His presence intensify all noble feeling, and encourage all noble effort, on the same principle that human sympathy is found a source of strength : the brave man feels braver when he knows that another stout heart is beating time with his ; the devoted woman who is wearing out her years in patient effort to alleviate suffering or save vice from the last stages of degradation, finds aid in the pressure of a friendly hand which tells her that there is one who understands her deeds, and in her place would do the like. The idea of a God who not only sympathizes with all we feel and endure for our fellow-men, but who will pour new life into our too languid love, and give firmness to our vacillating purpose, is an extension and multiplication of the effects produced by human sympathy ; and it has been intensified for the better spirits who have been under the influence of orthodox Christianity, by the contemplation of Jesus as "God manifest in the flesh." But Dr. Cumming's God is the very opposite of all this : he is a God who instead of sharing and aiding our human sympathies, is directly in collision with them ; who instead of strengthening the bond between man and man, by encouraging the sense that they are both alike the objects of His love and care, thrusts himself between them and forbids them to feel for each other except as they have relation to Him. He is a God who, instead of adding his solar force to swell the tide of those impulses that tend to give humanity a common life in which the good of one is the good of all, commands us to check those impulses, lest they should prevent us from thinking of His glory. It is in vain for Dr. Cumming to say that we are to love man for God's sake: with the conception of God which his teaching presents, the love of man for God's sake involves, as his writings abundantly show, a strong principle of hatred. We can only love one being for the sake of another when there is an habitual delight in associating the idea of those two beings—that is, when the object of our indirect love is a source of joy and honor to the object of our direct love; but according to Dr. Cumming's theory, the majority of mankind—the majority of his neighbors—are in precisely the opposite relation to God. His soul has no pleasure in them, they belong more to Satan than to Him, and if they contribute to His glory, it is against their will. Dr. Cumming then can only love *some* men for God's sake; the rest he must in consistency *hate* for God's sake.

There must be many, even in the circle of Dr. Cumming's admirers, who would be revolted by the doctrine we have just exposed, if their natural good sense and healthy feeling were not early stifled by dogmatic beliefs, and their reverence misled by pious phrases. But as it is, many a rational question, many a generous instinct, is repelled as the suggestion of a supernatural enemy, or as the ebullition of human pride and corruption. This state of inward contradiction can be put an end to only by the conviction that the free and diligent exertion of the intellect, instead of being a sin, is part of their responsibility—that Right and Reason are synonymous. The fundamental faith for man is, faith in the result of a brave, honest, and steady use of all his faculties:

"Let knowledge grow from more to more,
But more of reverence in us dwell;
That mind and soul according well
May make one music as before,
But vaster."

Before taking leave of Dr. Cumming, let us express a hope that we have in no case exaggerated the unfavorable character of the inferences to be drawn from his pages. His creed often obliges him to hope the worst of men, and exert himself in proving that the worst is true; but thus far we are happier than he. We have no theory which requires us to attribute unworthy motives to Dr. Cumming, no opinions, religious or irreligious, which can make it a gratification to us to detect him in delinquencies. On the contrary, the better we are able to think of him as a man, while we are obliged to disapprove him as a theologian, the stronger will be the evidence for our conviction, that the tendency toward good in human nature has a force which no creed can utterly counteract, and which insures the ultimate triumph of that tendency over all dogmatic perversions.

IV.

GERMAN WIT: HENRY HEINE.*

"NOTHING," says Goethe, "is more significant of men's character than what they find laughable." The truth of this observation would perhaps have been more apparent if he had said *culture* instead of character. The last thing in which the cultivated man can have community with the vulgar is their jocularity; and we can hardly exhibit more strikingly the wide gulf which separates him from them, than by comparing the object which shakes the diaphragm of a coal-heaver with the highly complex pleasure derived from a real witticism. That any high order of wit is exceedingly complex, and demands a ripe and strong mental development, has one evidence in the fact that we do not find it in boys at all in proportion to their manifestation of other powers. Clever boys generally aspire to the heroic and poetic rather than the comic, and the crudest of all their efforts are their jokes. Many a witty man will remember how in his school days a practical joke, more or less Rabelaisian, was for him the *ne plus ultra* of the ludicrous. It seems to have been the same with the boyhood of the human race. The history and literature of the ancient Hebrews gives the idea of a people who went about their business and their pleasure as gravely as a society of beavers; the smile and the laugh are often mentioned metaphorically, but the smile is one of complacency, the laugh is one of scorn. Nor can we imagine that the facetious element was very strong in the

* 1. "Heinrich Heine's Sämmtliche Werke." Philadelphia: John Weik. 1855. 2. "Vermischte Schriften von Heinrich Heine." Hamburg: Hoffman und Campe. 1854.

Egyptians; no laughter lurks in the wondering eyes and the broad calm lips of their statues. Still less can the Assyrians have had any genius for the comic: the round eyes and simpering satisfaction of their ideal faces belong to a type which is not witty, but the cause of wit in others. The fun of these early races was, we fancy, of the after-dinner kind—loud-throated laughter over the wine-cup, taken too little account of in sober moments to enter as an element into their Art, and differing as much from the laughter of a Chamfort or a Sheridan as the gastronomic enjoyment of an ancient Briton, whose dinner had no other "removes" than from acorns to beech-mast and back again to acorns, differed from the subtle pleasures of the palate experienced by his turtle-eating descendant. In fact they had to live seriously through the stages which to subsequent races were to become comedy, as those amiable-looking preadamite amphibia which Professor Owen has restored for us in effigy at Sydenham, took perfectly *au sérieux* the grotesque physiognomies of their kindred. Heavy experience in their case, as in every other, was the base from which the salt of future wit was to be made.

Humor is of earlier growth than Wit, and it is in accordance with this earlier growth that it has more affinity with the poetic tendencies, while Wit is more nearly allied to the ratiocinative intellect. Humor draws its materials from situations and characteristics; Wit seizes on unexpected and complex relations. Humor is chiefly representative and descriptive; it is diffuse, and flows along without any other law than its own fantastic will; or it flits about like a will-of-the-wisp, amazing us by its whimsical transitions. Wit is brief and sudden, and sharply defined as a crystal; it does not make pictures, it is not fantastic; but it detects an unsuspected analogy or suggests a startling or confounding inference. Every one who has had the opportunity of making the comparison will remember that the effect produced on him by some witticisms is closely akin to the effect produced on him by subtle reasoning which lays open a fallacy or absurdity, and there are persons whose delight in such reasoning always manifests itself in laughter. This affinity of wit with ratiocination is the more obvious in proportion as the species of wit is higher and deals less with less words and with superficialities than with the essential qualities of things. Some of Johnson's most admirable witticisms consist in the suggestion of an analogy which immediately exposes the absurdity of an action or proposition; and it is only their ingenuity, condensation, and instantaneousness which lift them from reasoning into Wit--they are *reasoning raised to a higher power*. On the other hand, Humor, in its higher forms, and in proportion as it associates itself with the sympathetic emotions, continually passes into poetry: nearly all great modern humorists may be called prose poets.

Some confusion as to the nature of Humor has been created by the fact that those who have written most eloquently on it have dwelt almost exclusively on its higher forms, and have defined humor in general as the *sympathetic* presentation of incongruous elements in human nature and life—a definition which only applies to its later development. A great deal of humor may coexist with a great deal of barbarism, as we see in the Middle Ages; but the strongest flavor of the humor in such cases will come, not from sympathy, but more probably from triumphant egoism or intolerance; at best it will be the love of the ludicrous exhibiting itself in illustrations of successful cunning and of the *lex talionis* as in *Reineke Fuchs*, or shaking off in a holiday mood the yoke of a too exacting faith, as in the old Mysteries. Again, it is impossible to deny a high degree of humor to many practical jokes, but no sympathetic nature can enjoy them. Strange as the genealogy may seem, the original parentage of that wonderful and delicious mixture of fun, fancy, philosophy, and feeling, which constitutes modern humor, was probably the cruel mockery of a savage at the writhings of a suffering enemy—such is the tendency of things toward the good and beautiful on this earth! Probably the reason why high culture demands more complete harmony with its moral sympathies in humor than in wit, is that humor is in its nature more prolix—that it has not the direct and irresistible force of wit. Wit is an electric shock, which takes us by violence, quite independently of our predominant mental disposition ; but humor approaches us more deliberately and leaves us masters of ourselves. Hence it is, that while coarse and cruel humor has almost disappeared from contemporary literature, coarse and cruel wit abounds ; even refined men cannot help laughing at a coarse *bon mot* or a lacerating personality, if the "shock" of the witticism is a powerful one ; while mere fun will have no power over them if it jar on their moral taste. Hence, too, it is, that while wit is perennial, humor is liable to become superannuated.

As is usual with definitions and classifications, however, this distinction between wit and humor does not exactly represent the actual fact. Like all other species, Wit and Humor overlap and blend with each other. There are *bon mots*, like many of Charles Lamb's, which are a sort of facetious hybrids, we hardly know whether to call them witty or humorous ; there are rather lengthy descriptions or narratives, which, like Voltaire's "Micromégas," would be more humorous if they were not so sparkling and antithetic, so pregnant with suggestion and satire, that we are obliged to call them witty. We rarely find wit untempered by humor, or humor without a spice of wit ; and sometimes we find them both united in the highest degree in the same mind, as in Shakespeare and Molière. A happy conjunction this, for wit is apt to be cold, and thin-lipped, and Mephistophelean in men who have no relish for humor, whose lungs do never crow like Chanticleer at fun and drollery ; and broad-faced, rollicking humor needs the refining influence of wit. Indeed, it may be said that there is no really fine writing in which wit has not an implicit, if not an explicit, action. The wit may never rise to the surface, it may never flame out into a witticism ; but it helps to give brightness and transparency, it warns off from flights and exaggerations which verge on the ridiculous—in every *genre* of writing it preserves a man from sinking into the *genre ennuyeux*. And it is eminently needed for this office in humorous writing; for as humor has no limits imposed on it by its material, no law but its own exuberance, it is apt to become preposterous and wearisome unless checked by wit, which is the enemy of all monotony, of all lengthiness, of all exaggeration.

Perhaps the nearest approach Nature has given us to a complete analysis, in which wit is as thoroughly exhausted of humor as possible, and humor as bare as possible of wit, is in the typical Frenchman and the typical German. Voltaire, the intensest example of pure wit, fails in most of his fictions from his lack of humor. "Micromégas" is a perfect tale, because, as it deals chiefly with philosophic ideas and does not touch the marrow of human feeling and life, the writer's wit and wisdom were all-sufficient for his purpose. Not so with "Candide." Here Voltaire had to give pictures of life as well as to convey philosophic truth and satire, and here we feel the want of humor. The sense of the ludicrous is continually defeated by disgust, and the scenes, instead of presenting us with an amusing or agreeable picture, are only the frame for a witticism. On the other hand, German humor generally shows no sense of measure, no instinctive tact; it is either floundering and clumsy as the antics of a leviathan, or laborious and interminable as a Lapland day, in which one loses all hope that the stars and quiet will ever come. For this reason, Jean Paul, the greatest of German humorists, is unendurable to many readers, and frequently tiresome to all. Here, as elsewhere, the German shows the absence of that delicate perception, that sensibility to gradation, which is the essence of tact and taste, and the necessary concomitant of wit. All his subtlety is reserved for the region of metaphysics. For *Identität* in the abstract no one can have an acuter vision, but in the concrete he is satisfied with a very loose approximation. He has the finest nose for *Empirismus* in philosophical doctrine, but the presence of more or less tobacco smoke in the air he breathes is imperceptible to him. To the typical German—*Vetter Michel*—it is indifferent whether his door-lock will catch, whether his teacup be more or less than an inch thick; whether or not his book have every other leaf unstitched; whether his neighbor's conversation be more or less of a shout; whether he pronounce *b* or *p*, *t* or *d*; whether or not his adored one's teeth be few and far between. He has the same sort of insensibility to gradations in time. A German comedy is like a German sentence: you see no reason in its structure why it should ever come to an end, and you accept the conclusion as an arrangement of Providence rather than of the author. We have heard Germans use the word *Langeweile*, the equivalent for ennui, and we have secretly wondered *what* it can be that produces ennui in a German. Not the longest of long tragedies, for we have known him to pronounce that *höchst fesselnd* (*so* enchaining!); not the heaviest of heavy books, for he delights in that as *gründlich* (deep, Sir, deep!); not the slowest of journeys in a *Postwagen*, for the slower the horses, the more cigars he can smoke before he reaches his journey's end. German ennui must be something as superlative as Barclay's treble X, which, we suppose, implies an extremely unknown quantity of stupefaction.

It is easy to see that this national deficiency in nicety of perception must have its effect on the national appreciation and exhibition of Humor. You find in Germany ardent admirers of Shakespeare, who tell you that what they think most admirable in him is his *Wortspiel*, his verbal quibbles; and one of these, a man of no slight culture and refinement, once cited to a friend of ours Proteus's joke in "The Two Gentlemen of Verona"—"Nod I? why that's Noddy," as a transcendant specimen of Shakespearian wit. German facetiousness is seldom comic to foreigners, and an Englishman with a swelled cheek might take up *Kladderadatsch*, the German Punch, without any danger of agitating his facial muscles. Indeed, it is a remarkable fact that, among the five great races concerned in modern civilization, the German race is the only one which, up to the present century, had contributed nothing classic to the common stock of European wit and humor; for *Reineke Fuchs* cannot be regarded as a peculiarly Teutonic product. Italy was the birthplace of Pantomime and the immortal Pulcinello; Spain had produced Cervantes; France had produced Rabelais and Molière, and classic wits innumerable; England had yielded Shakspeare and a host of humorists. But Germany had borne no great comic dramatist, no great satirist, and she has not yet repaired the omission; she had not even produced any humorist of a high order. Among her great writers, Lessing is the one who is the most specifically witty. We feel the implicit influence of wit—the "flavor of mind"—throughout his writings; and it is often concentrated into pungent satire, as every reader of the *Hamburgische Dramaturgie* remembers. Still Lessing's name has not become European through his wit, and his charming comedy, *Minna von Barnhelm*, has won no place on a foreign stage. Of course we do not pretend to an exhaustive acquaintance with German literature; we not only admit—we are sure that it includes much comic writing of which we know nothing. We simply state the fact, that no German production of that kind, before the present century, ranked as European; a fact which does not, indeed, determine the *amount* of the national facetiousness, but which is quite decisive as to its *quality*. Whatever may be the stock of fun which Germany yields for home consumption, she has provided little for the palate of other lands. All honor to her for the still greater things she has done for us! She has fought the hardest fight for freedom of thought, has produced the grandest inventions, has made magnificent contributions to science, has given us some of the divinest poetry, and quite the divinest music in the world. No one reveres and treasures the products of the German mind more than we do. To say that that mind is not fertile in wit is only like saying that excellent wheat land is not rich pasture; to say that we do not enjoy German facetiousness is no more than to say that, though the horse is the finest of quadrupeds, we do not like him to lay his hoof playfully on our shoulder. Still, as we have noticed that the pointless puns and stupid jocularity of the boy may ultimately be developed into the epigrammatic brilliancy and polished playfulness of the man; as we believe that racy wit and chastened delicate humor are inevitably the results of invigorated and refined mental activity, we can also believe that Germany will, one day, yield a crop of wits and humorists.

Perhaps there is already an earnest of that future crop in the existence of Heinrich Heine, a German born with the present century, who, to Teutonic imagination, sensibility, and humor, adds an amount of *esprit* that would make him brilliant among the most brilliant of Frenchmen. True, this unique German wit is half a Hebrew; but he and his ancestors spent their youth in German air, and were reared on *Wurst* and *Sauerkraut*, so that he is as much a German as a pheasant is an English bird, or a potato an Irish vegetable. But whatever else he may be, Heine is one of the most remarkable men of this age: no echo, but a real voice, and therefore, like all genuine things in this world, worth studying; a surpassing lyric poet, who has uttered our feelings for us in delicious song; a humorist, who touches leaden folly with the magic wand of his fancy, and transmutes it into the fine gold of art—who sheds his sunny smile on human tears, and makes them a beauteous rainbow on the cloudy background of life; a wit, who holds in his mighty hand the most scorching lightnings of satire; an artist in prose literature, who has shown even more completely than Goethe the possibilities of German prose; and—in spite of all charges against him, true as well as false—a lover of freedom, who has spoken wise and brave words on behalf of his fellow-men. He is, moreover, a suffering man, who, with all the highly-wrought sensibility of genius, has to endure terrible physical ills; and as such he calls forth more than an intellectual interest. It is true, alas! that there is a heavy weight in the other scale—that Heine's magnificent powers have often served only to give electric force to the expression of debased feeling, so that his works are no Phidian statue of gold, and ivory, and gems, but have not a little brass, and iron, and miry clay mingled with the precious metal. The audacity of his occasional coarseness and personality is unparalleled in contemporary literature, and has hardly been exceeded by the license of former days. Hence, before his volumes are put within the reach of immature minds, there is need of a friendly penknife to exercise a strict censorship. Yet, when all coarseness, all scurrility, all Mephistophelean contempt for the reverent feelings of other men, is removed, there will be a plenteous remainder of exquisite poetry, of wit, humor, and just thought. It is apparently too often a congenial task to write severe words about the transgressions committed by men of genius, especially when the censor has the advantage of being himself a man of *no* genius, so that those transgressions seem to him quite gratuitous; *he*, forsooth, never lacerated any one by his wit, or gave irresistible piquancy to a coarse allusion, and his indignation is not mitigated by any knowledge of the temptation that lies in transcendent power. We are also apt to measure what a gifted man has done by our arbitrary conception of what he might have done, rather than by a comparison of his actual doings with our own or those of other ordinary men. We make ourselves overzealous agents of heaven, and demand that our brother should bring usurious interest for his five Talents, forgetting that it is less easy to manage five Talents than two. Whatever benefit there may be in denouncing the evil, it is after all more edifying, and certainly more cheering, to appreciate the good. Hence, in endeavoring to give our readers some account of Heine and his works, we shall not dwell lengthily on his failings; we shall not hold the candle up to dusty, vermin-haunted corners, but let the light fall as much as possible on the nobler and more attractive details. Our sketch of Heine's life, which has been drawn from various sources, will be free from everything like intrusive gossip, and will derive its coloring chiefly from the autobiographical hints and descriptions scattered through his own writings. Those of our readers who happen to know nothing of Heine will in this way be making their acquaintance with the writer while they are learning the outline of his career.

We have said that Heine was born with the present century; but this statement is not precise, for we learn that, according to his certificate of baptism, he was born December 12th, 1799. However, as he himself says, the important point is that he was born, and born on the banks of the Rhine, at Düsseldorf, where his father was a merchant. In his "Reisebilder" he gives us some recollections, in his wild poetic way, of the dear old town where he spent his childhood, and of his schoolboy troubles there. We shall quote from these in butterfly fashion, sipping a little nectar here and there, without regard to any strict order:

"I first saw the light on the banks of that lovely stream, where Folly grows on the green hills, and in autumn is plucked, pressed, poured into casks, and sent into foreign lands. Believe me, I yesterday heard some one utter folly which, in anno 1811, lay in a bunch of grapes I then saw growing on the Johannisberg. . . . . Mon Dieu! if I had only such faith in me that I could remove mountains, the Johannisberg would be the very mountain I should send for wherever I might be; but as my faith is not so strong, imagination must help me, and it transports me at once to the lovely Rhine. . . . . I am again a child, and playing with other children on the Schlossplatz, at Düsseldorf on the Rhine. Yes, madam, there was I born; and I note this expressly, in case, after my death, seven cities—Schilda, Krähwinkel, Polkwitz, Bockum, Dülken, Göttingen, and Schöppenstädt—should contend for the honor of being my birthplace. Düsseldorf is a town on the Rhine; sixteen thousand men live there, and many hundred thousand men besides lie buried there. . . . . Among them, many of whom my mother says, that it would be better if they were still living; for example, my grandfather and my uncle, the old Herr von Geldern and the young Herr von Geldern, both such celebrated doctors, who saved so many men from death, and yet must die themselves. And the pious Ursula, who carried me in her arms when I was a child, also lies buried there and a rosebush grows on her grave; she loved the scent of roses so well in life, and her heart was pure rose-incense and goodness. The knowing old Canon, too, lies buried there. Heavens, what an object he looked when I last saw him! *He was made up of nothing but mind and plasters*, and nevertheless studied day and night, as if he were alarmed lest the worms should find an idea too little in his head. And the little William lies there, and for this I am to blame. We were schoolfellows in the Franciscan monastery, and were playing on that side of it where the Düssel flows between stone walls, and I said, 'William, fetch out the kitten that has just fallen in'—and merrily he went down on to the plank which lay across the brook, snatched the kitten out of the water, but fell in himself, and was dragged out dripping and dead. *The kitten lived to a good old age.* . . . . Princes in that day were not the tormented race as they are now; the crown grew firmly on their heads, and at night they drew a nightcap over it, and slept peacefully, and peacefully slept the people at their feet; and when the people waked in the morning, they said, 'Good morning, father!' and the princes answered, 'Good morning, dear children!' But it was suddenly quite otherwise; for when we awoke one morning at Düsseldorf, and were ready to say, 'Good morning, father!' lo! the father was gone away; and in the whole town there was nothing but dumb sorrow, everywhere a sort of funeral disposition; and people glided along silently to the market, and read the long placard placed on the door of the Town Hall. It was dismal weather; yet the lean tailor, Kilian, stood in his nankeen jacket which he usually wore only in the house, and his blue worsted stockings hung down so that his naked legs peeped out mournfully, and his thin lips trembled while he muttered the announcement to himself. And an old soldier read rather louder, and at many a word a crystal tear trickled down to his brave old mustache. I stood near him and wept in company, and asked him, '*Why we wept?*' He answered, 'The Elector has abdicated.' And then he read again, and at the words, 'for the long-manifested fidelity of my subjects,' and 'hereby set you free from your allegiance,' he wept more than ever. It is strangely touching to see an old man like that, with faded uniform and scarred face, weep so bitterly all of a sudden. While we were reading, the electoral arms were taken down from the Town Hall; everything had such a desolate air, that it was as if an eclipse of the sun were expected. . . . . I went home and wept, and wailed out, 'The Elector has abdicated!' In vain my mother took a world of trouble to explain the thing to me. I knew what I knew; I was not to be persuaded, but went crying to bed, and in the night dreamed that the world was at an end."

The next morning, however, the sun rises as usual, and Joachim Murat is proclaimed Grand Duke, whereupon there is a holiday at the public school, and Heinrich (or Harry, for that was his baptismal name, which he afterward had the good taste to change), perched on the bronze horse of the Electoral statue, sees quite a different scene from yesterday's :

> "The next day the world was again all in order, and we had school as before, and things were got by heart as before—the Roman emperors, chronology, the nouns in *im*, the *verba irregularia*, Greek, Hebrew, geography, mental arithmetic !—heavens ! my head is still dizzy with it—all must be learned by heart ! And a great deal of this came very conveniently for me in after life. For if I had not known the Roman kings by heart, it would subsequently have been quite indifferent to me whether Niebuhr had proved or had not proved that they never really existed. . . . But oh ! the trouble I had at school with the endless dates. And with arithmetic it was still worse. What I understood best was subtraction, for that has a very practical rule : 'Four can't be taken from three, therefore I must borrow one.' But I advise every one in such a case to borrow a few extra pence, for no one can tell what may happen. . . . As for Latin, you have no idea, madam, what a complicated affair it is. The Romans would never have found time to conquer the world if they had first had to learn Latin. Luckily for them, they already knew in their cradles what nouns have their accusative in *im*. I, on the contrary, had to learn them by heart in the sweat of my brow ; nevertheless, it is fortunate for me that I know them . . . and the fact that I have them at my finger-ends if I should ever happen to want them suddenly, affords me much inward repose and consolation in many troubled hours of life. . . . Of Greek I will not say a word, I should get too much irritated. The monks in the Middle Ages were not so far wrong when they maintained that Greek was an invention of the devil. God knows the suffering I endured over it. . . . With Hebrew it went somewhat better, for I had always a great liking for the Jews, though to this very hour they crucify my good name ; but I could never get on so far in Hebrew as my watch, which had much familiar intercourse with pawnbrokers, and in this way contracted many Jewish habits—for example, it wouldn't go on Saturdays."

Heine's parents were apparently not wealthy, but his education was cared for by his uncle, Solomon Heine, a great banker in Hamburg, so that he had no early pecuniary disadvantages to struggle with. He seems to have been very happy in his mother, who was not of Hebrew but of Teutonic blood ; he often mentions her with reverence and affection, and in the

"Buch der Lieder" there are two exquisite sonnets addressed to her, which tell how his proud spirit was always subdued by the charm of her presence, and how her love was the home of his heart after restless weary ramblings:

> "Wie mächtig auch mein stolzer Muth sich blähe,
> In deiner selig süssen, trauten Nahe
> Ergreift mich oft ein demuthvolles Zagen.
>
> * * * * *
>
> Und immer irrte ich nach Liebe, immer
> Nach Liebe, doch die Liebe fand ich nimmer,
> Und kehrte um nach Hause, krank und trübe.
> Doch da bist du entgegen mir gekommen,
> Und ach! was da in deinem Aug' geschwommen,
> Das war die süsse, langgesuchte Liebe."

He was at first destined for a mercantile life, but Nature declared too strongly against this plan. "God knows," he has lately said in conversation with his brother, "I would willingly have become a banker, but I could never bring myself to that pass. I very early discerned that bankers would one day be the rulers of the world." So commerce was at length given up for law, the study of which he began in 1819 at the University of Bonn. He had already published some poems in the corner of a newspaper, and among them was one on Napoleon, the object of his youthful enthusiasm. This poem, he says in a letter to St. Réné Taillandier, was written when he was only sixteen. It is still to be found in the "Buch der Lieder" under the title "Die Grenadiere," and it proves that even in its earliest efforts his genius showed a strongly specific character.

It will be easily imagined that the germs of poetry sprouted too vigorously in Heine's brain for jurisprudence to find much room there. Lectures on history and literature, we are told, were more diligently attended than lectures on law. He had taken care, too, to furnish his trunk with abundant editions of the poets, and the poet he especially studied at that time was Byron. At a later period we find his taste taking another direction, for he writes, "Of all authors, Byron is precisely the one who excites in me the most intolerable emotion; whereas Scott, in every one of his works, gladdens my heart, soothes, and invigorates me." Another indication of his bent in these Bonn days was a newspaper essay, in which he attacked the Romantic school; and here also he went through that chicken-pox of authorship—the production of a tragedy. Heine's tragedy—*Almansor*—is, as might be expected, better than the majority of these youthful mistakes. The tragic collision lies in the conflict between natural affection and the deadly hatred of religion and of race—in the sacrifice of youthful lovers to the strife between Moor and Spaniard, Moslem and Christian. Some of the situations are striking, and there are passages of considerable poetic merit; but the characters are little more than shadowy vehicles for the poetry, and there is a want of clearness and probability in the structure. It was published two years later, in company with another tragedy, in one act, called *William Ratcliffe*, in which there is rather a feeble use of the Scotch second-sight after the manner of the Fate in the Greek tragedy. We smile to find Heine saying of his tragedies, in a letter to a friend soon after their publication: "I know they will be terribly cut up, but I will confess to you in confidence that they are very good, better than my collection of poems, which are not worth a shot." Elsewhere he tells us, that when, after one of Paganini's concerts, he was passionately complimenting the great master on his violin-playing. Paganini interrupted him thus: "But how were you pleased with my *bows?*"

In 1820 Heine left Bonn for Göttingen. He there pursued his omission of law studies, and at the end of three months he was rusticated for a breach of the laws against duelling. While there, he had attempted a negotiation with Brockhaus for the printing of a volume of poems, and had endured the first ordeal of lovers and poets—a refusal. It was not until a year after that he found a Berlin publisher for his first volume of poems, subsequently transformed, with additions, into the "Buch der Lieder." He remained between two and three years at Berlin, and the society he found there seems to have made these years an important epoch in his culture. He was one of the youngest members of a circle which assembled at the house of the poetess Elise von Hohenhausen, the translator of Byron—a circle which included Chamisso, Varnhagen, and Rahel (Varnhagen's wife). For Rahel, Heine had a profound admiration and regard; he afterward dedicated to her the poems included under the title "Heimkehr;" and he frequently refers to her or quotes her in a way that indicates how he valued her influence. According to his friend F. von Hohenhausen, the opinions concerning Heine's talent were very various among his Berlin friends, and it was only a small minority that had any presentiment of his future fame. In this minority was Elise von Hohenhausen, who proclaimed Heine as the Byron of Germany; but her opinion was met with much head-shaking and opposition. We can imagine how precious was such a recognition as hers to the young poet, then only two or three and twenty, and with by no means an impressive personality for superficial eyes. Perhaps even the deep-sighted were far from detecting in that small, blonde, pale young man, with quiet, gentle manners, the latent powers of ridicule and sarcasm—the terrible talons that were one day to be thrust out from the velvet paw of the young leopard.

It was apparently during this residence in Berlin that Heine united himself with the Lutheran Church. He would willingly, like many of his friends, he tells us, have remained free from all ecclesiastical ties if the authorities there had not forbidden residence in Prussia, and especially in Berlin, to every one who did not belong to one of the positive religions recognized by the State.

"As Henry IV. once laughingly said, '*Paris vaut bien une messe,*' so I might with reason say, '*Berlin vaut bien une prêche;*' and I could afterward, as before, accommodate myself to the very enlightened Christianity, filtrated from all superstition, which could then be had in the churches of Berlin, and which was even free from the divinity of Christ, like turtle-soup without turtle."

At the same period, too, Heine became acquainted with Hegel. In his lately published "Geständnisse" (Confessions) he throws on Hegel's influence over him the blue light of demoniacal wit, and confounds us by the most bewildering double-edged sarcasms; but that influence seems to have been at least more wholesome than the one which produced the mocking retractations of the "Geständnisse." Through all his self-satire, we discern that in those days he had something like real earnestness and enthusiasm, which are certainly not apparent in his present theistic confession of faith.

"On the whole, I never felt a strong enthusiasm for this philosophy, and conviction on the subject was out of question. I never was an abstract thinker, and I accepted the synthesis of the Hegelian doctrine without demanding any proof, since its consequences flattered my vanity. I was young and proud, and it pleased my vainglory when I learned from Hegel that the true God was not, as my grandmother believed, the God who lives in heaven, but myself here upon earth. This foolish pride had not in the least a pernicious influence on my feelings; on the contrary, it heightened these to the pitch of heroism. I was at that time so lavish in generosity and self-sacrifice that I must assuredly have eclipsed the most brilliant deeds of those good *bourgeois* of virtue who acted merely from a sense of duty, and simply obeyed the laws of morality."

His sketch of Hegel is irresistibly amusing; but we must warn the reader that Heine's anecdotes are often mere devices of style by which he conveys his satire or opinions. The reader will see that he does not neglect an opportunity of giving a sarcastic lash or two, in passing, to Meyerbeer, for whose music he has a great contempt. The sarcasm conveyed in the substitution of *reputation* for *music* and *journalists* for *musicians*, might perhaps escape any one unfamiliar with the sly and unexpected turns of Heine's ridicule.

"To speak frankly, I seldom understood him, and only arrived at the meaning of his words by subsequent reflection. I believe he wished not to be understood; and hence his practice of sprinkling his discourse with modifying parentheses; hence, perhaps, his preference for persons of whom he knew that they did not understand him, and to whom he all the more willingly granted the honor of his familiar acquaintance. Thus every one in Berlin wondered at the intimate companionship of the profound Hegel with the late Heinrich Beer, a brother of Giacomo Meyerbeer, who is universally known by his reputation, and who has been celebrated by the cleverest journalists. This Beer, namely Heinrich, was a thoroughly stupid fellow, and indeed was afterward actually declared imbecile by his family, and placed under guardianship, because instead of making a name for himself in art or in science by means of his great fortune, he squandered his money on childish trifles ; and, for example, one day bought six thousand thalers' worth of walking-sticks. This poor man, who had no wish to pass either for a great tragic dramatist, or for a great star-gazer, or for a laurel-crowned musical genius, a rival of Mozart and Rossini, and preferred giving his money for walking-sticks—this degenerate Beer enjoyed Hegel's most confidential society ; he was the philosopher's bosom friend, his Pylades, and accompanied him everywhere like his shadow. The equally witty and gifted Felix Mendelssohn once sought to explain this phenomenon, by maintaining that Hegel did not understand Heinrich Beer. I now believe, however, that the real ground of that intimacy consisted in this—Hegel was convinced that no word of what he said was understood by Heinrich Beer ; and he could therefore, in his presence, give himself up to all the intellectual outpourings of the moment. In general, Hegel's conversation was a sort of monologue, sighed forth by starts in a noiseless voice ; the odd roughness of his expressions often struck me, and many of them have remained in my memory. One beautiful starlight evening we stood together at the window, and I, a young man of one-and-twenty, having just had a good dinner and finished my coffee, spoke with enthusiasm of the stars, and called them the habitations of the departed. But the master muttered to himself, 'The stars ! hum ! hum ! The stars are only a brilliant leprosy on the face of the heavens.' 'For God's sake,' I cried, 'is there, then, no happy place above, where virtue is rewarded after death ?' But he, staring at me with his pale eyes, said, cuttingly, 'So you want a bonus for having taken care of your sick mother, and refrained from poisoning your worthy brother ?' At these words he looked anxiously round, but appeared immediately set at rest when he observed that it was only Heinrich Beer, who had approached to invite him to a game at whist."

In 1823 Heine returned to Göttingen to complete his career as a law-student, and this time he gave evidence of advanced mental maturity, not only by producing many of the charming poems subsequently included in the "Reisebilder," but also by prosecuting his professional studies diligently enough to leave Göttingen, in 1825, as *Doctor juris*. Hereupon he settled at Hamburg as an advocate, but his profession seems to have been the least pressing of his occupations. In those days a small blonde young man, with the brim of his hat drawn over his nose, his coat flying open, and his hands stuck in his trousers pockets, might be seen stumbling along the streets of Hamburg, staring from side to side, and appearing to have small regard to the figure he made in the eyes of the good citizens. Occasionally an inhabitant more literary than usual would point out this young man to his companion as *Heinrich Heine*; but in general the young poet had not to endure the inconveniences of being a lion. His poems were devoured, but he was not asked to devour flattery in return. Whether because the fair Hamburgers acted in the spirit of Johnson's advice to Hannah More—to "consider what her flattery was worth before she choked him with it"—or for some other reason, Heine, according to the testimony of August Lewald, to whom we owe these particulars of his Hamburg life, was left free from the persecution of tea-parties. Not, however, from another persecution of Genius—nervous headaches, which some persons, we are told, regarded as an improbable fiction, intended as a pretext for raising a delicate white hand to his forehead. It is probable that the sceptical persons alluded to were themselves untroubled with nervous headaches, and that their hands were *not* delicate. Slight details, these, but worth telling about a man of genius, because they help us to keep in mind that he is, after all, our brother, having to endure the petty every-day ills of life as we have; with this difference, that his heightened sensibility converts what are mere insect stings for us into scorpion stings for him.

It was, perhaps, in these Hamburg days that Heine paid the visit to Goethe, of which he gives us this charming little picture:

"When I visited him in Weimar, and stood before him, I involuntarily glanced at his side to see whether the eagle was not there with the lightning in his beak. I was nearly speaking Greek to him; but, as I observed that he understood German, I stated to him in German that the plums on the road between Jena and Weimar were very good. I had for so many long winter nights thought over what lofty and profound things I would say to Goethe, if ever I saw him. And when I saw him at last, I said to him, that the Saxon plums were very good! And Goethe smiled."

During the next few years Heine produced the most popular of all his works—those which have won him his place as the greatest of living German poets and humorists. Between 1826 and 1829 appeared the four volumes of the "Reisebilder" (Pictures of Travel) and the "Buch der Lieder" (Book of Songs), a volume of lyrics, of which it is hard to say whether their greatest charm is the lightness and finish of their style, their vivid and original imaginativeness, or their simple, pure sensibility. In his "Reisebilder" Heine carries us with him to the Hartz, to the isle of Norderney, to his native town Düsseldorf, to Italy, and to England, sketching scenery and character, now with the wildest, most fantastic humor, now with the finest idyllic sensibility—letting his thoughts wander from poetry to politics, from criticism to dreamy reverie, and blending fun, imagination, reflection, and satire in a sort of exquisite, ever-varying shimmer, like the hues of the opal.

Heine's journey to England did not at all heighten his regard for the English. He calls our language the "hiss of egoism (*Zischlaute des Egoismus*); and his ridicule of English awkwardness is as merciless as—English ridicule of German awkwardness. His antipathy toward us seems to have grown in intensity, like many of his other antipathies; and in his "Vermischte Schriften" he is more bitter than ever. Let us quote one of his philippics, since bitters are understood to be wholesome:

"It is certainly a frightful injustice to pronounce sentence of condemnation on an entire people. But with regard to the English, momentary disgust might betray me into this injustice; and on looking at the mass I easily forget the many brave and noble men who distinguished themselves by intellect and love of freedom. But these, especially the British poets, were always all the more glaringly in contrast with the rest of the nation; they were isolated martyrs to their national relations; and, besides, great geniuses do not belong to the particular land of their birth: they scarcely belong to this earth, the Golgotha of their sufferings. The mass—the English blockheads, God forgive me!—are hateful to me in my inmost soul; and I often regard them not at all as my fellow-men, but as miserable automata—machines, whose motive power is egoism. In these moods, it seems to me as if I heard the whizzing wheelwork by which they think, feel, reckon, digest, and pray: their praying, their mechanical Anglican church-going, with the gilt Prayer-book under their arms, their stupid, tiresome Sunday, their awkward piety, is most of all odious to me. I am firmly convinced that a blaspheming Frenchman is a more pleasing sight for the Divinity than a praying Englishman."

On his return from England Heine was employed at Munich in editing the *Allgemeinen Politischen Annalen*, but in 1830 he was again in the north, and the news of the July Revolution surprised him on the island of Heligoland. He has given us a graphic picture of his democratic enthusiasm in those days in some letters, apparently written from Heligoland, which he has inserted in his book on Börne. We quote some passages, not only for their biographic interest as showing a phase of Heine's mental history, but because they are a specimen of his power in that kind of dithyrambic writing which, in less masterly hands, easily becomes ridiculous:

"The thick packet of newspapers arrived from the Continent with these warm, glowing-hot tidings. They were sunbeams wrapped up in packing-paper, and they inflamed my soul till it burst into the wildest conflagration. . . . It is all like a dream to me; especially the name Lafayette sounds to me like a legend out of my earliest childhood. Does he really sit again on horseback, commanding the National Guard? I almost fear it may not be true, for it is in print. I will myself go to Paris, to be convinced of it with my bodily eyes. . . . It must be splendid, when he rides through the street, the citizen of two worlds, the godlike old man, with his silver locks streaming down his sacred shoulder. . . . He greets, with his dear old eyes, the grandchildren of those who once fought with him for freedom and equality. . . . It is now sixty years since he returned from America with the Declaration of Human Rights, the decalogue of the world's new creed, which was revealed to him amid the thunders and lightnings of cannon. . . . And the tricolored flag waves again on the towers of Paris, and its streets resound with the Marseillaise! . . . It is all over with my yearning for repose. I now knew again what I will do, what I ought to do, what I must do. . . . I am the son of the Revolution, and seize again the hallowed weapons on which my mother pronounced her magic benediction. . . . Flowers! flowers! I will crown my head for the death-fight. And the lyre too, reach me the lyre, that I may sing a battle-song. . . . Words like flaming stars, that shoot down from the heavens, and burn up the palaces, and illuminate the huts. . . . Words like bright javelins, that whirr up to the seventh heaven and strike the pious hypocrites who have skulked into the Holy of Holies. . . . I am all joy and song, all sword and flame! Perhaps, too, all delirium. . . . One of those sunbeams wrapped in brown paper has flown to my brain, and set my thoughts aglow. In vain I dip my head into the sea. No water extinguishes this Greek fire. . . . Even the poor Heligolanders shout for joy, although they have only a sort of dim instinct of what has occurred. The fisherman who yesterday took me over to the little sand island, which is the bathing-place here, said to me smilingly, 'The poor people have won!' Yes; instinctively the people comprehend such events, perhaps, better than we, with all our means of knowledge. Thus Frau von Varnhagen once told me that when the issue of the Battle of Leipzig was not yet known, the maid-servant suddenly rushed into the room with the sorrowful cry, 'The nobles have won!' . . . This morning another packet of newspapers is come. I devour them like manna. Child that I am, affecting details touch me yet more than the momentous whole. Oh, if I could but see the dog Medor. . . . The dog Medor brought his master his gun and cartridge-box, and when his master fell, and was buried with his fellow-heroes in the Court of the Louvre, there stayed the poor dog like a monument of faithfulness, sitting motionless on the grave, day and night, eating but little of the food that was offered him—burying the greater part of it in the earth, perhaps as nourishment for his buried master!"

The enthusiasm which was kept thus at boiling heat by imagination, cooled down rapidly when brought into contact with reality. In the same book he indicates, in his caustic way, the commencement of that change in his political *temperature*—for it cannot be called a change in opinion—which has drawn down on him immense vituperation from some of the patriotic party, but which seems to have resulted simply from the essential antagonism between keen wit and fanaticism.

"On the very first days of my arrival in Paris I observed that things wore, in reality, quite different colors from those which had been shed on them, when in perspective, by the light of my enthusiasm. The silver locks which I saw fluttering so majestically on the shoulders of Lafayette, the hero of two worlds, were metamorphosed into a brown perruque, which made a pitiable covering for a narrow skull. And even the dog Medor, which I visited in the Court of the Louvre, and which, encamped under tricolored flags and trophies, very quietly allowed himself to be fed—he was not at all the right dog, but quite an ordinary brute, who assumed to himself merits not his own, as often happens with the French; and, like many others, he made a profit out of the glory of the Revolution. . . . He was pampered and patronized, perhaps promoted to the highest posts, while the true Medor, some days after the battle, modestly slunk out of sight, like the true people who created the Revolution."

That it was not merely interest in French politics which sent Heine to Paris in 1831, but also a perception that German air was not friendly to sympathizers in July revolutions, is humorously intimated in the "Geständnisse."

"I had done much and suffered much, and when the sun of the July Revolution arose in France, I had become very weary, and needed some recreation. Also, my native air was every day more unhealthy for me, and it was time I should seriously think of a change of climate. I had visions: the clouds terrified me, and made all sorts of ugly faces at me. It often seemed to me as if the sun were a Prussian cockade; at night I dreamed of a hideous black eagle, which gnawed my liver; and I was very melancholy. Add to this, I had become acquainted with an old Berlin Justizrath, who had spent many years in the fortress of Spandau, and he related to me how unpleasant it is when one is obliged to wear irons in winter. For myself I thought it very unchristian that the irons were not warmed a trifle. If the irons were warmed a little for us they would not make so unpleasant an impression, and even chilly natures might then bear them very well; it would be only proper consideration, too, if the fetters were perfumed with essence of roses and laurels, as is the case in this country (France). I asked my Justizrath whether he often got oysters to eat at Spandau? He said, No; Spandau was too far from the sea. Moreover, he said meat was very scarce there, and there was no kind of *volaille* except flies, which fell into one's soup. . . . Now, as I really needed some recreation, and as Spandau is too far from the sea for oysters to be got there, and the Spandau fly-soup did not seem very appetizing to me, as, besides all this, the Prussian chains are very cold in winter, and could not be conducive to my health, I resolved to visit Paris."

Since this time Paris has been Heine's home, and his best prose works have been written either to inform the Germans on French affairs or to inform the French on German philosophy and literature. He became a correspondent of the *Allgemeine Zeitung*, and his correspondence, which extends, with an interruption of several years, from 1831 to 1844, forms the volume entitled "Französische Zustände" (French Affairs), and the second and third volume of his "Vermischte Schriften." It is a witty and often wise commentary on public men and public events: Louis Philippe, Casimir Périer, Thiers, Guizot, Rothschild, the Catholic party, the Socialist party, have their turn of satire and appreciation, for Heine deals out both with an impartiality which made his less favorable critics—Börne, for example—charge him with the rather incompatible sins of reckless caprice and venality. Literature and art alternate with politics: we have now a sketch of George Sand or a description of one of Horace Vernet's pictures; now a criticism of Victor Hugo or of Liszt; now an irresistible caricature of Spontini or Kalkbrenner; and occasionally the predominant satire is relieved by a fine saying or a genial word of admiration. And all is done with that airy lightness, yet precision of touch, which distinguishes Heine beyond any living writer. The charge of venality was loudly made against Heine in Germany: first, it was said that he was paid to write; then, that he was paid to abstain from writing;

and the accusations were supposed to have an irrefragable basis in the fact that he accepted a stipend from the French government. He has never attempted to conceal the reception of that stipend, and we think his statement (in the "Vermischte Schriften") of the circumstances under which it was offered and received, is a sufficient vindication of himself and M. Guizot from any dishonor in the matter.

It may be readily imagined that Heine, with so large a share of the Gallic element as he has in his composition, was soon at his ease in Parisian society, and the years here were bright with intellectual activity and social enjoyment. "His wit," wrote August Lewald, "is a perpetual gushing fountain; he throws off the most delicious descriptions with amazing facility, and sketches the most comic characters in conversations." Such a man could not be neglected in Paris, and Heine was sought on all sides—as a guest in distinguished salons, as a possible proselyte in the circle of the Saint Simonians. His literary productiveness seems to have been furthered by his congenial life, which, however, was soon to some extent embittered by the sense of exile; for since 1835 both his works and his person have been the object of denunciation by the German governments. Between 1833 and 1845 appeared the four volumes of the "Salon," "Die Romantische Schule" (both written, in the first instance, in French), the book on Börne, "Atta Troll," a romantic poem, "Deutschland," an exquisitely humorous poem, describing his last visit to Germany, and containing some grand passages of serious writing; and the "Neue Gedichte," a collection of lyrical poems. Among the most interesting of his prose works are the second volume of the "Salon," which contains a survey of religion and philosophy in Germany, and the "Romantische Schule," a delightful introduction to that phase of German literature known as the Romantic school. The book on Börne, which appeared in 1840, two years after the death of that writer, excited great indignation in Germany, as a wreaking of vengeance on the dead, an insult to the memory of a man who had worked and suffered in the cause of freedom—a cause which was Heine's own. Börne, we may observe parenthetically for the information of those who are not familiar with recent German literature, was a remarkable political writer of the ultra-liberal party in Germany, who resided in Paris at the same time with Heine: a man of stern, uncompromising partisanship and bitter humor. Without justifying Heine's production of this book, we see excuses for him which should temper the condemnation passed on it. There was a radical opposition of nature between him and Börne; to use his own distinction, Heine is a Hellene—sensuous, realistic, exquisitely alive to the beautiful; while Börne was a Nazarene—ascetic, spiritualistic, despising the pure artist as destitute of earnestness. Heine has too keen a perception of practical absurdities and damaging exaggerations ever to become a thoroughgoing partisan; and with a love of freedom, a faith in the ultimate triumph of democratic principles, of which we see no just reason to doubt the genuineness and consistency, he has been unable to satisfy more zealous and one-sided liberals by giving his adhesion to their views and measures, or by adopting a denunciatory tone against those in the opposite ranks. Börne could not forgive what he regarded as Heine's epicurean indifference and artistic dalliance, and he at length gave vent to his antipathy in savage attacks on him through the press, accusing him of utterly lacking character and principle, and even of writing under the influence of venal motives. To these attacks Heine remained absolutely mute—from contempt according to his own account; but the retort, which he resolutely refrained from making during Börne's life, comes in this volume published after his death with the concentrated force of long-gathering thunder. The utterly inexcusable part of the book is the caricature of Börne's friend, Madame Wohl, and the scurrilous insinuations concerning Börne's domestic life. It is said, we know not with how much truth, that Heine had to answer for these in a duel with Madame Wohl's husband, and that, after receiving a serious wound, he promised to withdraw the offensive matter from a future edition. That edition, however, has not been called for. Whatever else we may think of the book, it is impossible to deny its transcendent talent—the dramatic vigor with which Börne is made present to us, the critical acumen with which he is characterized, and the wonderful play of wit, pathos, and thought which runs through the whole. But we will let Heine speak for himself, and first we will give part of his graphic description of the way in which Börne's mind and manners grated on his taste :

"To the disgust which, in intercourse with Börne, I was in danger of feeling toward those who surrounded him, was added the annoyance I felt from his perpetual talk about politics. Nothing but political argument, and again political argument, even at table, where he managed to hunt me out. At dinner, when I so gladly forget all the vexations of the world, he spoiled the best dishes for me by his patriotic gall, which he poured as a bitter sauce over everything. Calf's feet, *à la maître d'hôtel*, then my innocent *bonne bouche*, he completely spoiled for me by Job's tidings from Germany, which he scraped together out of the most unreliable newspapers. And then his accursed remarks, which spoiled one's appetite! . . . This was a sort of table-talk which did not greatly exhilarate me, and I avenged myself by affecting an excessive, almost impassioned indifference for the object of Börne's enthusiasm. For example, Börne was indignant that immediately on my arrival in Paris I had nothing better to do than to write for German papers a long account of the Exhibition of Pictures. I omit all discussion as to whether that interest in Art which induced me to undertake this work was so utterly irreconcilable with the revolutionary interests of the day ; but Börne saw in it a proof of my indifference toward the sacred cause of humanity, and I could in my turn spoil the taste of his patriotic *sauerkraut* for him by talking all dinner-time of nothing but pictures, of Robert's 'Reapers,' Horace Vernet's 'Judith,' and Scheffer's 'Faust.' . . . That I never thought it worth while to discuss my political principles with him it is needless to say ; and once when he declared that he had found a contradiction in my writings, I satisfied myself with the ironical answer, 'You are mistaken, *mon cher ;* such contradictions never occur in my works, for always before I begin to write, I read over the statement of my political principles in my previous writings, that I may not contradict myself, and that no one may be able to reproach me with apostasy from my liberal principles.'"

And here is his own account of the spirit in which the book was written:

"I was never Börne's friend, nor was I ever his enemy. The displeasure which he could often excite in me was never very important, and he atoned for it sufficiently by the cold silence which I opposed to all his accusations and raillery. While he lived I wrote not a line against him, I never thought about him, I ignored him completely; and that enraged him beyond measure. If I now speak of him, I do so neither out of enthusiasm nor out of uneasiness; I am conscious of the coolest impartiality. I write here neither an apology nor a critique, and as in painting the man I go on my own observation, the image I present of him ought perhaps to be regarded as a real portrait. And such a monument is due to him—to the great wrestler who, in the arena of our political games, wrestled so courageously, and earned, if not the laurel, certainly the crown of oak leaves. I give an image with his true features, without idealization—the more like him the more honorable for his memory. He was neither a genius nor a hero; he was no Olympian god. He was a man, a denizen of this earth; he was a good writer and a great patriot. . . . Beautiful, delicious peace, which I feel at this moment in the depths of my soul! Thou rewardest me sufficiently for everything I have done and for everything I have despised. . . . I shall defend myself neither from the reproach of indifference nor from the suspicion of venality. I have for years, during the life of the insinuator, held such self-justification unworthy of me; now even decency demands silence. That would be a frightful spectacle!—polemics between Death and Exile! Dost thou stretch out to me a beseeching hand from the grave? Without rancor I reach mine toward thee. . . . See how noble it is and pure! It was never soiled by pressing the hands of the mob, any more than by the impure gold of the people's enemy. In reality thou hast never injured me. . . . In all thy insinuations there is not a *louis d'or's* worth of truth."

In one of these years Heine was married, and, in deference to the sentiments of his wife, married according to the rites of the Catholic Church. On this fact busy rumor afterward founded the story of his conversion to Catholicism, and could of course name the day and spot on which he abjured Protestanism. In his "Geständnisse" Heine publishes a denial of this rumor; less, he says, for the sake of depriving the Catholics of the solace they may derive from their belief in a new convert, than in order to cut off from another party the more spiteful satisfaction of bewailing his instability :

"That statement of time and place was entirely correct. I was actually on the specified day in the specified church, which was, moreover, a Jesuit church, namely, St. Sulpice ; and I then went through a religious act. But this act was no odious abjuration, but a very innocent conjugation ; that is to say, my marriage, already performed, according to the civil law there received the ecclesiastical consecration, because my wife, whose family are staunch Catholics, would not have thought her marriage sacred enough without such a ceremony. And I would on no account cause this beloved being any uneasiness or disturbance in her religious views."

For sixteen years—from 1831 to 1847—Heine lived that rapid concentrated life which is known only in Paris ; but then, alas ! stole on the "days of darkness," and they were to be many. In 1847 he felt the approach of the terrible spinal disease which has for seven years chained him to his bed in acute suffering. The last time he went out of doors, he tells us, was in May, 1848 :

"With difficulty I dragged myself to the Louvre, and I almost sank down as I entered the magnificent hall where the ever-blessed goddess of beauty, our beloved Lady of Milo, stands on her pedestal. At her feet I lay long, and wept so bitterly that a stone must have pitied me. The goddess looked compassionately on me, but at the same time disconsolately, as if she would say, Dost thou not see, then, that I have no arms, and thus cannot help thee ?"

Since 1848, then, this poet, whom the lovely objects of Nature have always "haunted like a passion," has not descended from the second story of a Parisian house ; this man of hungry intellect has been shut out from all direct observation of life, all contact with society, except such as is derived from visitors to his sick-room. The terrible nervous disease has affected his eyes ; the sight of one is utterly gone, and he can only raise the lid of the other by lifting it with his finger. Opium alone is the beneficent genius that stills his pain. We hardly know whether to call it an alleviation or an intensification of the torture that Heine retains his mental vigor, his poetic imagination, and his incisive wit; for if this intellectual activity fills up a blank, it widens the sphere of suffering. His brother described him in 1851 as still, in moments when the hand of pain was not too heavy on him, the same Heinrich Heine, poet and satirist by turns. In such moments he would narrate the strangest things in the gravest manner. But when he came to an end, he would roguishly lift up the lid of his right eye with his finger to see the impression he had produced; and if his audience had been listening with a serious face, he would break into Homeric laughter. We have other proof than personal testimony that Heine's disease allows his genius to retain much of its energy, in the "Romanzero," a volume of poems published in 1851, and written chiefly during the three first years of his illness; and in the first volume of the "Vermischte Schriften," also the product of recent years. Very plaintive is the poet's own description of his condition, in the epilogue to the "Romanzero:"

"Do I really exist? My body is so shrunken that I am hardly anything but a voice; and my bed reminds me of the singing grave of the magician Merlin, which lies in the forest of Brozeliand, in Brittany, under tall oaks whose tops soar like green flames toward heaven. Alas! I envy thee those trees and the fresh breeze that moves their branches, brother Merlin, for no green leaf rustles about my mattress-grave in Paris, where early and late I hear nothing but the rolling of vehicles, hammering, quarrelling, and piano-strumming. A grave without repose, death without the privileges of the dead, who have no debts to pay, and need write neither letters nor books—that is a piteous condition. Long ago the measure has been taken for my coffin and for my necrology, but I die so slowly that the process is tedious for me as well as my friends. But patience: everything has an end. You will one day find the booth closed where the puppet-show of my humor has so often delighted you."

As early as 1850 it was rumored that since Heine's illness a change had taken place in his religious views; and as rumor seldom stops short of extremes, it was soon said that he had become a thorough pietist, Catholics and Protestants by turns claiming him as a convert. Such a change in so uncompromising an iconoclast, in a man who had been so zealous in his negations as Heine, naturally excited considerable sensation in the camp he was supposed to have quitted, as well as in that he was supposed to have joined. In the second volume of the "Salon," and in the "Romantische Schule," written in 1834 and '35, the doctrine of Pantheism is dwelt on with a fervor and unmixed seriousness which show that Pantheism was then an animating faith to Heine, and he attacks what he considers the false spiritualism and asceticism of Christianity as the enemy of true beauty in Art, and of social well-being. Now, however, is was said that Heine had recanted all his heresies; but from the fact that visitors to his sick-room brought away very various impressions as to his actual religious views, it seemed probable that his love of mystification had found a tempting opportunity for exercise on this subject, and that, as one of his friends said, he was not inclined to pour out unmixed wine to those who asked for a sample out of mere curiosity. At length, in the epilogue to the "Romanzero," dated 1851, there appeared, amid much mystifying banter, a declaration that he had embraced Theism and the belief in a future life, and what chiefly lent an air of seriousness and reliability to this affirmation was the fact that he took care to accompany it with certain negations:

"As concerns myself, I can boast of no particular progress in politics; I adhered (after 1848) to the same democratic principles which had the homage of my youth, and for which I have ever since glowed with increasing fervor. In theology, on the contrary, I must accuse myself of retrogression, since, as I have already confessed, I returned to the old superstition—to a personal God. This fact is, once for all, not to be stifled, as many enlightened and well-meaning friends would fain have had it. But I must expressly contradict the report that my retrograde movement has carried me as far as to the threshold of a Church, and that I have even been received into her lap. No: my religious convictions and views have remained free from any tincture of ecclesiasticism; no chiming of bells has allured me, no altar candles have dazzled me. I have dallied with no dogmas, and have not utterly renounced my reason."

This sounds like a serious statement. But what shall we say to a convert who plays with his newly-acquired belief in a future life, as Heine does in the very next page? He says to his reader:

"Console thyself; we shall meet again in a better world, where I also mean to write thee better books. I take for granted that my health will there be improved, and that Swedenborg has not deceived me. He relates, namely, with great confidence, that we shall peacefully carry on our old occupations in the other world, just as we have done in this; that we shall there preserve our individuality unaltered, and that death will produce no particular change in our organic development. Swedenborg is a thoroughly honorable fellow, and quite worthy of credit in what he tells us about the other world, where he saw with his own eyes the persons who had played a great part on our earth. Most of them, he says, remained unchanged, and busied themselves with the same things as formerly; they remained stationary, were old-fashioned, *rococo*—which now and then produced a ludicrous effect. For example, our dear Dr. Martin Luther kept fast by his doctrine of Grace, about which he had for three hundred years daily written down the same mouldy arguments—just in the same way as the late Baron Ekstein, who during twenty years printed in the *Allgemeine Zeitung* one and the same article, perpetually chewing over again the old cud of Jesuitical doctrine. But, as we have said, all persons who once figured here below were not found by Swedenborg in such a state of fossil immutability: many had considerably developed their character, both for good and evil, in the other world; and this gave rise to some singular results. Some who had been heroes and saints on earth had *there* sunk into scamps and good-for-nothings; and there were examples, too, of a contrary transformation. For instance, the fumes of self-conceit mounted to Saint Anthony's head when he learned what immense veneration and adoration had been paid to him by all Christendom; and he who here below withstood the most terrible temptations was now quite an impertinent rascal and dissolute gallows-bird, who vied with his pig in rolling himself in the mud. The chaste Susanna, from having been excessively vain of her virtue, which she thought indomitable, came to a shameful fall, and she who once so gloriously resisted the two old men, was a victim to the seductions of the young Absalom, the son of David. On the contrary, Lot's daughters had in the lapse of time become very virtuous, and passed in the other world for models of propriety: the old man, alas! had stuck to the wine-flask."

In his "Geständnisse," the retractation of former opinions and profession of Theism are renewed, but in a strain of irony that repels our sympathy and baffles our psychology. Yet what strange, deep pathos is mingled with the audacity of the following passage!

"What avails it me, that enthusiastic youths and maidens crown my marble bust with laurel, when the withered hands of an aged nurse are pressing Spanish flies behind my ears? What avails it me, that all the roses of Shiraz glow and waft incense for me? Alas! Shiraz is two thousand miles from the Rue d'Amsterdam, where, in the wearisome loneliness of my sick-room, I get no scent, except it be, perhaps, the perfume of warmed towels. Alas! God's satire weighs heavily on me. The great Author of the universe, the Aristophanes of Heaven, was bent on demonstrating, with crushing force, to me, the little, earthly, German Aristophanes, how my wittiest sarcasms are only pitiful attempts at jesting in comparison with His, and how miserably I am beneath him in humor, in colossal mockery."

For our own part, we regard the paradoxical irreverence with which Heine professes his theoretical reverence as pathological, as the diseased exhibition of a predominant tendency urged into anomalous action by the pressure of pain and mental privation—as a delirium of wit starved of its proper nourishment. It is not for us to condemn, who have never had the same burden laid on us; it is not for pigmies at their ease to criticise the writhings of the Titan chained to the rock.

On one other point we must touch before quitting Heine's personal history. There is a standing accusation against him in some quarters of wanting political principle, of wishing to denationalize himself, and of indulging in insults against his native country. Whatever ground may exist for these accusations, that ground is not, so far as we see, to be found in his writings. He may not have much faith in German revolutions and revolutionists; experience, in his case as in that of others, may have thrown his millennial anticipations into more distant perspective; but we see no evidence that he has ever swerved from his attachment to the principles of freedom, or written anything which to a philosophic mind is incompatible with true patriotism. He has expressly denied the report that he wished to become naturalized in France; and his yearning toward his native land and the accents of his native language is expressed with a pathos the more reliable from the fact that he is sparing in such effusions. We do not see why Heine's satire of the blunders and foibles of his fellow-countrymen should be denounced as a crime of *lèse-patrie*, any more than the political caricatures of any other satirist. The real offences of Heine are his occasional coarseness and his unscrupulous personalities, which are reprehensible, not because they are directed against his fellow-countrymen, but because they are *personalities*. That these offences have their precedents in men whose memory the world delights to honor does not remove their turpitude, but it is a fact which should modify our condemnation in a particular case; unless, indeed, we are to deliver our judgments on a principle of compensation—making up for our indulgence in one direction by our severity in another. On this ground of coarseness and personality, a true bill may be found against Heine; *not*, we think, on the ground that he has laughed at what is laughable in his compatriots. Here is a specimen of the satire under which we suppose German patriots wince:

"Rhenish Bavaria was to be the starting-point of the German revolution. Zweibrücken was the Bethlehem in which the infant Saviour—Freedom—lay in the cradle, and gave whimpering promise of redeeming the world. Near his cradle bellowed many an ox, who afterward, when his horns were reckoned on, showed himself a very harmless brute. It was confidently believed that the German revolution would begin in Zweibrücken, and everything was there ripe for an outbreak. But, as has been hinted, the tender-heartedness of some persons frustrated that illegal undertaking. For example, among the Bipontine conspirators there was a tremendous braggart, who was always loudest in his rage, who boiled over with the hatred of tyranny, and this man was fixed on to strike the first blow, by cutting down a sentinel who kept an important post. . . . . 'What!' cried the man, when this order was given him—'What!—me! Can you expect so horrible, so bloodthirsty an act of me? I—*I*, kill an innocent sentinel? I, who am the father of a family! And this sentinel is perhaps also father of a family. One father of a family kill another father of a family? Yes. Kill—murder!'"

In political matters Heine, like all men whose intellect and taste predominate too far over their impulses to allow of their becoming partisans, is offensive alike to the aristocrat and the democrat. By the one he is denounced as a man who holds incendiary principles, by the other as a half-hearted "trimmer." He has no sympathy, as he says, with "that vague, barren pathos, that useless effervescence of enthusiasm, which plunges, with the spirit of a martyr, into an ocean of generalities, and which always reminds me of the American sailor, who had so fervent an enthusiasm for General Jackson, that he at last sprang from the top of a mast into the sea, crying, "*I die for General Jackson!*"

"But thou liest, Brutus, thou liest, Cassius, and thou, too, liest, Asinius, in maintaining that my ridicule attacks those ideas which are the precious acquisition of Humanity, and for which I myself have so striven and suffered. No! for the very reason that those ideas constantly hover before the poet in glorious splendor and majesty, he is the more irresistibly overcome by laughter when he sees how rudely, awkwardly, and clumsily those ideas are seized and mirrored in the contracted minds of contemporaries. . . . There are mirrors which have so rough a surface that even an Apollo reflected in them becomes a caricature, and excites our laughter. *But we laugh then only at the caricature, not at the god.*"

For the rest, why should we demand of Heine that he should be a hero, a patriot, a solemn prophet, any more than we should demand of a gazelle that it should draw well in harness? Nature has not made him of her sterner stuff—not of iron and adamant, but of pollen of flowers, the juice of the grape, and Puck's mischievous brain, plenteously mixing also the dews of kindly affection and the gold-dust of noble thoughts. It is, after all, a *tribute* which his enemies pay him when they utter their bitterest dictum, namely, that he is "*nur Dichter*"—only a poet. Let us accept this point of view for the present, and, leaving all consideration of him as a man, look at him simply as a poet and literary artist.

Heine is essentially a lyric poet. The finest products of his genius are

> "Short swallow flights of song that dip
> Their wings in tears, and skim away;"

and they are so emphatically songs that, in reading them, we feel as if each must have a twin melody born in the same moment and by the same inspiration. Heine is too impressible and mercurial for any sustained production; even in his short lyrics his tears sometimes pass into laughter and his laughter into tears; and his longer poems, "Atta Troll" and "Deutschland," are full of Ariosto-like transitions. His song has a wide compass of notes; he can take us to the shores of the Northern Sea and thrill us by the sombre sublimity of his pictures and dreamy fancies; he can draw forth our tears by the voice he gives to our own sorrows, or to the sorrows of "Poor Peter;" he can throw a cold shudder over us by a mysterious legend, a ghost story, or a still more ghastly rendering of hard reality; he can charm us by a quiet idyl, shake us with laughter at his overflowing fun, or give us a piquant sensation of surprise by the ingenuity of his transitions from the lofty to the ludicrous. This last power is not, indeed, essentially poetical; but only a poet can use it with the same success as Heine, for only a poet can poise our emotion and expectation at such a height as to give effect to the sudden fall. Heine's greatest power as a poet lies in his simple pathos, in the ever-varied but always natural expression he has given to the tender emotions. We may perhaps indicate this phase of his genius by referring to Wordsworth's beautiful little poem, "She dwelt among the untrodden ways;" the conclusion—

> "She dwelt alone, and few could know
> When Lucy ceased to be;
> But she is in her grave, and, oh!
> The difference to me"—

is entirely in Heine's manner; and so is Tennyson's poem of a dozen lines, call "Circumstance." Both these poems have Heine's pregnant simplicity. But, lest this comparison should mislead, we must say that there is no general resemblance between either Wordsworth, or Tennyson, and Heine. Their greatest qualities lie quite a way from the light, delicate lucidity, the easy, rippling music, of Heine's style. The distinctive charm of his lyrics may best be seen by comparing them with Goethe's. Both have the same masterly, finished simplicity and rhythmic grace; but there is more thought mingled with Goethe's feeling—his lyrical genius is a vessel that draws more water than Heine's, and, though it seems to glide along with equal ease, we have a sense of greater weight and force, accompanying the grace of its movements.

But for this very reason Heine touches our hearts more strongly; his songs are all music and feeling—they are like birds that not only enchant us with their delicious notes, but nestle against us with their soft breasts, and make us feel the agitated beating of their hearts. He indicates a whole sad history in a single quatrain; there is not an image in it, not a thought; but it is beautiful, simple, and perfect as a "big round tear"—it is pure feeling, breathed in pure music:

"Anfangs wollt' ich fast verzagen
Und ich glaubt' ich trug es nie,
Und ich hab' es doch getragen—
Aber fragt mich nur nicht, wie." *

He excels equally in the more imaginative expression of feeling: he represents it by a brief image, like a finely cut cameo; he expands it into a mysterious dream, or dramatizes it in a little story, half ballad, half idyl; and in all these forms his art is so perfect that we never have a sense of artificiality or of unsuccessful effort; but all seems to have developed itself by the same beautiful necessity that brings forth vine-leaves and

* At first I was almost in despair, and I thought I could never bear it, and yet I have borne it—only do not ask me *how?*

grapes and the natural curls of childhood. Of Heine's humorous poetry, "Deutschland" is the most charming specimen—charming, especially, because its wit and humor grow out of a rich loam of thought. "Atta Troll" is more original, more various, more fantastic; but it is too great a strain on the imagination to be a general favorite. We have said that feeling is the element in which Heine's poetic genius habitually floats; but he can occasionally soar to a higher region, and impart deep significance to picturesque symbolism; he can flash a sublime thought over the past and into the future; he can pour forth a lofty strain of hope or indignation. Few could forget, after once hearing them, the stanzas at the close of "Deutschland," in which he warns the King of Prussia not to incur the irredeemable hell which the injured poet can create for him—the *singing flames* of a Dante's *terza rima!*

"Kennst du die Hölle des Dante nicht,
Die schrecklichen Terzetten?
Wen da der Dichter hineingesperrt
Den kann kein Gott mehr retten.

"Kein Gott, kein Heiland, erlöst ihn je
Aus diesen singenden Flammen!
Nimm dich in Acht, das wir dich nicht
Zu solcher Hölle verdammen." *

As a prosaist, Heine is, in one point of view, even more distinguished than as a poet. The German language easily lends itself to all the purposes of poetry; like the ladies of the Middle Ages, it is gracious and compliant to the Troubadours. But as these same ladies were often crusty and repulsive to their

* It is not fair to the English reader to indulge in German quotations, but in our opinion poetical translations are usually worse than valueless. For those who think differently, however, we may mention that Mr. Stores Smith has published a modest little book, containing "Selections from the Poetry of Heinrich Heine," and that a meritorious (American) translation of Heine's complete works, by Charles Leland, is now appearing in shilling numbers.

unmusical mates, so the German language generally appears awkward and unmanageable in the hands of prose writers. Indeed, the number of really fine German prosaists before Heine would hardly have exceeded the numerating powers of a New Hollander, who can count three and no more. Persons the most familiar with German prose testify that there is an extra fatigue in reading it, just as we feel an extra fatigue from our walk when it takes us over ploughed clay. But in Heine's hands German prose, usually so heavy, so clumsy, so dull, becomes, like clay in the hands of the chemist, compact, metallic, brilliant; it is German in an *allotropic* condition. No dreary labyrinthine sentences in which you find "no end in wandering mazes lost;" no chains of adjectives in linked harshness long drawn out; no digressions thrown in as parentheses; but crystalline definiteness and clearness, fine and varied rhythm, and all that delicate precision, all those felicities of word and cadence, which belong to the highest order of prose. And Heine has proved—what Madame de Stäel seems to have doubted—that it is possible to be witty in German; indeed, in reading him, you might imagine that German was pre-eminently the language of wit, so flexible, so subtle, so piquant does it become under his management. He is far more an artist in prose than Goethe. He has not the breadth and repose, and the calm development which belong to Goethe's style, for they are foreign to his mental character; but he excels Goethe in susceptibility to the manifold qualities of prose, and in mastery over its effects. Heine is full of variety, of light and shadow: he alternates between epigrammatic pith, imaginative grace, sly allusion, and daring piquancy; and athwart all these there runs a vein of sadness, tenderness, and grandeur which reveals the poet. He continually throws out those finely chiselled sayings which stamp themselves on the memory, and become familiar by quotation. For example: "The People have time enough, they are immortal; kings only are mortal." —"Wherever a great soul utters its thoughts, there is Golgotha."—"Nature wanted to see how she looked, and she created Goethe."—"Only the man who has known bodily suffering is truly a *man*; his limbs have their Passion history, they are spiritualized." He calls Rubens "this Flemish Titan, the wings of whose genius were so strong that he soared as high as the sun, in spite of the hundred-weight of Dutch cheeses that hung on his legs." Speaking of Börne's dislike to the calm creations of the true artist, he says, "He was like a child which, insensible to the glowing significance of a Greek statue, only touches the marble and complains of cold."

The most poetic and specifically humorous of Heine's prose writings are the "Reisebilder." The comparison with Sterne is inevitable here; but Heine does not suffer from it, for if he falls below Sterne in raciness of humor, he is far above him in poetic sensibility and in reach and variety of thought. Heine's humor is never persistent, it never flows on long in easy gayety and drollery; where it is not swelled by the tide of poetic feeling, it is continually dashing down the precipice of a witticism. It is not broad and unctuous; it is aërial and sprite-like, a momentary resting-place between his poetry and his wit. In the "Reisebilder" he runs through the whole gamut of his powers, and gives us every hue of thought, from the wildly droll and fantastic to the sombre and the terrible. Here is a passage almost Dantesque in conception:

"Alas! one ought in truth to write against no one in this world. Each of us is sick enough in this great lazaretto, and many a polemical writing reminds me involuntarily of a revolting quarrel, in a little hospital at Cracow, of which I chanced to be a witness, and where it was horrible to hear how the patients mockingly reproached each other with their infirmities: how one who was wasted by consumption jeered at another who was bloated by dropsy; how one laughed at another's cancer in the nose, and this one again at his neighbor's locked-jaw or squint, until at last the delirious fever-patient sprang out of bed and tore away the coverings from the wounded bodies of his companions, and nothing was to be seen but hideous misery and mutilation."

And how fine is the transition in the very next chapter,

where, after quoting the Homeric description of the feasting gods, he says :

"Then suddenly approached, panting, a pale Jew, with drops of blood on his brow, with a crown of thorns on his head, and a great cross laid on his shoulders ; and he threw the cross on the high table of the gods, so that the golden cups tottered, and the gods became dumb and pale, and grew ever paler, till they at last melted away into vapor."

The richest specimens of Heine's wit are perhaps to be found in the works which have appeared since the "Reisebilder." The years, if they have intensified his satirical bitterness, have also given his wit a finer edge and polish. His sarcasms are so subtly prepared and so slily allusive, that they may often escape readers whose sense of wit is not very acute ; but for those who delight in the subtle and delicate flavors of style, there can hardly be any wit more irresistible than Heine's. We may measure its force by the degree in which it has subdued the German language to its purposes, and made that language brilliant in spite of a long hereditary transmission of dulness. As one of the most harmless examples of his satire, take this on a man who has certainly had his share of adulation :

"Assuredly it is far from my purpose to depreciate M. Victor Cousin. The titles of this celebrated philosopher even lay me under an obligation to praise him. He belongs to that living pantheon of France which we call the peerage, and his intelligent legs rest on the velvet benches of the Luxembourg. I must indeed sternly repress all private feelings which might seduce me into an excessive enthusiasm. Otherwise I might be suspected of servility ; for M. Cousin is very influential in the State by means of his position and his tongue. This consideration might even move me to speak of his faults as frankly as of his virtues. Will he himself disapprove of this? Assuredly not. I know that we cannot do higher honor to great minds than when we throw as strong a light on their demerits as on their merits. When we sing the praises of a Hercules, we must also mention that he once laid aside the lion's skin and sat down to the distaff : what then? he remains notwithstanding a Hercules! So when we relate similar circumstances concerning M. Cousin, we must nevertheless add, with discriminating eulogy: *M. Cousin, if he has sometimes sat twaddling at the distaff, has never laid aside the lion's skin.* . . . It is true that, having been suspected of demagogy, he spent some time in a German prison, just as Lafayette and Richard Cœur de Lion. But that M. Cousin there in his leisure hours studied Kant's 'Critique of Pure Reason' is to be doubted on three grounds. First, this book is written in German. Secondly, in order to read this book, a man must understand German. Thirdly, M. Cousin does not understand German. . . . I fear I am passing unawares from the sweet waters of praise into the bitter ocean of blame. Yes, on one account I cannot refrain from bitterly blaming M. Cousin—namely, that he who loves truth far more than he loves Plato and Tenneman is unjust to himself when he wants to persuade us that he has borrowed something from the philosophy of Schelling and Hegel. Against this self-accusation I must take M. Cousin under my protection. On my word and conscience! this honorable man has not stolen a jot from Schelling and Hegel, and if he brought home anything of theirs, it was merely their friendship. That does honor to his heart. But there are many instances of such false self-accusation in psychology. I knew a man who declared that he had stolen silver spoons at the king's table; and yet we all knew that the poor devil had never been presented at court, and accused himself of stealing these spoons to make us believe that he had been a guest at the palace. No! In German philosophy M. Cousin has always kept the sixth commandment; here he has never pocketed a single idea, not so much as a salt-spoon of an idea. All witnesses agree in attesting that in this respect M. Cousin is honor itself. . . . I prophesy to you that the renown of M. Cousin, like the French Revolution, will go round the world! I hear some one wickedly add: Undeniably the renown of M. Cousin is going round the world, and *it has already taken its departure from France.*"

The following "symbolical myth" about Louis Philippe is very characteristic of Heine's manner:

"I remember very well that immediately on my arrival (in Paris) I hastened to the Palais Royal to see Louis Philippe. The friend who conducted me told me that the king now appeared on the terrace only at stated hours, but that formerly he was to be seen at any time for five francs. 'For five francs!' I cried with amazement; 'does he then show himself for money?' 'No, but he is shown for money, and it happens in this way: There is a society of *claqueurs, marchands de contremarques,* and such riff-raff, who offered every foreigner to show him the king for five francs: if he would give ten francs, he might see the king raise his eyes to heaven, and lay his hand protestingly on his heart; if he would give twenty francs, the king would sing the Marseillaise. If the foreigner gave five francs, they raised a loud cheering under the king's windows, and His Majesty appeared on the terrace, bowed, and retired. If ten francs, they shouted still louder, and gesticulated as if they had been possessed, when the king appeared, who then, as a sign of silent emotion, raised his eyes to heaven and laid his hand on his heart. English visitors, however, would sometimes spend as much as twenty francs, and then the enthusiasm mounted to the highest pitch; no sooner did the king appear on the terrace than the Marseillaise was struck up and roared out frightfully, until Louis Philippe, perhaps only for the sake of putting an end to the singing, bowed, laid his hand on his heart, and joined in the Marseillaise. Whether, as is asserted, he beat time with his foot, I cannot say.'"

One more quotation, and it must be our last:

"Oh the women! We must forgive them much, for they love much—and many. Their hate is properly only love turned inside out. Sometimes they attribute some delinquency to us, because they think they can in this way gratify another man. When they write, they have always one eye on the paper and the other on a man; and this is true of all authoresses, except the Countess Hahn-Hahn, who has only one eye."

V.

THE NATURAL HISTORY OF GERMAN LIFE.*

It is an interesting branch of psychological observation to note the images that are habitually associated with abstract or collective terms—what may be called the picture-writing of the mind, which it carries on concurrently with the more subtle symbolism of language. Perhaps the fixity or variety of these associated images would furnish a tolerably fair test of the amount of concrete knowledge and experience which a given word represents, in the minds of two persons who use it with equal familiarity. The word *railways*, for example, will probably call up, in the mind of a man who is not highly locomotive, the image either of a "Bradshaw," or of the station with which he is most familiar, or of an indefinite length of tramroad; he will alternate between these three images, which represent his stock of concrete acquaintance with railways. But suppose a man to have had successively the experience of a "navvy," an engineer, a traveller, a railway director and shareholder, and a landed proprietor in treaty with a railway company, and it is probable that the range of images which would by turns present themselves to his mind at the mention of the *word* "railways," would include all the essential facts in the existence and relations of the *thing*. Now it is possible for the first-mentioned personage to entertain very expanded views as to the multiplication of railways in the abstract, and their ultimate function in civilization. He may talk of a vast

* 1. "Die Bürgerliche Gesellschaft." Von W. H. Riehl. Dritte Auflage. 1855. 2. "Land und Leute." Von W. H. Riehl. Dritte Auflage. 1856.

net-work of railways stretching over the globe, of future "lines" in Madagascar, and elegant refreshment-rooms in the Sandwich Islands, with none the less glibness because his distinct conceptions on the subject do not extend beyond his one station and his indefinite length of tram-road. But it is evident that if we want a railway to be made, or its affairs to be managed, this man of wide views and narrow observation will not serve our purpose.

Probably, if we could ascertain the images called up by the terms "the people," "the masses," "the proletariat," "the peasantry," by many who theorize on those bodies with eloquence, or who legislate without eloquence, we should find that they indicate almost as small an amount of concrete knowledge—that they are as far from completely representing the complex facts summed up in the collective term, as the railway images of our non-locomotive gentleman. How little the real characteristics of the working-classes are known to those who are outside them, how little their natural history has been studied, is sufficiently disclosed by our Art as well as by our political and social theories. Where, in our picture exhibitions, shall we find a group of true peasantry? What English artist even attempts to rival in truthfulness such studies of popular life as the pictures of Teniers or the ragged boys of Murillo? Even one of the greatest painters of the pre-eminently realistic school, while, in his picture of "The Hireling Shepherd," he gave us a landscape of marvellous truthfulness, placed a pair of peasants in the foreground who were not much more real than the idyllic swains and damsels of our chimney ornaments. Only a total absence of acquaintance and sympathy with our peasantry could give a moment's popularity to such a picture as "Cross Purposes," where we have a peasant girl who looks as if she knew L. E. L.'s poems by heart, and English rustics, whose costume seems to indicate that they are meant for ploughmen, with exotic features that remind us of a handsome *primo tenore*. Rather than such cockney sentimentality as this, as an education for the taste and sympathies, we prefer the most crapulous group of boors that Teniers ever painted. But even those among our painters who aim at giving the rustic type of features, who are far above the effeminate feebleness of the "Keepsake" style, treat their subjects under the influence of traditions and prepossessions rather than of direct observation. The notion that peasants are joyous, that the typical moment to represent a man in a smock-frock is when he is cracking a joke and showing a row of sound teeth, that cottage matrons are usually buxom, and village children necessarily rosy and merry, are prejudices difficult to dislodge from the artistic mind, which looks for its subjects into literature instead of life. The painter is still under the influence of idyllic literature, which has always expressed the imagination of the cultivated and town-bred, rather than the truth of rustic life. Idyllic ploughmen are jocund when they drive their team afield; idyllic shepherds make bashful love under hawthorn bushes; idyllic villagers dance in the checkered shade and refresh themselves, not immoderately, with spicy nut-brown ale. But no one who has seen much of actual ploughmen thinks them jocund; no one who is well acquainted with the English peasantry can pronounce them merry. The slow gaze, in which no sense of beauty beams, no humor twinkles, the slow utterance, and the heavy, slouching walk, remind one rather of that melancholy animal the camel than of the sturdy countryman, with striped stockings, red waistcoat, and hat aside, who represents the traditional English peasant. Observe a company of haymakers. When you see them at a distance, tossing up the forkfuls of hay in the golden light, while the wagon creeps slowly with its increasing burden over the meadow, and the bright green space which tells of work done gets larger and larger, you pronounce the scene "smiling," and you think these companions in labor must be as bright and cheerful as the picture to which they give animation. Approach nearer, and you will certainly find that haymaking time is a time for joking, especially if there are women among the laborers; but the coarse laugh that bursts out every now and then, and expresses the triumphant taunt, is as far as possible from your conception of idyllic merriment. That delicious effervescence of the mind which we call fun has no equivalent for the northern peasant, except tipsy revelry ; the only realm of fancy and imagination for the English clown exists at the bottom of the third quart pot.

The conventional countryman of the stage, who picks up pocket-books and never looks into them, and who is too simple even to know that honesty has its opposite, represents the still lingering mistake, that an unintelligible dialect is a guarantee for ingenuousness, and that slouching shoulders indicate an upright disposition. It is quite true that a thresher is likely to be innocent of any adroit arithmetical cheating, but he is not the less likely to carry home his master's corn in his shoes and pocket ; a reaper is not given to writing begging-letters, but he is quite capable of cajoling the dairymaid into filling his small-beer bottle with ale. The selfish instincts are not subdued by the sight of buttercups, nor is integrity in the least established by that classic rural occupation, sheep-washing. To make men moral something more is requisite than to turn them out to grass.

Opera peasants, whose unreality excites Mr. Ruskin's indignation, are surely too frank an idealization to be misleading ; and since popular chorus is one of the most effective elements of the opera, we can hardly object to lyric rustics in elegant laced boddices and picturesque motley, unless we are prepared to advocate a chorus of colliers in their pit costume, or a ballet of charwomen and stocking-weavers. But our social novels profess to represent the people as they are, and the unreality of their representations is a grave evil. The greatest benefit we owe to the artist, whether painter, poet, or novelist, is the extension of our sympathies. Appeals founded on generalizations and statistics require a sympathy ready-made, a moral sentiment already in activity ; but a picture of human life such as a great artist can give, surprises even the trivial and the selfish into that attention to what is a part from themselves, which may be called the raw material of moral sentiment. When Scott takes us into Luckie Mucklebackit's cottage, or tells the story of "The Two Drovers;" when Wordsworth sings to us the reverie of "Poor Susan;" when Kingsley shows us Alton Locke gazing yearningly over the gate which leads from the highway into the first wood he ever saw; when Hornung paints a group of chimney-sweepers—more is done toward linking the higher classes with the lower, toward obliterating the vulgarity of exclusiveness, than by hundreds of sermons and philosophical dissertations. Art is the nearest thing to life; it is a mode of amplifying experience and extending our contact with our fellow-men beyond the bounds of our personal lot. All the more sacred is the task of the artist when he undertakes to paint the life of the People. Falsification here is far more pernicious than in the more artificial aspects of life. It is not so very serious that we should have false ideas about evanescent fashions—about the manners and conversation of beaux and duchesses; but it *is* serious that our sympathy with the perennial joys and struggles, the toil, the tragedy, and the humor in the life of our more heavily laden fellow-men, should be perverted, and turned toward a false object instead of the true one.

This perversion is not the less fatal because the misrepresentation which give rise to it has what the artist considers a moral end. The thing for mankind to know is, not what are the motives and influences which the moralist thinks *ought* to act on the laborer or the artisan, but what are the motives and influences which *do* act on him. We want to be taught to feel, not for the heroic artisan or the sentimental peasant, but for the peasant in all his coarse apathy, and the artisan in all his suspicious selfishness.

We have one great novelist who is gifted with the utmost power of rendering the external traits of our town population; and if he could give us their psychological character—their conception of life, and their emotions—with the same truth as their idiom and manners, his books would be the greatest contribution Art has ever made to the awakening of social sympathies. But while he can copy Mrs. Plornish's colloquial style with the delicate accuracy of a sun-picture, while there is the same startling inspiration in his description of the gestures and phrases of "Boots," as in the speeches of Shakespeare's mobs or numskulls, he scarcely ever passes from the humorous and external to the emotional and tragic, without becoming as transcendent in his unreality as he was a moment before in his artistic truthfulness. But for the precious salt of his humor, which compels him to reproduce external traits that serve in some degree as a corrective to his frequently false psychology, his preternaturally virtuous poor children and artisans, his melodramatic boatmen and courtesans, would be as obnoxious as Eugène Sue's idealized proletaires, in encouraging the miserable fallacy that high morality and refined sentiment can grow out of harsh social relations, ignorance, and want; or that the working-classes are in a condition to enter at once into a millennial state of *altruism*, wherein every one is caring for everyone else, and no one for himself.

If we need a true conception of the popular character to guide our sympathies rightly, we need it equally to check our theories, and direct us in their application. The tendency created by the splendid conquests of modern generalization, to believe that all social questions are merged in economical science, and that the relations of men to their neighbors may be settled by algebraic equations—the dream that the uncultured classes are prepared for a condition which appeals principally to their moral sensibilities—the aristocractic dilettantism which attempts to restore the "good old times" by a sort of idyllic masquerading, and to grow feudal fidelity and veneration as we grow prize turnips, by an artificial system of culture—none of these diverging mistakes can coexist with a real knowledge of the people, with a thorough study of their habits, their ideas, their motives. The landholder, the clergyman, the mill-owner, the mining-agent, have each an opportunity for making precious observations on different sections of the working-classes, but unfortunately their experience is too often not registered at all, or its results are too scattered to be available as a source of information and stimulus to the public mind generally. If any man of sufficient moral and intellectual breadth, whose observations would not be vitiated by a foregone conclusion, or by a professional point of view, would devote himself to studying the natural history of our social classes, especially of the small shopkeepers, artisans, and peasantry—the degree in which they are influenced by local conditions, their maxims and habits, the points of view from which they regard their religious teachers, and the degree in which they are influenced by religious doctrines, the interaction of the various classes on each other, and what are the tendencies in their position toward disintegration or toward development—and if, after all this study, he would give us the result of his observation in a book well nourished with specific facts, his work would be a valuable aid to the social and political reformer.

What we are desiring for ourselves has been in some degree done for the Germans by Riehl, the author of the very remarkable books, the titles of which are placed at the head of this article; and we wish to make these books known to our readers, not only for the sake of the interesting matter they contain, and the important reflections they suggest, but also as a model for some future or actual student of our own people. By way of introducing Riehl to those who are unacquainted with his writings, we will give a rapid sketch from his picture of the German Peasantry, and perhaps this indication of the mode in which he treats a particular branch of his subject may prepare them to follow us with more interest when we enter on the general purpose and contents of his works.

In England, at present, when we speak of the peasantry we mean scarcely more than the class of farm-servants and farm-laborers; and it is only in the most primitive districts, as in Wales, for example, that farmers are included under the term. In order to appreciate what Riehl says of the German peasantry, we must remember what the tenant-farmers and small proprietors were in England half a century ago, when the master helped to milk his own cows, and the daughters got up at one o'clock in the morning to brew—when the family dined in the kitchen with the servants, and sat with them round the kitchen fire in the evening. In those days, the quarried parlor was innocent of a carpet, and its only specimens of art were a framed sampler and the best tea-board; the daughters even of substantial farmers had often no greater accomplishment in writing and spelling than they could procure at a dame-school; and, instead of carrying on sentimental correspondence, they were spinning their future table-linen, and looking after every saving in butter and eggs that might enable them to add to the little stock of plate and china which they were laying in against their marriage. In our own day, setting aside the superior order of farmers, whose style of living and mental culture are often equal to that of the professional class in provincial towns, we can hardly enter the least imposing farm-house without finding a bad piano in the "drawing-room," and some old annuals, disposed with a symmetrical imitation of negligence, on the table; though the daughters may still drop their *h's*, their vowels are studiously narrow; and it is only in very primitive regions that they will consent to sit in a covered vehicle without springs, which was once thought an advance in luxury on the pillion.

The condition of the tenant-farmers and small proprietors in Germany is, we imagine, about on a par, not, certainly, in material prosperity, but in mental culture and habits, with that of the English farmers who were beginning to be thought old-fashioned nearly fifty years ago, and if we add to these the farm servants and laborers we shall have a class approximating in its characteristics to the *Bauernthum*, or peasantry, described by Riehl.

In Germany, perhaps more than in any other country, it is among the peasantry that we must look for the historical type of the national *physique*. In the towns this type has become so modified to express the personality of the individual that even "family likeness" is often but faintly marked. But the peasants may still be distinguished into groups, by their physical peculiarities. In one part of the country we find a longer-legged, in another a broader-shouldered race, which has inherited these peculiarities for centuries. For example, in certain districts of Hesse are seen long faces, with high foreheads, long, straight noses, and small eyes, with arched eyebrows and large eyelids. On comparing these physiognomies with the sculptures in the church of St. Elizabeth, at Marburg, executed in the thirteenth century, it will be found that the same old Hessian type of face has subsisted unchanged, with this distinction only, that the sculptures represent princes and nobles, whose features then bore the stamp of their race, while that stamp is now to be found only among the peasants. A painter who wants to draw mediæval characters with historic truth must seek his models among the peasantry. This explains why the old German painters gave the heads of their subjects a greater uniformity of type than the painters of our day; the race had not attained to a high degree of individualization in features and expression. It indicates, too, that the cultured man acts more as an individual, the peasant more as one of a group. Hans drives the plough, lives, and thinks just as Kunz does; and it is this fact that many thousands of men are as like each other in thoughts and habits as so many sheep or oysters, which constitutes the weight of the peasantry in the social and political scale.

In the cultivated world each individual has his style of speaking and writing. But among the peasantry it is the race, the district, the province, that has its style—namely, its dialect, its phraseology, its proverbs, and its songs, which belong alike to the entire body of the people. This provincial style of the peasant is again, like his *physique*, a remnant of history, to which he clings with the utmost tenacity. In certain parts of Hungary there are still descendants of German colonists of the twelfth and thirteenth centuries, who go about the country as reapers, retaining their old Saxon songs and manners, while the more cultivated German emigrants in a very short time forget their own language, and speak Hungarian. Another remarkable case of the same kind is that of the Wends, a Slavonic race settled in Lusatia, whose numbers amount to 200,000, living either scattered among the German population or in separate parishes. They have their own schools and churches, and are taught in the Slavonic tongue. The Catholics among them are rigid adherents of the Pope; the Protestants not less rigid adherents of Luther, or *Doctor* Luther, as they are particular in calling him—a custom which a hundred years ago was universal in Protestant Germany. The Wend clings tenaciously to the usages of his Church, and perhaps this may contribute not a little to the purity in which he maintains the specific characteristics of his race. German education, German law and government, service in the standing army, and many other agencies, are in antagonism to his national exclusiveness; but the *wives* and *mothers* here, as elsewhere, are a conservative influence, and the habits temporarily laid aside in the outer world are recovered by the fireside. The Wends form several stout regiments in the Saxon army; they are sought far and wide, as diligent and honest servants; and many a weakly Dresden or Leipzig child becomes thriving under the care of a Wendish nurse. In their villages they have the air and habits of genuine sturdy peasants, and all their customs indicate that they have been from the first an agricultural people. For example, they have traditional modes of treating their domestic animals. Each cow has its own name, generally chosen carefully, so as to express the special qualities of the animal; and all important family events are narrated to the *bees*—a custom which is found also in Westphalia. Whether by the help of the bees or not, the Wend farming is especially prosperous; and when a poor Bohemian peasant has a son born to him he binds him to the end of a long pole and turns his face toward Lusatia, that he may be as lucky as the Wends, who live there.

The peculiarity of the peasant's language consists chiefly in his retention of historical peculiarities, which gradually disappear under the friction of cultivated circles. He prefers any proper name that may be given to a day in the calendar, rather than the abstract date, by which he very rarely reckons. In the baptismal names of his children he is guided by the old custom of the country, not at all by whim and fancy. Many old baptismal names, formerly common in Germany, would have become extinct but for their preservation among the peasantry, especially in North Germany; and so firmly have they adhered to local tradition in this matter that it would be possible to give a sort of topographical statistics of proper names, and distinguish a district by its rustic names as we do by its Flora and Fauna. The continuous inheritance of certain favorite proper names in a family, in some districts, forces the peasant to adopt the princely custom of attaching a numeral to the name, and saying, when three generations are living at once, Hans I., II., and III.; or—in the more antique fashion—Hans the elder, the middle, and the younger. In some of our English counties there is a similar adherence to a narrow range of proper names, and a mode of distinguishing collateral branches in the same family, you will hear of Jonathan's Bess, Thomas's Bess, and Samuel's Bess—the three Bessies being cousins.

The peasant's adherence to the traditional has much greater inconvenience than that entailed by a paucity of proper names. In the Black Forest and in Hüttenberg you will see him in the dog-days wearing a thick fur cap, because it is an historical fur cap—a cap worn by his grandfather. In the Wetterau, that peasant girl is considered the handsomest who wears the most petticoats. To go to field-labor in seven petticoats can be anything but convenient or agreeable, but it is the traditionally correct thing, and a German peasant girl would think herself as unfavorably conspicuous in an untraditional costume as an English servant-girl would now think herself in a "linsey-wolsey" apron or a thick muslin cap. In many districts no medical advice would induce the rustic to renounce the tight leather belt with which he injures his digestive functions; you could more easily persuade him to smile on a new communal system than on the unhistorical invention of braces. In the eighteenth century, in spite of the philanthropic preachers of potatoes, the peasant for years threw his potatoes to the pigs and the dogs, before he could be persuaded to put them on his own table. However, the unwillingness of the peasant to adopt innovations has a not unreasonable foundation in the fact that for him experiments are practical, not theoretical, and must be made with expense of money instead of brains—a fact that is not, perhaps, sufficiently taken into account by agricultural theorists, who complain of the farmer's obstinacy. The peasant has the smallest possible faith in theoretic knowledge; he thinks it rather dangerous than otherwise, as is well indicated by a Lower Rhenish proverb—"One is never too old to learn, said an old woman; so she learned to be a witch."

Between many villages an historical feud, once perhaps the occasion of much bloodshed, is still kept up under the milder form of an occasional round of cudgelling and the launching of traditional nicknames. An historical feud of this kind still exists, for example, among many villages on the Rhine and more inland places in the neighborhood. *Rheinschnacke* (of which the equivalent is perhaps "water-snake") is the standing term of ignominy for the inhabitant of the Rhine village, who repays it in kind by the epithet "karst" (mattock), or "kukuk" (cuckoo), according as the object of his hereditary hatred belongs to the field or the forest. If any Romeo among the "mattocks" were to marry a Juliet among the "water-snakes," there would be no lack of Tybalts and Mercutios to carry the conflict from words to blows, though neither side knows a reason for the enmity.

A droll instance of peasant conservatism is told of a village on the Taunus, whose inhabitants, from time immemorial, had been famous for impromptu cudgelling. For this historical offence the magistrates of the district had always inflicted the equally historical punishment of shutting up the most incorrigible offenders, not in prison, but in their own pig-sty. In recent times, however, the government, wishing to correct the rudeness of these peasants, appointed an "enlightened" man as a magistrate, who at once abolished the original penalty above mentioned. But this relaxation of punishment was so far from being welcome to the villagers that they presented a petition praying that a more energetic man might be given them as a magistrate, who would have the courage to punish according to law and justice, "as had been beforetime." And the magistrate who abolished incarceration in the pig-sty could never obtain the respect of the neighborhood. This happened no longer ago than the beginning of the present century.

But it must not be supposed that the historical piety of the German peasant extends to anything not immediately connected with himself. He has the warmest piety toward the old tumble-down house which his grandfather built, and which nothing will induce him to improve, but toward the venerable ruins of the old castle that overlooks his village he has no piety at all, and carries off its stones to make a fence for his garden, or tears down the gothic carving of the old monastic church, which is "nothing to him," to mark off a foot-path through his field. It is the same with historical traditions. The peasant has them fresh in his memory, so far as they relate to himself. In districts where the peasantry are unadulterated, you can discern the remnants of the feudal relations in innumerable customs and phrases, but you will ask in vain for historical traditions concerning the empire, or even concerning the particular princely house to which the peasant is subject. He can tell you what "half people and whole people" mean; in Hesse you will still hear of "four horses making a whole peasant," or of "four-day and three-day peasants;" but you will ask in vain about Charlemagne and Frederic Barbarossa.

Riehl well observes that the feudal system, which made the peasant the bondman of his lord, was an immense benefit in a country, the greater part of which had still to be colonized—rescued the peasant from vagabondage, and laid the foundation of persistency and endurance in future generations. If a free German peasantry belongs only to modern times, it is to his ancestor who was a serf, and even, in the earliest times, a slave, that the peasant owes the foundation of his independence, namely, his capability of a settled existence—nay, his unreasoning persistency, which has its important function in the development of the race.

Perhaps the very worst result of that unreasoning persistency is the peasant's inveterate habit of litigation. Every one remembers the immortal description of Dandie Dinmont's importunate application to Lawyer Pleydell to manage his "bit lawsuit," till at length Pleydell consents to help him to ruin himself, on the ground that Dandie may fall into worse hands. It seems this is a scene which has many parallels in Germany. The farmer's lawsuit is his point of honor; and he will carry it through, though he knows from the very first day that he shall get nothing by it. The litigious peasant piques himself, like Mr. Saddletree, on his knowledge of the law, and this vanity is the chief impulse to many a lawsuit. To the mind of the peasant, law presents itself as the "custom of the country," and it is his pride to be versed in all customs. *Custom with him holds the place of sentiment, of theory, and in many cases of affection.* Riehl justly urges the importance of simplifying law proceedings, so as to cut off this vanity at its source, and also of encouraging, by every possible means, the practice of arbitration.

The peasant never begins his lawsuit in summer, for the same reason that he does not make love and marry in summer—because he has no time for that sort of thing. Anything is easier to him than to move out of his habitual course, and he is attached even to his privations. Some years ago a peasant youth, out of the poorest and remotest region of the Westerwald, was enlisted as a recruit, at Weilburg in Nassau. The lad, having never in his life slept in a bed, when he had got into one for the first time began to cry like a child; and he deserted twice because he could not reconcile himself to sleeping in a bed, and to the "fine" life of the barracks: he was homesick at the thought of his accustomed poverty and his thatched hut. A strong contrast, this, with the feeling of the poor in towns, who would be far enough from deserting because their condition was too much improved! The genuine peasant is never ashamed of his rank and calling; he is rather inclined to look down on every one who does not wear a smock frock, and thinks a man who has the manners of the gentry is likely to be rather windy and unsubstantial. In some places, even in French districts, this feeling is strongly symbolized by the practice of the peasantry, on certain festival days, to dress the images of the saints in peasant's clothing. History tells us of all kinds of peasant insurrections, the object of which was to obtain relief for the peasants from some of their many oppressions; but of an effort on their part to step out of their hereditary rank and calling, to become gentry, to leave the plough and carry on the easier business of capitalists or government functionaries, there is no example.

The German novelists who undertake to give pictures of peasant-life fall into the same mistake as our English novelists: they transfer their own feelings to ploughmen and woodcutters, and give them both joys and sorrows of which they know nothing. The peasant never questions the obligation of family ties—he questions *no custom*—but tender affection, as it exists among the refined part of mankind, is almost as foreign to him as white hands and filbert-shaped nails. That the aged father who has given up his property to his children on condition of their maintaining him for the remainder of his life, is very far from meeting with delicate attentions, is indicated by the proverb current among the peasantry—"Don't take your clothes off before you go to bed." Among rustic moral tales and parables, not one is more universal than the story of the ungrateful children, who made their gray-headed father, dependent on them for a maintenance, eat at a wooden trough because he shook the food out of his trembling hands. Then these same ungrateful children observed one day that their own little boy was making a tiny wooden trough; and when they asked him what it was for, he answered—that his father and mother might eat out of it, when he was a man and had to keep them.

Marriage is a very prudential affair, especially among the peasants who have the largest share of property. Politic marriages are as common among them as among princes; and when a peasant-heiress in Westphalia marries, her husband adopts her name, and places his own after it with the prefix *geborner* (*née*). The girls marry young, and the rapidity with which they get old and ugly is one among the many proofs that the early years of marriage are fuller of hardships than of conjugal tenderness. "When our writers of village stories," says Riehl, "transferred their own emotional life to the peasant, they obliterated what is precisely his most predominant characteristic, namely, that with him general custom holds the place of individual feeling."

We pay for greater emotional susceptibility too often by nervous diseases of which the peasant knows nothing. To him headache is the least of physical evils, because he thinks head-work the easiest and least indispensable of all labor. Happily, many of the younger sons in peasant families, by going to seek their living in the towns, carry their hardy nervous system to amalgamate with the overwrought nerves of our town population, and refresh them with a little rude vigor. And a return to the habits of peasant life is the best remedy for many moral as well as physical diseases induced by perverted civilization. Riehl points to colonization as presenting the true field for this regenerative process. On the other side of the ocean a man will have the courage to begin life again as a peasant, while at home, perhaps, opportunity as well as courage will fail him. *Apropos* of this subject of emigration, he remarks the striking fact, that the native shrewdness and mother-wit of the German peasant seem to forsake him entirely when he has to apply them under new circumstances, and on relations foreign to his experience. Hence it is that the German peasant who emigrates, so constantly falls a victim to unprincipled adventurers in the preliminaries to emigration; but if once he gets his foot on the American soil he exhibits all the first-rate qualities of an agricultural colonist; and among all German emigrants the peasant class are the most successful.

But many disintegrating forces have been at work on the peasant character, and degeneration is unhappily going on at a greater pace than development. In the wine districts especially, the inability of the small proprietors to bear up under the vicissitudes of the market, or to insure a high quality of wine by running the risks of a late vintage and the competition of beer and cider with the inferior wines, have tended to produce that uncertainty of gain which, with the peasant, is the inevitable cause of demoralization. The small peasant proprietors are not a new class in Germany, but many of the evils of their position are new. They are more dependent on ready money than formerly; thus, where a peasant used to get his wood for building and firing from the common forest, he has now to pay for it with hard cash; he used to thatch his own house, with the help perhaps of a neighbor, but now he pays a man to do it for him; he used to pay taxes in kind, he now pays them in money. The chances of the market have to be discounted, and the peasant falls into the hands of money-lenders. Here is one of the cases in which social policy clashes with a purely economical policy.

Political vicissitudes have added their influence to that of economical changes in disturbing that dim instinct, that reverence for traditional custom, which is the peasant's principle of action. He is in the midst of novelties for which he knows no reason—changes in political geography, changes of the government to which he owes fealty, changes in bureaucratic management and police regulations. He finds himself in a new element before an apparatus for breathing in it is developed in him. His only knowledge of modern history is in some of its results—for instance, that he has to pay heavier taxes from year to year. His chief idea of a government is of a power that raises his taxes, opposes his harmless customs, and torments him with new formalities. The source of all this is the false system of "enlightening" the peasant which has been adopted by the bureaucratic governments. A system which disregards the traditions and hereditary attachments of the peasant, and appeals only to a logical understanding which is not yet developed in him, is simply disintegrating and ruinous to the peasant character. The interference with the communal regulations has been of this fatal character. Instead of endeavoring to promote to the utmost the healthy life of the Commune, as an organism the conditions of which are bound up with the historical characteristics of the peasant, the bureaucratic plan of government is bent on improvement by its patent machinery of state-appointed functionaries and off-hand regulations in accordance with modern enlightenment. The spirit of communal exclusiveness—the resistance to the indiscriminate establishment of strangers, is an intense traditional feeling in the peasant. "This gallows is for us and our children," is the typical motto of this spirit. But such exclusiveness is highly irrational and repugnant to modern liberalism; therefore a bureaucratic government at once opposes it, and encourages to the utmost the introduction of new inhabitants in the provincial communes. Instead of allowing the peasants to manage their own affairs, and, if they happen to believe that five and four make eleven, to unlearn the prejudice by their own experience in calculation, so that they may gradually understand processes, and not merely see results, bureaucracy comes with its "Ready Reckoner" and works all the peasant's sums for him—the surest way of maintaining him in his stupidity, however it may shake his prejudice.

Another questionable plan for elevating the peasant is the supposed elevation of the clerical character by preventing the clergyman from cultivating more than a trifling part of the land attached to his benefice; that he may be as much as possible of a scientific theologian, and as little as possible of a peasant. In this, Riehl observes, lies one great source of weakness to the Protestant Church as compared with the Catholic, which finds the great majority of its priests among the lower orders; and we have had the opportunity of making an analogous comparison in England, where many of us can remember country districts in which the great mass of the people were christianized by illiterate Methodist and Independent ministers, while the influence of the parish clergyman among the poor did not extend much beyond a few old women in scarlet cloaks and a few exceptional church-going laborers.

Bearing in mind the general characteristics of the German peasant, it is easy to understand his relation to the revolutionary ideas and revolutionary movements of modern times. The peasant, in Germany as elsewhere, is a born grumbler. He has always plenty of grievances in his pocket, but he does not generalize those grievances; he does not complain of "government" or "society," probably because he has good reason to complain of the burgomaster. When a few sparks from the first French Revolution fell among the German peasantry, and in certain villages of Saxony the country people assembled together to write down their demands, there was no glimpse in their petition of the "universal rights of man," but simply of their own particular affairs as Saxon peasants. Again, after the July revolution of 1830, there were many insignificant peasant insurrections; but the object of almost all was the removal of local grievances. Toll-houses were pulled down; stamped paper was destroyed; in some places there was a persecution of wild boars, in others, of that plentiful tame animal, the German *Rath*, or councillor who is never called into council. But in 1848 it seemed as if the movements of the peasants had taken a new character; in the small western states of Germany it seemed as if the whole class of peasantry was in insurrection. But, in fact, the peasant did not know the meaning of the part he was playing. He had heard that everything was being set right in the towns, and that wonderful things were happening there, so he tied up his bundle and set off. Without any distinct object or resolution, the country people presented themselves on the scene of commotion, and were warmly received by the party leaders. But, seen from the windows of ducal palaces and ministerial hotels, these swarms of peasants had quite another aspect, and it was imagined that they had a common plan of co-operation. This, however, the peasants have never had. Systematic co-operation implies general conceptions, and a provisional subordination of egoism, to which even the artisans of towns have rarely shown themselves equal, and which are as foreign to the mind of the peasant as logarithms or the doctrine of chemical proportions. And the revolutionary fervor of the peasant was soon cooled. The old mistrust of the towns was reawakened on the spot. The Tyrolese peasants saw no great good in the freedom of the press and the constitution, because these changes "seemed to please the gentry so much." Peasants who had given their voices stormily for a German parliament asked afterward, with a doubtful look, whether it were to consist of infantry or cavalry. When royal domains were declared the property of the State, the peasants in some small principalities rejoiced over this, because they interpreted it to mean that every one would have his share in them, after the manner of the old common and forest rights.

The very practical views of the peasants with regard to the demands of the people were in amusing contrast with the abstract theorizing of the educated townsmen. The peasant continually withheld all State payments until he saw how matters would turn out, and was disposed to reckon up the solid benefit, in the form of land or money, that might come to him from the changes obtained. While the townsman was heating his brains about representation on the broadest basis, the peasant asked if the relation between tenant and landlord would continue as before, and whether the removal of the "feudal obligations' meant that the farmer should become owner of the land!

It is in the same naïve way that Communism is interpreted by the German peasantry. The wide spread among them of communistic doctrines, the eagerness with which they listened to a plan for the partition of property, seemed to countenance the notion that it was a delusion to suppose the peasant would be secured from this intoxication by his love of secure possession and peaceful earnings. But, in fact, the peasant contemplated "partition" by the light of an historical reminiscence rather than of novel theory. The golden age, in the imagination of the peasant, was the time when every member of the commune had a right to as much wood from the forest as would enable him to sell some, after using what he wanted in firing—in which the communal possessions were so profitable that, instead of his having to pay rates at the end of the year, each member of the commune was something in pocket. Hence the peasants in general understood by "partition," that the State lands, especially the forests, would be divided among the communes, and that, by some political legerdemain or other, everybody would have free fire-wood, free grazing for his cattle, and over and above that, a piece of gold without working for it. That he should give up a single clod of his own to further the general "partition" had never entered the mind of the peasant communist; and the perception that this was an essential preliminary to "partition" was often a sufficient cure for his Communism.

In villages lying in the neighborhood of large towns, however, where the circumstances of the peasantry are very different, quite another interpretation of Communism is prevalent. Here the peasant is generally sunk to the position of the proletaire living from hand to mouth: he has nothing to lose, but everything to gain by "partition." The coarse nature of the peasant has here been corrupted into bestiality by the disturbance of his instincts, while he is as yet incapable of principles; and in this type of the degenerate peasant is seen the worst example of ignorance intoxicated by theory.

A significant hint as to the interpretation the peasants put on revolutionary theories may be drawn from the way they employed the few weeks in which their movements were unchecked. They felled the forest trees and shot the game; they withheld taxes; they shook off the imaginary or real burdens imposed on them by their mediatized princes, by presenting their "demands" in a very rough way before the ducal or princely "Schloss;" they set their faces against the bureaucratic management of the communes, deposed the government functionaries who had been placed over them as burgomasters and magistrates, and abolished the whole bureaucratic system of procedure, simply by taking no notice of its regulations, and recurring to some tradition—some old order or disorder of things. In all this it is clear that they were animated not in the least by the spirit of modern revolution, but by a purely narrow and personal impulse toward reaction.

The idea of constitutional government lies quite beyond the range of the German peasant's conceptions. His only notion of representation is that of a representation of ranks—of classes; his only notion of a deputy is of one who takes care, not of the national welfare, but of the interests of his own order. Herein lay the great mistake of the democratic party, in common with the bureaucratic governments, that they entirely omitted the peculiar character of the peasant from their political calculations. They talked of the "people," and forgot that the peasants were included in the term. Only a baseless misconception of the peasant's character could induce the supposition that he would feel the slightest enthusiasm about the principles involved in the reconstitution of the Empire, or even about the reconstitution itself. He has no zeal for a written law, as such, but only so far as it takes the form of a living law—a tradition. It was the external authority which the revolutionary party had won in Baden that attracted the peasants into a participation of the struggle.

Such, Riehl tells us, are the general characteristics of the German peasantry—characteristics which subsist amid a wide variety of circumstances. In Mecklenburg, Pomerania, and Brandenburg the peasant lives on extensive estates; in Westphalia he lives in large isolated homesteads; in the Westerwald and in Sauerland, in little groups of villages and hamlets; on the Rhine land is for the most part parcelled out among small proprietors, who live together in large villages. Then, of course, the diversified physical geography of Germany gives rise to equally diversified methods of land-culture; and out of these various circumstances grow numerous specific differences in manner and character. But the generic character of the German peasant is everywhere the same; in the clean mountain hamlet and in the dirty fishing village on the coast; in the plains of North Germany and in the backwoods of America. "Everywhere he has the same historical character—everywhere custom is his supreme law. Where religion and patriotism are still a naïve instinct, are still a sacred *custom*, there begins the class of the German Peasantry."

Our readers will perhaps already have gathered from the foregoing portrait of the German peasant that Riehl is not a man who looks at objects through the spectacles either of the doctrinaire or the dreamer; and they will be ready to believe what he tells us in his Preface, namely, that years ago he began his wanderings over the hills and plains of Germany for the sake of obtaining, in immediate intercourse with the people, that completion of his historical, political, and economical studies which he was unable to find in books. He began his investigations with no party prepossessions, and his present views were evolved entirely from his own gradually amassed observations. He was, first of all, a pedestrian, and only in the second place a political author. The views at which he has arrived by this inductive process, he sums up in the term—*social-political-conservatism*; but his conservatism is, we conceive, of a thoroughly philosophical kind. He sees in European society *incarnate history*, and any attempt to disengage it from its historical elements must, he believes, be simply destructive of social vitality.* What has grown up historically can only die out historically, by the gradual operation of necessary laws. The external conditions which society has inherited from the past are but the manifestation of inherited internal conditions in the human beings who compose it; the internal conditions and the external are related to each other as the organism and its medium, and development can take place only by the gradual consentaneous development of both. Take the familiar example of attempts to abolish titles, which have been about as effective as the process of cutting off poppy-heads in a corn-field. *Jedem Menschem*, says Riehl, *ist sein Zopf angeboren, warum soll denn der sociale Sprachgebrauch nicht auch sein Zopf haben?*—which we may render—"As long as snobism runs in the blood, why should it not run in our speech?" As a necessary preliminary to a purely rational society, you must obtain purely rational men, free from the sweet and bitter prejudices of hereditary affection and antipathy; which is as easy as to get running streams without springs, or the leafy shade of the forest without the secular growth of trunk and branch.

The historical conditions of society may be compared with those of language. It must be admitted that the language of cultivated nations is in anything but a rational state; the great sections of the civilized world are only approximatively intelligible to each other, and even that only at the cost of long study; one word stands for many things, and many words for one thing; the subtle shades of meaning, and still subtler echoes of association, make language an instrument which scarcely anything short of genius can wield with definiteness and certainty. Suppose, then, that the effect which has been again and again made to construct a universal language on a rational basis has at length succeeded, and that you have a language which has no uncertainty, no whims of idiom, no cumbrous forms, no fitful simmer of many-hued significance,

* Throughout this article in our statement of Riehl's opinions we must be understood not as quoting Riehl, but as interpreting and illustrating him.

no hoary archaisms "familiar with forgotten years"—a patent deodorized and non-resonant language, which effects the purpose of communication as perfectly and rapidly as algebraic signs. Your language may be a perfect medium of expression to science, but will never express *life*, which is a great deal more than science. With the anomalies and inconveniences of historical language you will have parted with its music and its passions, and its vital qualities as an expression of individual character, with its subtle capabilities of wit, with everything that gives it power over the imagination; and the next step in simplification will be the invention of a talking watch, which will achieve the utmost facility and despatch in the communication of ideas by a graduated adjustment of ticks, to be represented in writing by a corresponding arrangement of dots. A melancholy "language of the future!" The sensory and motor nerves that run in the same sheath are scarcely bound together by a more necessary and delicate union than that which binds men's affections, imagination, wit and humor, with the subtle ramifications of historical language. Language must be left to grow in precision, completeness, and unity, as minds grow in clearness, comprehensiveness, and sympathy. And there is an analogous relation between the moral tendencies of men and the social conditions they have inherited. The nature of European men has its roots intertwined with the past, and can only be developed by allowing those roots to remain undisturbed while the process of development is going on until that perfect ripeness of the seed which carries with it a life independent of the root. This vital connection with the past is much more vividly felt on the Continent than in England, where we have to recall it by an effort of memory and reflection; for though our English life is in its core intensely traditional, Protestantism and commerce have modernized the face of the land and the aspects of society in a far greater degree than in any continental country:

"Abroad," says Ruskin, "a building of the eighth or tenth century stands ruinous in the open streets; the children play round it the peasants heap their corn in it, the buildings of yesterday nestle about it, and fit their new stones in its rents, and tremble in sympathy as it trembles. No one wonders at it, or thinks of it as separate, and of another time; we feel the ancient world to be a real thing, and one with the new; antiquity is no dream; it is rather the children playing about the old stones that are the dream. But all is continuous; and the words 'from generation to generation'' understandable here.''

This conception of European society as incarnate history is the fundamental idea of Riehl's books. After the notable failure of revolutionary attempts conducted from the point of view of abstract democratic and socialistic theories, after the practical demonstration of the evils resulting from a bureaucratic system, which governs by an undiscriminating, dead mechanism, Riehl wishes to urge on the consideration of his countrymen a social policy founded on the special study of the people as they are—on the natural history of the various social ranks. He thinks it wise to pause a little from theorizing, and see what is the material actually present for theory to work upon. It is the glory of the Socialists—in contrast with the democratic doctrinaires who have been too much occupied with the general idea of "the people" to inquire particularly into the actual life of the people—that they have thrown themselves with enthusiastic zeal into the study at least of one social group, namely, the factory operatives; and here lies the secret of their partial success. But, unfortunately, they have made this special duty of a single fragment of society the basis of a theory which quietly substitutes for the small group of Parisian proletaires or English factory-workers the society of all Europe—nay, of the whole world. And in this way they have lost the best fruit of their investigations. For, says Riehl, the more deeply we penetrate into the knowledge of society in its details, the more thoroughly we shall be convinced that *a universal social policy has no validity except on paper*, and can never be carried into successful practice. The conditions of German society are altogether different from those of French, of English, or of Italian society; and to apply the same social theory to these nations indiscriminately is about as wise a procedure as Triptolemus Yellowley's application of the agricultural directions in Virgil's "Georgics" to his farm in the Shetland Isles.

It is the clear and strong light in which Riehl places this important position that in our opinion constitutes the suggestive value of his books for foreign as well as German readers. It has not been sufficiently insisted on, that in the various branches of Social Science there is an advance from the general to the special, from the simple to the complex, analogous with that which is found in the series of the sciences, from Mathematics to Biology. To the laws of quantity comprised in Mathematics and Physics are superadded, in Chemistry, laws of quality; to these again are added, in Biology, laws of life; and lastly, the conditions of life in general branch out into its special conditions, or Natural History, on the one hand, and into its abnormal conditions, or Pathology, on the other. And in this series or ramification of the sciences, the more general science will not suffice to solve the problems of the more special. Chemistry embraces phenomena which are not explicable by Physics; Biology embraces phenomena which are not explicable by Chemistry; and no biological generalization will enable us to predict the infinite specialities produced by the complexity of vital conditions. So Social Science, while it has departments which in their fundamental generality correspond to mathematics and physics, namely, those grand and simple generalizations which trace out the inevitable march of the human race as a whole, and, as a ramification of these, the laws of economical science, has also, in the departments of government and jurisprudence, which embrace the conditions of social life in all their complexity, what may be called its Biology, carrying us on to innumerable special phenomena which outlie the sphere of science, and belong to Natural History. And just as the most thorough acquaintance with physics, or chemistry, or general physiology, will not enable you at once to establish the balance of life in your private vivarium, so that your particular society of zoophytes, mollusks, and echinoderms may feel themselves, as the Germans say, at ease in their skin ; so the most complete equipment of theory will not enable a statesman or a political and social reformer to adjust his measures wisely, in the absence of a special acquaintance with the section of society for which he legislates, with the peculiar characteristics of the nation, the province, the class whose well-being he has to consult. In other words, a wise social policy must be based not simply on abstract social science, but on the natural history of social bodies.

Riehl's books are not dedicated merely to the argumentative maintenance of this or of any other position ; they are intended chiefly as a contribution to that knowledge of the German people on the importance of which he insists. He is less occupied with urging his own conclusions than with impressing on his readers the facts which have led him to those conclusions. In the volume entitled "Land und Leute," which, though published last, is properly an introduction to the volume entitled "Die Bürgerliche Gesellschaft," he considers the German people in their physical geographical relations ; he compares the natural divisions of the race, as determined by land and climate, and social traditions, with the artificial divisions which are based on diplomacy ; and he traces the genesis and influences of what we may call the ecclesiastical geography of Germany—its partition between Catholicism and Protestantism. He shows that the ordinary antithesis of North and South Germany represents no real ethnographical distinction, and that the natural divisions of Germany, founded on its physical geography are threefold—namely, the low plains, the middle mountain region, and the high mountain region, or Lower, Middle, and Upper Germany ; and on this primary natural division all the other broad ethnographical distinctions of Germany will be found to rest. The plains of North or Lower Germany include all the seaboard the nation possesses ; and this, together with the fact that they are traversed to the depth of 600 miles by navigable rivers, makes them the natural seat of a trading race. Quite different is the geographical character of

Middle Germany. While the northern plains are marked off into great divisions, by such rivers as the Lower Rhine, the Weser, and the Oder, running almost in parallel lines, this central region is cut up like a mosaic by the capricious lines of valleys and rivers. Here is the region in which you find those famous roofs from which the rain-water runs toward two different seas, and the mountain-tops from which you may look into eight or ten German states. The abundance of water-power and the presence of extensive coal-mines allow of a very diversified industrial development in Middle Germany. In Upper Germany, or the high mountain region, we find the same symmetry in the lines of the rivers as in the north ; almost all the great Alpine streams flow parallel with the Danube. But the majority of these rivers are neither navigable nor available for industrial objects, and instead of serving for communication they shut off one great tract from another. The slow development, the simple peasant life of many districts is here determined by the mountain and the river. In the south-east, however, industrial activity spreads through Bohemia toward Austria, and forms a sort of balance to the industrial districts of the Lower Rhine. Of course, the boundaries of these three regions cannot be very strictly defined ; but an approximation to the limits of Middle Germany may be obtained by regarding it as a triangle, of which one angle lies in Silesia, another in Aix-la-Chapelle, and a third at Lake Constance.

This triple division corresponds with the broad distinctions of climate. In the northern plains the atmosphere is damp and heavy ; in the southern mountain region it is dry and rare, and there are abrupt changes of temperature, sharp contrasts between the seasons, and devastating storms ; but in both these zones men are hardened by conflict with the roughness of the climate. In Middle Germany, on the contrary, there is little of this struggle ; the seasons are more equable, and the mild, soft air of the valleys tends to make the inhabitants luxurious and sensitive to hardships. It is only in exceptional mountain districts that one is here reminded of the rough, bracing air on the heights of Southern Germany. It is a curious fact that, as the air becomes gradually lighter and rarer from the North German coast toward Upper Germany, the average of suicides regularly decreases. Mecklenburg has the highest number, then Prussia, while the fewest suicides occur in Bavaria and Austria.

Both the northern and southern regions have still a large extent of waste lands, downs, morasses, and heaths; and to these are added, in the south, abundance of snow-fields and naked rock; while in Middle Germany culture has almost overspread the face of the land, and there are no large tracts of waste. There is the same proportion in the distribution of forests. Again, in the north we see a monotonous continuity of wheat-fields, potato-grounds, meadow-lands, and vast heaths, and there is the same uniformity of culture over large surfaces in the southern table-lands and the Alpine pastures. In Middle Germany, on the contrary, there is a perpetual variety of crops within a short space; the diversity of land surface and the corresponding variety in the species of plants are an invitation to the splitting up of estates, and this again encourages to the utmost the motley character of the cultivation.

According to this threefold division, it appears that there are certain features common to North and South Germany in which they differ from Central Germany, and the nature of this difference Riehl indicates by distinguishing the former as *Centralized Land* and the latter as *Individualized Land*; a distinction which is well symbolized by the fact that North and South Germany possess the great lines of railway which are the medium for the traffic of the world, while Middle Germany is far richer in lines for local communication, and possesses the greatest length of railway within the smallest space. Disregarding superficialities, the East Frieslanders, the Schleswig-Holsteiners, the Mecklenburghers, and the Pomeranians are much more nearly allied to the old Bavarians, the Tyrolese, and the Styrians than any of these are allied to the Saxons, the Thuringians, or the Rhinelanders. Both in North and

South Germany original races are still found in large masses, and popular dialects are spoken ; you still find there thoroughly peasant districts, thorough villages, and also, at great intervals, thorough cities ; you still find there a sense of rank. In Middle Germany, on the contrary, the original races are fused together or sprinkled hither and thither ; the peculiarities of the popular dialects are worn down or confused ; there is no very strict line of demarkation between the country and the town population, hundreds of small towns and large villages being hardly distinguishable in their characteristics ; and the sense of rank, as part of the organic structure of society, is almost extinguished. Again, both in the north and south there is still a strong ecclesiastical spirit in the people, and the Pomeranian sees Antichrist in the Pope as clearly as the Tyrolese sees him in Doctor Luther ; while in Middle Germany the confessions are mingled, they exist peaceably side by side in very narrow space, and tolerance or indifference has spread itself widely even in the popular mind. And the analogy, or rather the causal relation between the physical geography of the three regions and the development of the population goes still further :

"For," observes Riehl, "the striking connection which has been pointed out between the local geological formations in Germany and the revolutionary disposition of the people has more than a metaphorical significance. Where the primeval physical revolutions of the globe have been the wildest in their effcts, and the most multiform strata have been tossed together or thrown one upon the other, it is a very intelligible consequence that on a land surface thus broken up, the population should sooner develop itself into small communities, and that the more intense life generated in these smaller communities should become the most favorable nidus for the reception of modern culture, and with this a susceptibility for its revolutionary ideas ; while a people settled in a region where its groups are spread over a large space will persist much more obstinately in the retention of its original character. The people of Middle Germany have none of that exclusive one-sidedness which determines the peculiar genius of great national groups, just as this one-sidedness or uniformity is wanting to the geological and geographical character of their land."

This ethnographical outline Riehl fills up with special and typical descriptions, and then makes it the starting-point for a criticism of the actual political condition of Germany. The volume is full of vivid pictures, as well as penetrating glances into the maladies and tendencies of modern society. It would be fascinating as literature if it were not important for its facts and philosophy. But we can only commend it to our readers, and pass on to the volume entitled "Die Bürgerliche Gesellschaft," from which we have drawn our sketch of the German peasantry. Here Riehl gives us a series of studies in that natural history of the people which he regards as the proper basis of social policy. He holds that, in European society, there are *three natural ranks or estates:* the hereditary landed aristocracy, the citizens or commercial class, and the peasantry or agricultural class. By *natural ranks* he means ranks which have their roots deep in the historical structure of society, and are still, in the present, showing vitality above ground; he means those great social groups which are not only distinguished externally by their vocation, but essentially by their mental character, their habits, their mode of life—by the principle they represent in the historical development of society. In his conception of the "Fourth Estate" he differs from the usual interpretation, according to which it is simply equivalent to the Proletariat, or those who are dependent on daily wages, whose only capital is their skill or bodily strength—factory operatives, artisans, agricultural laborers, to whom might be added, especially in Germany, the day-laborers with the quill, the literary proletariat. This, Riehl observes, is a valid basis of economical classification, but not of social classification. In his view, the Fourth Estate is a stratum produced by the perpetual abrasion of the other great social groups; it is the sign and result of the decomposition which is commencing in the organic constitution of society. Its elements are derived alike from the aristocracy, the bourgeoisie, and the peasantry. It assembles under its banner the deserters of historical society, and forms them into a terrible army, which is only just awaking to the consciousness of its corporate power. The tendency of this Fourth Estate, by the very process of its formation, is to do away with the distinctive historical character of the other estates, and to resolve their peculiar rank and vocation into a uniform social relation founded on an abstract conception of society. According to Riehl's classification, the day-laborers, whom the political economist designates as the Fourth Estate, belong partly to the peasantry or agricultural class, and partly to the citizens or commercial class.

Riehl considers, in the first place, the peasantry and aristocracy as the "Forces of social persistence," and, in the second, the bourgeoisie and the "Fourth Estate" as the "Forces of social movement."

The aristocracy, he observes, is the only one among these four groups which is denied by others besides Socialists to have any natural basis as a separate rank. It is admitted that there was once an aristocracy which had an intrinsic ground of existence, but now, it is alleged, this is an historical fossil, an antiquarian relic, venerable because gray with age. It what, it is asked, can consist the peculiar vocation of the aristocracy, since it has no longer the monopoly of the land, of the higher military functions, and of government offices, and since the service of the court has no longer any political importance? To this Riehl replies, that in great revolutionary crises, the "men of progress" have more than once "abolished" the aristocracy. But, remarkably enough, the aristocracy has always reappeared. This measure of abolition showed that the nobility were no longer regarded as a real class, for to abolish a real class would be an absurdity. It is quite possible to contemplate a voluntary breaking up of the peasant or citizen class in the socialistic sense, but no man in his senses would think of straightway "abolishing" citizens and peasants. The aristocracy, then, was regarded as a sort of cancer, or excrescence of society. Nevertheless, not only has it been found impossible to annihilate an hereditary nobility by decree, but also the aristocracy of the eighteenth century outlived even the self-destructive acts of its own perversity. A life which was entirely without object, entirely destitute of functions, would not, says Riehl, be so persistent. He has an acute criticism of those who conduct a polemic against the idea of an hereditary aristocracy while they are proposing an "aristocracy of talent," which after all is based on the principle of inheritance. The Socialists are, therefore, only consistent in declaring against an aristocracy of talent. "But when they have turned the world into a great Foundling Hospital they will still be unable to eradicate the 'privileges of birth.'" We must not follow him in his criticism, however; nor can we afford to do more than mention hastily his interesting sketch of the mediæval aristocracy, and his admonition to the German aristocracy of the present day, that the vitality of their class is not to be sustained by romantic attempts to revive mediæval forms and sentiments, but only by the exercise of functions as real and salutary for actual society as those of the mediæval aristocracy were for the feudal age. "In modern society the divisions of rank indicate *division of labor*, according to that distribution of functions in the social organism which the historical constitution of society has determined. In this way the principle of differentiation and the principle of unity are identical."

The elaborate study of the German bourgeoisie, which forms the next division of the volume, must be passed over, but we may pause a moment to note Riehl's definition of the social *Philister* (Philistine), an epithet for which we have no equivalent, not at all, however, for want of the object it represents. Most people who read a little German know that the epithet *Philister* originated in the *Burschen-leben*, or Student-life of Germany, and that the antithesis of *Bursch* and *Philister* was equivalent to the antithesis of "gown" and "town;" but since the word has passed into ordinary language it has assumed several shades of significance which have not yet been merged into a single, absolute meaning; and one of the questions which an English visitor in Germany will probably take an opportunity of asking is, "What is the strict meaning of the word *Philister?*" Riehl's answer is, that the *Philister* "is one who is indifferent to all social interests, all public life, as distinguished from selfish and private interests; he has no sympathy with political and social events except as they affect his own comfort and prosperity, as they offer him material for amusement or opportunity for gratifying his vanity. He has no social or political creed, but is always of the opinion which is most convenient for the moment. He is always in the majority, and is the main element of unreason and stupidity in the judgment of a "discerning public." It seems presumptuous in us to dispute Riehl's interpretation of a German word, but we must think that, in literature, the epithet *Philister* has usually a wider meaning than this—includes his definition and something more. We imagine the *Philister* is the personification of the spirit which judges everything from a lower point of view than the subject demands; which judges the affairs of the parish from the egotistic or purely personal point of view; which judges the affairs of the nation from the parochial point of view, and does not hesitate to measure the merits of the universe from the human point of view. At least this must surely be the spirit to which Goethe alludes in a passage cited by Riehl himself, where he says that the Germans need not be ashamed of erecting a monument to him as well as to Blucher; for if Blucher had freed them from the French, he (Goethe) had freed them from the nets of the *Philister:*

> "Ihr mögt mirimmer ungescheut
> Gleich Blüchern Denkmal setzen!
> Von Franzosen hat er euch befreit,
> Ich von Philister-netzen."

Goethe could hardly claim to be the apostle of public spirit; but he is eminently the man who helps us to rise to a lofty point of observation, so that we may see things in their relative proportions.

The most interesting chapters in the description of the

"Fourth Estate," which concludes the volume, are those on the "Aristocratic Proletariat" and the "Intellectual Proletariat." The Fourth Estate in Germany, says Riehl, has its centre of gravity not, as in England and France, in the day laborers and factory operatives, and still less in the degenerate peasantry. In Germany the *educated* proletariat is the leaven that sets the mass in fermentation; the dangerous classes there go about, not in blouses, but in frock coats; they begin with the impoverished prince and end in the hungriest *littérateur*. The custom that all the sons of a nobleman shall inherit their father's title necessarily goes on multiplying that class of aristocrats who are not only without function but without adequate provision, and who shrink from entering the ranks of the citizens by adopting some honest calling. The younger son of a prince, says Riehl, is usually obliged to remain without any vocation; and however zealously he may study music, painting, literature, or science, he can never be a regular musician, painter, or man of science; his pursuit will be called a "passion," not a "calling," and to the end of his days he remains a dilettante. "But the ardent pursuit of a fixed practical calling can alone satisfy the active man." Direct legislation cannot remedy this evil. The inheritance of titles by younger sons is the universal custom, and custom is stronger than law. But if all government preference for the "aristocratic proletariat" were withdrawn, the sensible men among them would prefer emigration, or the pursuit of some profession, to the hungry distinction of a title without rents.

The intellectual proletaires Riehl calls the "church militant" of the Fourth Estate in Germany. In no other country are they so numerous; in no other country is the trade in material and industrial capital so far exceeded by the wholesale and retail trade, the traffic and the usury, in the intellectual capital of the nation. *Germany yields more intellectual produce than it can use and pay for.*

"This over-production, which is not transient but permanent, nay, is constantly on the increase, evidences a diseased state of the national industry, a perverted application of industrial powers, and is a far more pungent satire on the national condition than all the poverty of operatives and peasants. . . . Other nations need not envy us the preponderance of the intellectual proletariat over the proletaires of manual labor. For man more easily becomes diseased from over-study than from the labor of the hands; and it is precisely in the intellectual proletariat that there are the most dangerous seeds of disease. This is the group in which the opposition between earnings and wants, between the ideal social position and the real, is the most hopelessly irreconcilable."

We must unwillingly leave our readers to make acquaintance for themselves with the graphic details with which Riehl follows up this general statement; but before quitting these admirable volumes, let us say, lest our inevitable omissions should have left room for a different conclusion, that Riehl's conservatism is not in the least tinged with the partisanship of a class, with a poetic fanaticism for the past, or with the prejudice of a mind incapable of discerning the grander evolution of things to which all social forms are but temporarily subservient. It is the conservatism of a clear-eyed, practical, but withal large-minded man—a little caustic, perhaps, now and then in his epigrams on democratic doctrinaires who have their nostrum for all political and social diseases, and on communistic theories which he regards as "the despair of the individual in his own manhood, reduced to a system," but nevertheless able and willing to do justice to the elements of fact and reason in every shade of opinion and every form of effort. He is as far as possible from the folly of supposing that the sun will go backward on the dial because we put the hands of our clock backward; he only contends against the opposite folly of decreeing that it shall be mid-day while in fact the sun is only just touching the mountain-tops, and all along the valley men are stumbling in the twilight.

VI.

SILLY NOVELS BY LADY NOVELISTS.

Silly Novels by Lady Novelists are a genus with many species, determined by the particular quality of silliness that predominates in them—the frothy, the prosy, the pious, or the pedantic. But it is a mixture of all these—a composite order of feminine fatuity—that produces the largest class of such novels, which we shall distinguish as the *mind-and-millinery* species. The heroine is usually an heiress, probably a peeress in her own right, with perhaps a vicious baronet, an amiable duke, and an irresistible younger son of a marquis as lovers in the foreground, a clergyman and a poet sighing for her in the middle distance, and a crowd of undefined adorers dimly indicated beyond. Her eyes and her wit are both dazzling; her nose and her morals are alike free from any tendency to irregularity; she has a superb *contralto* and a superb intellect; she is perfectly well dressed and perfectly religious; she dances like a sylph, and reads the Bible in the original tongues. Or it may be that the heroine is not an heiress—that rank and wealth are the only things in which she is deficient; but she infallibly gets into high society, she has the triumph of refusing many matches and securing the best, and she wears some family jewels or other as a sort of crown of righteousness at the end. Rakish men either bite their lips in impotent confusion at her repartees, or are touched to penitence by her reproofs, which, on appropriate occasions, rise to a lofty strain of rhetoric; indeed, there is a general propensity in her to make speeches, and to rhapsodize at some length when she retires to her bedroom. In her recorded conversations she is amazingly eloquent, and in her unrecorded conversations amazingly witty. She is understood to have a depth of insight that looks through and through the shallow theories of philosophers, and her superior instincts are a sort of dial by which men have only to set their clocks and watches, and all will go well. The men play a very subordinate part by her side. You are consoled now and then by a hint that they have affairs, which keeps you in mind that the working-day business of the world is somehow being carried on, but ostensibly the final cause of their existence is that they may accompany the heroine on her "starring" expedition through life. They see her at a ball, and they are dazzled; at a flower-show, and they are fascinated; on a riding excursion, and they are witched by her noble horsemanship; at church, and they are awed by the sweet solemnity of her demeanor. She is the ideal woman in feelings, faculties, and flounces. For all this she as often as not marries the wrong person to begin with, and she suffers terribly from the plots and intrigues of the vicious baronet; but even death has a soft place in his heart for such a paragon, and remedies all mistakes for her just at the right moment. The vicious baronet is sure to be killed in a duel, and the tedious husband dies in his bed requesting his wife, as a particular favor to him, to marry the man she loves best, and having already dispatched a note to the lover informing him of the comfortable arrangement. Before matters arrive at this desirable issue our feelings are tried by seeing the noble, lovely, and gifted heroine pass through many *mauvais moments*, but we have the satisfaction of knowing that her sorrows are wept into embroidered pocket-handkerchiefs, that her fainting form reclines on the very best upholstery, and that whatever vicissitudes she may undergo, from being dashed out of her carriage to having her head shaved in a fever, she comes out of them all with a complexion more blooming and locks more redundant than ever.

We may remark, by the way, that we have been relieved from a serious scruple by discovering that silly novels by lady novelists rarely introduce us into any other than very lofty and fashionable society. We had imagined that destitute women turned novelists, as they turned governesses, because they had no other "ladylike" means of getting their bread. On this supposition, vacillating syntax, and improbable incident had a certain pathos for us, like the extremely supererogatory pincushions and ill-devised nightcaps that are offered for sale by a blind man. We felt the commodity to be a nuisance, but we were glad to think that the money went to relieve the necessitous, and we pictured to ourselves lonely women struggling for a maintenance, or wives and daughters devoting themselves to the production of "copy" out of pure heroism—perhaps to pay their husband's debts or to purchase luxuries for a sick father. Under these impressions we shrank from criticising a lady's novel: her English might be faulty, but we said to ourselves her motives are irreproachable; her imagination may be uninventive, but her patience is untiring. Empty writing was excused by an empty stomach, and twaddle was consecrated by tears. But no! This theory of ours, like many other pretty theories, has had to give way before observation. Women's silly novels, we are now convinced, are written under totally different circumstances. The fair writers have evidently never talked to a tradesman except from a carriage window; they have no notion of the working-classes except as "dependents;" they think five hundred a year a miserable pittance; Belgravia and "baronial halls" are their primary truths; and they have no idea of feeling interest in any man who is not at least a great landed proprietor, if not a prime minister. It is clear that they write in elegant boudoirs, with violet-colored ink and a ruby pen; that they must be entirely indifferent to publishers' accounts, and inexperienced in every form of poverty except poverty of brains. It is true that we are constantly struck with the want of verisimilitude in their representations of the high society in which they seem to live; but then they betray no closer acquaintance with any other form of life. If their peers and peeresses are improbable, their literary men, tradespeople, and cottagers are impossible; and their intellect seems to have the peculiar impartiality of reproducing both what they *have* seen and heard, and what they have *not* seen and heard, with equal unfaithfulness.

There are few women, we suppose, who have not seen something of children under five years of age, yet in "Compensation," a recent novel of the mind-and-millinery species, which calls itself a "story of real life," we have a child of four and a half years old talking in this Ossianic fashion:

"'Oh, I am so happy, dear gran'mamma;—I have seen—I have seen such a delightful person; he is like everything beautiful—like the smell of sweet flowers, and the view from Ben Lemond;—or no, *better than that*—he is like what I think of and see when I am very, very happy; and he is really like mamma, too, when she sings; and his forehead is like *that distant sea*,' she continued, pointing to the blue Mediterranean; 'there seems no end—no end; or like the clusters of stars I like best to look at on a warm fine night. . . . Don't look so . . . your forehead is like Loch Lomond, when the wind is blowing and the sun is gone in; I like the sunshine best when the lake is smooth. . . . So now—I like it better than ever . . . It is more beautiful still from the dark cloud that has gone over it, *when the sun suddenly lights up all the colors of the forests and shining purple rocks, and it is all reflected in the waters below.*'"

We are not surprised to learn that the mother of this infant phenomenon, who exhibits symptoms so alarmingly like those of adolescence repressed by gin, is herself a phœnix. We are assured, again and again, that she had a remarkably original in mind, that she was a genius, and "conscious of her originality," and she was fortunate enough to have a lover who was also a genius and a man of "most original mind."

This lover, we read, though "wonderfully similar" to her "in powers and capacity," was "infinitely superior to her in faith and development," and she saw in him "'Agape'—so rare to find—of which she had read and admired the meaning in her Greek Testament; having, *from her great facility in learning languages*, read the Scriptures in their original *tongues*." Of course! Greek and Hebrew are mere play to a heroine ; Sanscrit is no more than *a b c* to her ; and she can talk with perfect correctness in any language, except English. She is a polking polyglot, a Creuzer in crinoline. Poor men . There are so few of you who know even Hebrew ; you think it something to boast of if, like Bolingbroke, you only " understand that sort of learning and what is writ about it ;" and you are perhaps adoring women who can think slightingly of you in all the Semitic languages successively. But, then, as we are almost invariably told that a heroine has a " beautifully small head," and as her intellect has probably been early invigorated by an attention to costume and deportment, we may conclude that she can pick up the Oriental tongues, to say nothing of their dialects, with the same aërial facility that the butterfly sips nectar. Besides, there can be no difficulty in conceiving the depth of the heroine's erudition when that of the authoress is so evident.

In " Laura Gay," another novel of the same school, the heroine seems less at home in Greek and Hebrew but she makes up for the deficiency by a quite playful familiarity with the Latin classics—with the " dear old Virgil," " the graceful Horace, the humane Cicero, and the pleasant Livy ;" indeed, it is such a matter of course with her to quote Latin that she does it at a picnic in a very mixed company of ladies and gentlemen, having, we are told, " no conception that the nobler sex were capable of jealousy on this subject. And if, indeed," continues the biographer of Laura Gay, " the wisest and noblest portion of that sex were in the majority, no such sentiment would exist ; but while Miss Wyndhams and Mr. Redfords abound, great sacrifices must be made to their existence." Such sacrifices, we presume, as abstaining from Latin quotations, of extremely moderate interest and applicability, which the wise and noble minority of the other sex would be quite as willing to dispense with as the foolish and ignoble majority. It is as little the custom of well-bred men as of well-bred women to quote Latin in mixed parties ; they can contain their familiarity with " the humane Cicero" without allowing it to boil over in ordinary conversation, and even references to "the pleasant Livy" are not absolutely irrepressible. But Ciceronian Latin is the mildest form of Miss Gay's conversational power. Being on the Palatine with a party of sightseers, she falls into the following vein of well-rounded remark: "Truth can only be pure objectively, for even in the creeds where it predominates, being subjective, and parcelled out into portions, each of these necessarily receives a hue of idiosyncrasy, that is, a taint of superstition more or less strong; while in such creeds as the Roman Catholic, ignorance, interest, the basis of ancient idolatries, and the force of authority, have gradually accumulated on the pure truth, and transformed it, at last, into a mass of superstition for the majority of its votaries; and how few are there, alas! whose zeal, courage, and intellectual energy are equal to the analysis of this accumulation, and to the discovery of the pearl of great price which lies hidden beneath this heap of rubbish." We have often met with women much more novel and profound in their observations than Laura Gay, but rarely with any so inopportunely long-winded. A clerical lord, who is half in love with her, is alarmed by the daring remarks just quoted, and begins to suspect that she is inclined to free-thinking. But he is mistaken; when in a moment of sorrow he delicately begs leave to "recall to her memory, a *depôt* of strength and consolation under affliction, which, until we are hard pressed by the trials of life, we are too apt to forget," we learn that she really has "recurrence to that sacred depôt," together with the tea-pot. There is a certain flavor of orthodoxy mixed with the parade of fortunes and fine carriages in "Laura Gay," but it is an orthodoxy mitigated by study of "the humane Cicero," and by an "intellectual disposition to analyze."

"Compensation" is much more heavily dosed with doctrine, but then it has a treble amount of snobbish worldliness and absurd incident to tickle the palate of pious frivolity. Linda, the heroine, is still more speculative and spiritual than Laura Gay, but she has been "presented," and has more and far grander lovers; very wicked and fascinating women are introduced—even a French *lionne;* and no expense is spared to get up as exciting a story as you will find in the most immoral novels. In fact, it is a wonderful *pot pourri* of Almack's, Scotch second-sight, Mr. Rogers's breakfasts, Italian brigands, death-bed conversions, superior authoresses, Italian mistresses, and attempts at poisoning old ladies, the whole served up with a garnish of talk about "faith and development" and "most original minds." Even Miss Susan Barton, the superior authoress, whose pen moves in a "quick, decided manner when she is composing," declines the finest opportunities of marriage; and though old enough to be Linda's mother (since we are told that she refused Linda's father), has her hand sought by a young earl, the heroine's rejected lover. Of course, genius and morality must be backed by eligible offers, or they would seem rather a dull affair; and piety, like other things, in order to be *comme il faut,* must be in "society," and have admittance to the best circles.

"Rank and Beauty" is a more frothy and less religious variety of the mind-and-millinery species. The heroine, we are told, "if she inherited her father's pride of birth and her mother's beauty of person, had in herself a tone of enthusiastic feeling that, perhaps, belongs to her age even in the lowly born, but which is refined into the high spirit of wild romance only in the far descended, who feel that it is their best inheritance." This enthusiastic young lady, by dint of reading the newspaper to her father, falls in love with the *prime minister,* who, through the medium of leading articles and "the *resumé* of the debates," shines upon her imagination as a bright particular star, which has no parallax for her living in the country as simple Miss Wyndham. But she forthwith becomes Baroness Umfraville in her own right, astonishes the world with her beauty and accomplishments when she bursts upon it from her mansion in Spring Gardens, and, as you foresee, will presently come into contact with the unseen *objet aimé.* Perhaps the words "prime minister" suggest to you a wrinkled or obese sexagenarian; but pray dismiss the image. Lord Rupert Conway has been "called while still almost a youth to the first situation which a subject can hold in the *universe*," and even leading articles and a *resumé* of the debates have not conjured up a dream that surpasses the fact.

"The door opened again, and Lord Rupert Conway entered. Evelyn gave one glance. It was enough; she was not disappointed. It seemed as if a picture on which she had long gazed was suddenly instinct with life, and had stepped from its frame before her. His tall figure, the distinguished simplicity of his air—it was a living Vandyke, a cavalier, one of his noble cavalier ancestors, or one to whom her fancy had always likened him, who long of yore had with an Umfraville fought the Paynim far beyond the sea. Was this reality?"

Very little like it, certainly.

By and by it becomes evident that the ministerial heart is touched. Lady Umfraville is on a visit to the Queen at Windsor, and—

"The last evening of her stay, when they returned from riding, Mr. Wyndham took her and a large party to the top of the Keep, to see the view. She was leaning on the battlements, gazing from that 'stately height' at the prospect beneath her, when Lord Rupert was by her side. 'What an unrivalled view!' exclaimed she.

"'Yes, it would have been wrong to go without having been up here. You are pleased with your visit?'

"'Enchanted! A Queen to live and die under, to live and die for!'

"'Ha!' cried he, with sudden emotion, and with a *eureka* expression of countenance, as if he had *indeed found a heart in unison with his own*.'"

The "*eureka* expression of countenance" you see at once to be prophetic of marriage at the end of the third volume; but before that desirable consummation there are very complicated misunderstandings, arising chiefly from the vindictive plotting of Sir Luttrel Wycherley, who is a genius, a poet, and in every way a most remarkable character indeed. He is not only a romantic poet, but a hardened rake and a cynical wit; yet his deep passion for Lady Umfraville has so impoverished his epigrammatic talent that he cuts an extremely poor figure in conversation. When she rejects him, he rushes into the shrubbery and rolls himself in the dirt; and on recovering, devotes himself to the most diabolical and laborious schemes of vengeance, in the course of which he disguises himself as a quack physician and enters into general practice, foreseeing that Evelyn will fall ill, and that he shall be called in to attend her. At last, when all his schemes are frustrated, he takes leave of her in a long letter, written, as you will perceive from the following passage, entirely in the style of an eminent literary man:

"Oh, lady, nursed in pomp and pleasure, will you ever cast one thought upon the miserable being who addresses you? Will you ever, as your gilded galley is floating down the unruffled stream of prosperity, will you ever, while lulled by the sweetest music—thine own praises—hear the far-off sigh from that world to which I am going?"

On the whole, however, frothy as it is, we rather prefer "Rank and Beauty" to the two other novels we have mentioned. The dialogue is more natural and spirited; there is some frank ignorance and no pedantry; and you are allowed to take the heroine's astounding intellect upon trust, without being called on to read her conversational refutations of sceptics and philosophers, or her rhetorical solutions of the mysteries of the universe.

Writers of the mind-and-millinery school are remarkably unanimous in their choice of diction. In their novels there is usually a lady or gentleman who is more or less of a upas tree; the lover has a manly breast; minds are redolent of various things; hearts are hollow; events are utilized; friends are consigned to the tomb; infancy is an engaging period; the sun is a luminary that goes to his western couch, or gathers the rain-drops into his refulgent bosom; life is a melancholy boon; Albion and Scotia are conversational epithets. There is a striking resemblance, too, in the character of their moral comments, such, for instance, as that "It is a fact, no less true than melancholy, that all people, more or less, richer or poorer, are swayed by bad example;" that "Books, however trivial, contain some subjects from which useful information may be drawn;" that "Vice can too often borrow the language of virtue;" that "Merit and nobility of nature must exist, to be accepted, for clamor and pretension cannot impose upon those too well read in human nature to be easily deceived;" and that "In order to forgive, we must have been injured." There is doubtless a class of readers to whom these remarks appear peculiarly pointed and pungent; for we often find them doubly and trebly scored with the pencil, and delicate hands giving in their determined adhesion to these hardy novelties by a distinct *très vrai*, emphasized by many notes of exclamation. The colloquial style of these novels is often marked by much ingenious inversion, and a careful avoidance of such cheap phraseology as can be heard every day. Angry young gentlemen exclaim, "'Tis ever thus, methinks;" and in the half hour before dinner a young lady informs her next neighbor that the first day she read Shakespeare she "stole away into the park, and beneath the shadow of the greenwood tree, devoured with rapture the inspired page of the great magician." But the most remarkable efforts of the mind-and-millinery writers lie in their philosophic reflections. The authoress of "Laura Gay," for example, having married her hero and heroine, improves the event by observing that "if those sceptics, whose eyes have so long gazed on matter that they can no longer see aught else in man, could once enter with heart and soul, into such bliss as this, they would come to say that the soul of man and the polypus are not of common origin, or of the same texture." Lady novelists, it appears, can see something else besides matter; they are not limited to phenomena, but can relieve their eyesight by occasional glimpses of the *noumenon*, and are, therefore, naturally better able than any one else to confound sceptics, even of that remarkable but to us unknown school which maintains that the soul of man is of the same texture as the polypus.

The most pitiable of all silly novels by lady novelists are what we may call the *oracular* species—novels intended to expound the writer's religious, philosophical, or moral theories. There seems to be a notion abroad among women, rather akin to the superstition that the speech and actions of idiots are inspired, and that the human being most entirely exhausted of common-sense is the fittest vehicle of revelation. To judge from their writings, there are certain ladies who think that an amazing ignorance, both of science and of life, is the best possible qualification for forming an opinion on the knottiest moral and speculative questions. Apparently, their recipe for solving all such difficulties is something like this: Take a woman's head, stuff it with a smattering of philosophy and literature chopped small, and with false notions of society baked hard, let it hang over a desk a few hours every day, and serve up hot in feeble English when not required. You will rarely meet with a lady novelist of the oracular class who is diffident of her ability to decide on theological questions—who has any suspicion that she is not capable of discriminating with the nicest accuracy between the good and evil in all church parties—who does not see precisely how it is that men have gone wrong hitherto—and pity philosophers in general that they have not had the opportunity of consulting her. Great writers, who have modestly contented themselves with putting their experience into fiction, and have thought it quite a sufficient task to exhibit men and things as they are, she sighs over as deplorably deficient in the application of their powers. "They have solved no great questions"—and she is ready to remedy their omission by setting before you a complete theory of life and manual of divinity in a love story, where ladies and gentlemen of good family go through genteel vicissitudes, to the utter confusion of Deists, Puseyites, and ultra-Protestants, and to the perfect establishment of that peculiar view of Christianity which either condenses itself into a sentence of small caps, or explodes into a cluster of stars on the three hundred and thirtieth page. It is true, the ladies and gentlemen will probably seem to you remarkably little like any you have had the fortune or misfortune to meet with, for, as a general rule, the ability of a lady novelist to describe actual life and her fellow-men is in inverse proportion to her confident eloquence about God and the other world, and the means by which she usually chooses to conduct you to true ideas of the invisible is a totally false picture of the visible.

As typical a novel of the oracular kind as we can hope to meet with, is "The Enigma: a Leaf from the Chronicles of the Wolchorley House." The "enigma" which this novel is to solve is certainly one that demands powers no less gigantic than those of a lady novelist, being neither more nor less than the existence of evil. The problem is stated and the answer dimly foreshadowed on the very first page. The spirited young lady, with raven hair, says, "All life is an inextricable confusion;" and the meek young lady, with auburn hair, looks at the picture of the Madonna which she is copying, and—"*There* seemed the solution of that mighty enigma." The style of this novel is quite as lofty as its purpose; indeed, some passages on which we have spent much patient study are quite beyond our reach, in spite of the illustrative aid of italics and small caps; and we must await further "development" in order to understand them. Of Ernest, the model young clergyman, who sets every one right on all occasions, we read that "he held not of marriage in the marketable kind, after a social desecration;" that, on one eventful night, "sleep had not visited his divided heart, where tumultuated, in varied type and combination, the aggregate feelings of grief and joy;" and that, "for the *marketable* human article he had no toleration, be it of what sort, or set for what value it might, whether for worship or class, his upright soul abhorred it, whose ultimatum, the self-deceiver, was to him THE *great spiritual lie*, 'living in a vain show, deceiving and being deceived;' since he did not suppose the phylactery and enlarged border on the garment to be *merely* a social trick." (The italics and small caps are the author's, and we hope they assist the reader's comprehension.) Of Sir Lionel, the model old gentleman, we are told that "the simple ideal of the middle age, apart from its anarchy and decadence, in him most truly seemed to live again, when the ties which knit men together were of heroic cast. The first-born colors of pristine faith and truth engraven on the common soul of man, and blent into the wide arch of brotherhood, where the primæval law of *order* grew and multiplied each perfect after his kind, and mutually interdependent." You see clearly, of course, how colors are first engraven on the soul, and then blent into a wide arch, on which arch of colors—apparently a rainbow—the law of order grew and multiplied, each—apparently the arch and the law—perfect after his kind? If, after this, you can possibly want any further aid toward knowing what Sir Lionel was, we can tell you that in his soul "the scientific combinations of thought could educe no fuller harmonies of the good and the true than lay in the primæval pulses which floated as an atmosphere around it!" and that, when he was sealing a letter, "Lo! the responsive throb in that good man's bosom echoed back in simple truth the honest witness of a heart that condemned him not, as his eye, bedewed with love, rested, too, with something of ancestral pride, on the undimmed motto of the family—'Loiauté.'"

The slightest matters have their vulgarity fumigated out of them by the same elevated style. Commonplace people would say that a copy of Shakespeare lay on a drawing-room table; but the authoress of "The Enigma," bent on edifying periphrasis, tells you that there lay on the table, "that fund of human thought and feeling, which teaches the heart through the little name, 'Shakespeare.'" A watchman sees a light burning in an upper window rather longer than usual, and thinks that people are foolish to sit up late when they have an opportunity of going to bed; but, lest this fact should seem too low and common, it is presented to us in the following striking and metaphysical manner: "He marvelled—as a man *will* think for others in a necessarily separate personality, consequently (though disallowing it) in false mental premise—how differently *he* should act, how gladly *he* should prize the rest so lightly held of within." A footman—an ordinary Jeames, with large calves and aspirated vowels—answers the door-bell, and the opportunity is seized to tell you that he was a "type of the large class of pampered menials, who follow the curse of Cain—'vagabonds' on the face of the earth, and whose estimate of the human class varies in the graduated scale of money and expenditure. . . . These, and such as these, O England, be the false lights of thy morbid civilization!" We have heard of various "false lights," from Dr. Cumming to Robert Owen, from Dr. Pusey to the Spirit-rappers, but we never before heard of the false light that emanates from plush and powder.

In the same way very ordinary events of civilized life are exalted into the most awful crises, and ladies in full skirts and *manches à la Chinoise*, conduct themselves not unlike the heroines of sanguinary melodramas. Mrs. Percy, a shallow woman of the world, wishes her son Horace to marry the auburn-haired Grace, she being an heiress; but he, after the manner of sons, falls in love with the raven-haired Kate, the heiress's portionless cousin; and, moreover, Grace herself shows every symptom of perfect indifference to Horace. In such cases sons are often sulky or fiery, mothers are alternately manœuvring and waspish, and the portionless young lady often lies awake at night and cries a good deal. We are getting used to these things now, just as we are used to eclipses of the moon, which no longer set us howling and beating tin kettles. We never heard of a lady in a fashionable "front" behaving like Mrs. Percy under these circumstances. Happening one day to see Horace talking to Grace at a window, without in the least knowing what they are talking about, or having the least reason to believe that Grace, who is mistress of the house and a person of dignity, would accept her son if he were to offer himself, she suddenly rushes up to them and clasps them both, saying, "with a flushed countenance and in an excited manner"—" This is indeed happiness ; for, may I not call you so, Grace ?—my Grace—my Horace's Grace !—my dear children !" Her son tells her she is mistaken, and that he is engaged to Kate, whereupon we have the following scene and tableau :

" Gathering herself up to an unprecedented height (!) her eyes lightening forth the fire of her anger :

" ' Wretched boy !' she said, hoarsely and scornfully, and clenching her hand, ' Take then the doom of your own choice ! Bow down your miserable head and let a mother's—'

" ' Curse not !' spake a deep low voice from behind, and Mrs. Percy started, scared, as though she had seen a heavenly visitant appear, to break upon her in the midst of her sin.

" Meantime Horace had fallen on his knees, at her feet, and hid his face in his hands.

" Who then, is she—who ! Truly his ' guardian spirit ' hath stepped between him and the fearful words, which, however unmerited, must have hung as a pall over his future existence ;—a spell which could not be unbound—which could not be unsaid.

" Of an earthly paleness, but calm with the still, iron-bound calmness of death—the only calm one there—Katherine stood ; and her words smote on the ear in tones whose appallingly slow and separate intonation rung on the heart like a chill, isolated tolling of some fatal knell.

" ' He would have plighted me his faith, but I did not accept it ; you cannot, therefore—you *dare* not curse him. And here,' she continued, raising her hand to heaven, whither her large dark eyes also rose with a chastened glow, which, for the first time, *suffering* had lighted in those passionate orbs—' here I promise, come weal, come woe, that Horace Wolchorley and I do never interchange vows without his mother's sanction —without his mother's blessing !' "

Here, and throughout the story, we see that confusion of purpose which is so characteristic of silly novels written by women. It is a story of quite modern drawing-room society

—a society in which polkas are played and Puseyism discussed; yet we have characters, and incidents, and traits of manner introduced, which are mere shreds from the most heterogeneous romances. We have a blind Irish harper, "relic of the picturesque bards of yore," startling us at a Sunday-school festival of tea and cake in an English village; we have a crazy gypsy, in a scarlet cloak, singing snatches of romantic song, and revealing a secret on her death-bed which, with the testimony of a dwarfish miserly merchant, who salutes strangers with a curse and a devilish laugh, goes to prove that Ernest, the model young clergyman, is Kate's brother; and we have an ultra-virtuous Irish Barney, discovering that a document is forged, by comparing the date of the paper with the date of the alleged signature, although the same document has passed through a court of law and occasioned a fatal decision. The "Hall" in which Sir Lionel lives is the venerable country-seat of an old family, and this, we suppose, sets the imagination of the authoress flying to donjons and battlements, where "lo! the warder blows his horn;" for, as the inhabitants are in their bedrooms on a night certainly within the recollection of Pleaceman X. and a breeze springs up, which we are at first told was faint, and then that it made the old cedars bow their branches to the greensward, she falls into this mediæval vein of description (the italics are ours): "The banner *unfurled it* at the sound, and shook its guardian wing above, while the startled owl *flapped her* in the ivy; the firmament looking down through her 'argus eyes'—

'Ministers of heaven's mute melodies.'

And lo! two strokes tolled from out the warder tower, and 'Two o'clock' re-echoed its interpreter below."

Such stories as this of "The Enigma" remind us of the pictures clever children sometimes draw "out of their own head," where you will see a modern villa on the right, two knights in helmets fighting in the foreground, and a tiger grinning in a jungle on the left, the several objects being brought together because the artist thinks each pretty, and perhaps still more because he remembers seeing them in other pictures.

But we like the authoress much better on her mediæval stilts than on her oracular ones—when she talks of the *Ich* and of "subjective" and "objective," and lays down the exact line of Christian verity, between "right-hand excesses and left-hand declensions." Persons who deviate from this line are introduced with a patronizing air of charity. Of a certain Miss Inshquine she informs us, with all the lucidity of italics and small caps, that "*function*, not *form*, AS *the inevitable outer expression of the spirit in this tabernacle age*, weakly engrossed her." And *à propos* of Miss Mayjar, an evangelical lady who is a little too apt to talk of her visits to sick women and the state of their souls, we are told that the model clergyman is "not one to disallow, through the *super* crust, the undercurrent toward good in the *subject*, or the positive benefits, nevertheless, to the *object*." We imagine the double-refined accent and protrusion of chin which are feebly represented by the italics in this lady's sentences! We abstain from quoting any of her oracular doctrinal passages, because they refer to matters too serious for our pages just now.

The epithet "silly" may seem impertinent, applied to a novel which indicates so much reading and intellectual activity as "The Enigma," but we use this epithet advisedly. If, as the world has long agreed, a very great amount of instruction will not make a wise man, still less will a very mediocre amount of instruction make a wise woman. And the most mischievous form of feminine silliness is the literary form, because it tends to confirm the popular prejudice against the more solid education of women.

When men see girls wasting their time in consultations about bonnets and ball dresses, and in giggling or sentimental love-confidences, or middle-aged women mismanaging their children, and solacing themselves with acrid gossip, they can hardly help saying, "For Heaven's sake, let girls be better educated; let them have some better objects of thought—some more solid occupations." But after a few hours' conversation with an oracular literary woman, or a few hours' reading of her books, they are likely enough to say, "After all, when a woman gets some knowledge, see what use she makes of it! Her knowledge remains acquisition instead of passing into culture; instead of being subdued into modesty and simplicity by a larger acquaintance with thought and fact, she has a feverish consciousness of her attainments; she keeps a sort of mental pocket-mirror, and is continually looking in it at her own 'intellectuality;' she spoils the taste of one's muffin by questions of metaphysics; 'puts down' men at a dinner-table with her superior information; and seizes the opportunity of a *soirée* to catechise us on the vital question of the relation between mind and matter. And then, look at her writings! She mistakes vagueness for depth, bombast for eloquence, and affectation for originality; she struts on one page, rolls her eyes on another, grimaces in a third, and is hysterical in a fourth. She may have read many writings of great men, and a few writings of great women; but she is as unable to discern the difference between her own style and theirs as a Yorkshireman is to discern the difference between his own English and a Londoner's: rhodomontade is the native accent of her intellect. No—the average nature of women is too shallow and feeble a soil to bear much tillage; it is only fit for the very lightest crops."

It is true that the men who come to such a decision on such very superficial and imperfect observation may not be among the wisest in the world; but we have not now to contest their opinion—we are only pointing out how it is unconsciously encouraged by many women who have volunteered themselves as representatives of the feminine intellect. We do not believe that a man was ever strengthened in such an opinion by associating with a woman of true culture, whose mind had absorbed her knowledge instead of being absorbed by it. A really cultured woman, like a really cultured man, is all the simpler and the less obtrusive for her knowledge; it has made her see herself and her opinions in something like just proportions; she does not make it a pedestal from which she flatters herself that she commands a complete view of men and things, but makes it a point of observation from which to form a right estimate of herself. She neither spouts poetry nor quotes Cicero on slight provocation; not because she thinks that a sacrifice must be made to the prejudices of men, but because that mode of exhibiting her memory and Latinity does not present itself to her as edifying or graceful. She does not write books to confound philosophers, perhaps because she is able to write books that delight them. In conversation she is the least formidable of women, because she understands you, without wanting to make you aware that you *can't* understand her. She does not give you information, which is the raw material of culture—she gives you sympathy, which is its subtlest essence.

A more numerous class of silly novels than the oracular (which are generally inspired by some form of High Church or transcendental Christianity) is what we may call the *white neck-cloth* species, which represent the tone of thought and feeling in the Evangelical party. This species is a kind of genteel tract on a large scale, intended as a sort of medicinal sweetmeat for Low Church young ladies; an Evangelical substitute for the fashionable novel, as the May Meetings are a substitute for the Opera. Even Quaker children, one would think, can hardly have been denied the indulgence of a doll; but it must be a doll dressed in a drab gown and a coal-scuttle-bonnet—not a worldly doll, in gauze and spangles. And there are no young ladies, we imagine—unless they belong to the Church of the United Brethren, in which people are married without any love-making—who can dispense with love stories. Thus, for Evangelical young ladies there are Evangelical love stories, in which the vicissitudes of the tender passion are sanctified by saving views of Regeneration and the Atonement. These novels differ from the oracular ones, as a Low Churchwoman often differs from a High Churchwoman: they are a little less supercilious and a great deal more ignorant, a little less correct in their syntax and a great deal more vulgar.

The Orlando of Evangelical literature is the young curate, looked at from the point of view of the middle class, where cambric bands are understood to have as thrilling an effect on the hearts of young ladies as epaulettes have in the classes above and below it. In the ordinary type of these novels the hero is almost sure to be a young curate, frowned upon, perhaps by worldly mammas, but carrying captive the hearts of their daughters, who can "never forget *that* sermon;" tender glances are seized from the pulpit stairs instead of the opera-box; *tête-à-têtes* are seasoned with quotations from Scripture instead of quotations from the poets; and questions as to the state of the heroine's affections are mingled with anxieties as to the state of her soul. The young curate always has a background of well-dressed and wealthy if not fashionable society—for Evangelical silliness is as snobbish as any other kind of silliness—and the Evangelical lady novelist, while she explains to you the type of the scapegoat on one page, is ambitious on another to represent the manners and conversations of aristocratic people. Her pictures of fashionable society are often curious studies, considered as efforts of the Evangelical imagination; but in one particular the novels of the White Neckcloth School are meritoriously realistic—their favorite hero, the Evangelical young curate, is always rather an insipid personage.

The most recent novel of this species that we happen to have before us is "The Old Grey Church." It is utterly tame and feeble; there is no one set of objects on which the writer seems to have a stronger grasp than on any other; and we should be entirely at a loss to conjecture among what phases of life her experience has been gained, but for certain vulgarisms of style which sufficiently indicate that she has had the advantage, though she has been unable to use it, of mingling chiefly with men and women whose manners and characters have not had all their bosses and angles rubbed down by refined conventionalism. It is less excusable in an Evangelical novelist than in any other, gratuitously to seek her subjects among titles and carriages. The real drama of Evangelicalism—and it has abundance of fine drama for any one who has genius enough to discern and reproduce it—lies among the middle and lower classes; and are not Evangelical opinions understood to give an especial interest in the weak things of the earth, rather than in the mighty? Why, then, cannot our Evangelical lady novelists show us the operation of their religious views among people (there really are many such in the world) who keep no carriage, "not so much as a brass-bound gig," who even manage to eat their dinner without a silver fork, and in whose mouths the authoress's questionable English would be strictly consistent? Why can we not have pictures of religious life among the industrial classes in England, as interesting as Mrs. Stowe's pictures of religious life among the negroes? Instead of this pious ladies nauseate us with novels which remind us of what we sometimes see in a worldly woman recently "converted;"—she is as fond of a fine dinner-table as before, but she invites clergymen instead of beaux; she thinks as much of her dress as before, but she adopts a more sober choice of colors and patterns; her conversation is as trivial as before, but the triviality is flavored with gospel instead of gossip. In "The Old Grey Church" we have the same sort of Evangelical travesty of the fashionable novel, and of course the vicious, intriguing baronet is not wanting. It is worth while to give a sample of the style of conversation attributed to this high-born rake—a style that, in its profuse italics and palpable innuendoes, is worthy of Miss Squeers. In an evening visit to the ruins of the Colosseum, Eustace, the young clergyman, has been withdrawing the heroine, Miss Lushington, from the rest of the party, for the sake of a *tête-à-tête*. The baronet is jealous, and vents his pique in this way:

"There they are, and Miss Lushington, no doubt, quite safe; for she is under the holy guidance of Pope Eustace the First, who has, of course, been delivering to her an edifying homily on the wickedness of the heathens of yore, who, as tradition tells us, in this very place let loose the wild *beastises* on poor St. Paul!—Oh, no! by the bye, I believe I am wrong, and betraying my want of clergy, and that it was not at all St. Paul, nor was it here. But no matter, it would equally serve as a text to preach from, and from which to diverge to the degenerate *heathen* Christians of the present day, and all their naughty practices, and so end with an exhortation to 'come out from among them, and be separate;'—and I am sure, Miss Lushington, you have most scrupulously conformed to that injunction this evening, for we have seen nothing of you since our arrival. But every one seems agreed it has been a *charming party of pleasure*, and I am sure we all feel *much indebted* to Mr. Gray for having *suggested* it; and as he seems so capital a cicerone, I hope he will think of something else equally agreeable to *all*."

This drivelling kind of dialogue, and equally drivelling narrative, which, like a bad drawing, represents nothing, and barely indicates what is meant to be represented, runs through the book; and we have no doubt is considered by the amiable authoress to constitute an improving novel, which Christian mothers will do well to put into the hands of their daughters. But everything is relative; we have met with American vegetarians whose normal diet was dry meal, and who, when their appetite wanted stimulating, tickled it with *wet* meal; and so, we can imagine that there are Evangelical circles in which "The Old Grey Church" is devoured as a powerful and interesting fiction.

But perhaps the least readable of silly women's novels are the *modern-antique* species, which unfold to us the domestic life of Jannes and Jambres, the private love affairs of Sennacherib, or the mental struggles and ultimate conversion of Demetrius the silversmith. From most silly novels we can at least extract a laugh; but those of the modern-antique school have a ponderous, a leaden kind of fatuity, under which we groan. What can be more demonstrative of the inability of literary women to measure their own powers than their frequent assumption of a task which can only be justified by the rarest concurrence of acquirement with genius? The finest effort to reanimate the past is of course only approximative—is always more or less an infusion of the modern spirit into the ancient form—

> Was ihr den Geist der Zeiten heisst,
> Das ist im Grund der Herren eigner Geist,
> In dem die Zeiten sich bespiegeln.

Admitting that genius which has familiarized itself with all the relics of an ancient period can sometimes, by the force of its sympathetic divination, restore the missing notes in the "music of humanity," and reconstruct the fragments into a whole which will really bring the remote past nearer to us, and interpret it to our duller apprehension—this form of imaginative power must always be among the very rarest, because it demands as much accurate and minute knowledge as creative vigor. Yet we find ladies constantly choosing to make their mental mediocrity more conspicuous by clothing it in a masquerade of ancient names; by putting their feeble sentimentality into the mouths of Roman vestals or Egyptian princesses, and attributing their rhetorical arguments to Jewish high-priests and Greek philosophers. A recent example of this heavy imbecility is "Adonijah, a Tale of the Jewish Dispersion," which forms part of a series, "uniting," we are told, "taste, humor, and sound principles." "Adonijah," we presume, exemplifies the tale of "sound principles;" the taste and humor are to be found in other members of the series. We are told on the cover that the incidents of this tale are "fraught with unusual interest," and the preface winds up thus: "To those who feel interested in the dispersed of Israel and Judea, these pages may afford, perhaps, information on an important subject, as well as amusement." Since the "important subject" on which this book is to afford information is not specified, it may possibly lie in some esoteric meaning to which we have no key; but if it has relation to the dispersed of Israel and Judea at any period of their history, we believe a tolerably well-informed school-girl already knows much more of it than she will find in this "Tale of the Jewish Dispersion." "Adonijah" is simply the feeblest kind of love story, supposed to be instructive, we presume, because the hero is a Jewish captive and the heroine a Roman vestal; because they and their friends are converted to Christianity after the shortest and easiest method approved by the "Society for Promoting the Conversion of the Jews;" and because, instead of being written in plain language, it is adorned with that peculiar style of grandiloquence which is held by some lady novelists to give an antique coloring, and which we recognize at once in such phrases as these:—"the splendid regnal talent, undoubtedly, possessed by the Emperor Nero"—"the expiring scion of a lofty stem"—"the virtuous partner of his couch"—"ah, by Vesta!"—and "I tell thee, Roman." Among the quotations which serve at once for instruction and ornament on the cover of this volume, there is one from Miss Sinclair, which informs us that "Works of imagination are *avowedly* read by men of science, wisdom, and piety;" from which we suppose the reader is to gather the cheering inference that Dr. Daubeny, Mr. Mill, or Mr. Maurice may openly indulge himself with the perusal of "Adonijah," without being obliged to secrete it among the sofa cushions, or read it by snatches under the dinner-table.

"Be not a baker if your head be made of butter," says a homely proverb, which, being interpreted, may mean, let no woman rush into print who is not prepared for the consequences. We are aware that our remarks are in a very different tone from that of the reviewers who, with perennial recurrence of precisely similar emotions, only paralleled, we imagine, in the experience of monthly nurses, tell one lady novelist after another that they "hail" her productions "with delight." We are aware that the ladies at whom our criticism is pointed are accustomed to be told, in the choicest phraseology of puffery, that their pictures of life are brilliant, their characters well drawn, their style fascinating, and their sentiments lofty. But if they are inclined to resent our plainness of speech, we ask them to reflect for a moment on the chary praise, and often captious blame, which their panegyrists give to writers whose works are on the way to become classics. No sooner does a woman show that she has genius or effective talent, than she receives the tribute of being moderately praised and severely criticised. By a peculiar thermometric adjustment, when a woman's talent is at zero, journalistic approbation is at the boiling pitch; when she attains mediocrity, it is already at no more than summer heat; and if ever she reaches excellence, critical enthusiasm drops to the freezing point. Harriet Martineau, Currer Bell, and Mrs. Gaskell have been treated as cavalierly as if they had been men. And every critic who forms a high estimate of the share women may ultimately take in literature, will on principle abstain from any exceptional indulgence toward the productions of literary women. For it must be plain to every one who looks impartially and extensively into feminine literature that its greatest deficiencies are due hardly more to the want of intellectual power than to the want of those moral qualities that contribute to literary excellence—patient diligence, a sense of the responsibility involved in publication, and an appreciation of the sacredness of the writer's art. In the majority of woman's books you see that kind of facility which springs from the absence of any high standard; that fertility in imbecile combination or feeble imitation which a little self-criticism would check and reduce to barrenness; just as with a total want of musical ear people will sing out of tune, while a degree more melodic sensibility would suffice to render them silent. The foolish vanity of wishing to appear in print, instead of being counterbalanced by any consciousness of the intellectual or moral derogation implied in futile authorship, seems to be encouraged by the extremely false impression that to write *at all* is a proof of superiority in a woman. On this ground we believe that the average intellect of women is unfairly represented by the mass of feminine literature, and that while the few women who write well are very far above the ordinary intellectual level of their sex, the many women who write ill are very far below it. So that, after all, the severer critics are fulfilling a chivalrous duty in depriving the mere fact of feminine authorship of any false prestige which may give it a delusive attraction, and in recommending women of mediocre faculties—as at least a negative service they can render their sex—to abstain from writing.

The standing apology for women who become writers without any special qualification is that society shuts them out from other spheres of occupation. Society is a very culpable entity, and has to answer for the manufacture of many unwholesome commodities, from bad pickles to bad poetry. But society, like "matter," and Her Majesty's Government, and other lofty abstractions, has its share of excessive blame as well as excessive praise. Where there is one woman who writes from necessity, we believe there are three women who write from vanity; and besides, there is something so antispetic in the mere healthy fact of working for one's bread, that the most trashy and rotten kind of feminine literature is not likely to have been produced under such circumstances. "In all labor there is profit;" but ladies' silly novels, we imagine, are less the result of labor than of busy idleness.

Happily, we are not dependent on argument to prove that Fiction is a department of literature in which women can, after their kind, fully equal men. A cluster of great names, both living and dead, rush to our memories in evidence that women can produce novels not only fine, but among the very finest—novels, too, that have a precious speciality, lying quite apart from masculine aptitudes and experience. No educational restrictions can shut women out from the materials of fiction, and there is no species of art which is so free from rigid requirements. Like crystalline masses, it may take any form, and yet be beautiful; we have only to pour in the right elements—genuine observation, humor, and passion. But it is precisely this absence of rigid requirement which constitutes the fatal seduction of novel-writing to incompetent women. Ladies are not wont to be very grossly deceived as to their power of playing on the piano; here certain positive difficulties of execution have to be conquered, and incompetence inevitably breaks down. Every art which has its absolute *technique* is, to a certain extent, guarded from the intrusions of mere left-handed imbecility. But in novel-writing there are no barriers for incapacity to stumble against, no external criteria to prevent a writer from mistaking foolish facility for mastery. And so we have again and again the old story of La Fontaine's ass, who puts his nose to the flute, and, finding that he elicits some sound, exclaims, "Moi, aussi, je joue de la flute"—a fable which we commend, at parting, to the consideration of any feminine reader who is in danger of adding to the number of "silly novels by lady novelists."

VII.

WORLDLINESS AND OTHER-WORLDLINESS: THE POET YOUNG.*

The study of men, as they have appeared in different ages and under various social conditions, may be considered as the natural history of the race. Let us, then, for a moment imagine ourselves, as students of this natural history, "dredging" the first half of the eighteenth century in search of specimens. About the year 1730 we have hauled up a remarkable individual of the species *divine*—a surprising name, considering the nature of the animal before us, but we are used to unsuitable names in natural history. Let us examine this individual at our leisure. He is on the verge of fifty, and has recently undergone his metamorphosis into the clerical form. Rather a paradoxical specimen, if you observe him narrowly: a sort of cross between a sycophant and a psalmist; a poet whose imagination is alternately fired by the "Last Day" and by a creation of peers, who fluctuates between rhapsodic applause of King George and rhapsodic applause of Jehovah. After spending "a foolish youth, the sport of peers and poets," after being a hanger-on of the profligate Duke of Wharton, after aiming in vain at a parliamentary career, and angling for pensions and preferment with fulsome dedications and fustian odes, he is a little disgusted with his imperfect success, and has determined to retire from the general men-

* 1. "Young's Works." 1767. 2. "Johnson's Lives of the Poets." Edited by Peter Cunningham Murray: 1854. 3. "Life of Edward Young, LL.D." By Dr. Doran. Prefixed to "Night Thoughts." Boutledge: 1853. 4. *Gentleman's Magazine*, 1782. 5. "Nichols's Literary Anecdotes." Vol. I. 6. "Spence's Anecdotes."

dicancy business to a particular branch; in other words, he has determined on that renunciation of the world implied in "taking orders," with the prospect of a good living and an advantageous matrimonial connection. And no man can be better fitted for an Established Church. He personifies completely her nice balance of temporalities and spiritualities. He is equally impressed with the momentousness of death and of burial fees; he languishes at once for immortal life and for "livings;" he has a fervid attachment to patrons in general, but on the whole prefers the Almighty. He will teach, with something more than official conviction, the nothingness of earthly things; and he will feel something more than private disgust if his meritorious efforts in directing men's attention to another world are not rewarded by substantial preferment in this. His secular man believes in cambric bands and silk stockings as characteristic attire for "an ornament of religion and virtue;" hopes courtiers will never forget to copy Sir Robert Walpole; and writes begging letters to the King's mistress. His spiritual man recognizes no motives more familiar than Golgotha and "the skies;" it walks in graveyards, or it soars among the stars. His religion exhausts itself in ejaculations and rebukes, and knows no medium between the ecstatic and the sententious. If it were not for the prospect of immortality, he considers, it would be wise and agreeable to be indecent or to murder one's father; and, heaven apart, it would be extremely irrational in any man not to be a knave. Man, he thinks, is a compound of the angel and the brute; the brute is to be humbled by being reminded of its "relation to the stalls," and frightened into moderation by the contemplation of death-beds and skulls; the angel is to be developed by vituperating this world and exalting the next; and by this double process you get the Christian—"the highest style of man." With all this, our new-made divine is an unmistakable poet. To a clay compounded chiefly of the worldling and the rhetorician, there is added a real spark of Promethean fire. He will one day clothe his apostrophes and objurgations, his astronomical religion and his charnel-house morality, in lasting verse, which will stand, like a Juggernaut made of gold and jewels, at once magnificent and repulsive: for this divine is Edward Young, the future author of the "Night Thoughts."

It would be extremely ill-bred in us to suppose that our readers are not acquainted with the facts of Young's life; they are among the things that "every one knows;" but we have observed that, with regard to these universally known matters, the majority of readers like to be treated after the plan suggested by Monsieur Jourdain. When that distinguished *bourgeois* was asked if he knew Latin, he replied, "Oui, mais faites comme si je ne le savais pas." Assuming, then, as a polite writer should, that our readers know everything about Young, it will be a direct *sequitur* from that assumption that we should proceed as if they knew nothing, and recall the incidents of his biography with as much particularity as we may without trenching on the space we shall need for our main purpose—the reconsideration of his character as a moral and religious poet.

Judging from Young's works, one might imagine that the preacher had been organized in him by hereditary transmission through a long line of clerical forefathers—that the diamonds of the "Night Thoughts" had been slowly condensed from the charcoal of ancestral sermons. Yet it was not so. His grandfather, apparently, wrote himself *gentleman*, not *clerk;* and there is no evidence that preaching had run in the family blood before it took that turn in the person of the poet's father, who was quadruply clerical, being at once rector, prebendary, court chaplain, and dean. Young was born at his father's rectory of Upham in 1681. We may confidently assume that even the author of the "Night Thoughts" came into the world without a wig; but, apart from Dr. Doran's authority, we should not have ventured to state that the excellent rector "kissed, *with dignified emotion*, his only son and intended namesake." Dr. Doran doubtless knows this, from his intimate acquaintance with clerical physiology and psychology. He has ascertained that the paternal emotions of prebendaries have a sacerdotal quality, and that the very chyme and chyle of a rector are conscious of the gown and band.

In due time the boy went to Winchester College, and subsequently, though not till he was twenty-two, to Oxford, where, for his father's sake, he was befriended by the wardens of two colleges, and in 1708, three years after his father's death, nominated by Archbishop Tenison to a law fellowship at All Souls. Of Young's life at Oxford in these years, hardly anything is known. His biographer, Croft, has nothing to tell us but the vague report that, when "Young found himself independent and his own master at All Souls, he was not the ornament to religion and morality that he afterward became," and the perhaps apocryphal anecdote, that Tindal, the atheist, confessed himself embarrassed by the originality of Young's arguments. Both the report and the anecdote, however, are borne out by indirect evidence. As to the latter, Young has left us sufficient proof that he was fond of arguing on the theological side, and that he had his own way of treating old subjects. As to the former, we learn that Pope, after saying other things which we know to be true of Young, added, that he passed "a foolish youth, the sport of peers and poets;" and, from all the indications we possess of his career till he was nearly fifty, we are inclined to think that Pope's statement only errs by defect, and that he should rather have said, "a foolish youth and *middle* age." It is not likely that Young was a very hard student, for he impressed Johnson, who saw him in his old age, as "not a great scholar," and as surprisingly ignorant of what Johnson thought "quite common maxims" in literature; and there is no evidence that he filled either his leisure or his purse by taking pupils. His career as an author did not commence till he was nearly thirty, even dating from the publication of a portion of the "Last Day," in the *Tatler;* so that he could hardly have been absorbed in composition. But where the fully developed insect is parasitic, we believe the larva is usually parasitic also, and we shall probably not be far wrong in supposing that Young at Oxford, as elsewhere, spent a good deal of his time in hanging about possible and actual patrons, and accommodating himself to the habits with considerable flexibility of conscience and of tongue; being none the less ready, upon occasion, to present himself as the champion of theology and to rhapsodize at convenient moments in the company of the skies or of skulls. That brilliant profligate, the Duke of Wharton, to whom Young afterward clung as his chief patron, was at this time a mere boy; and, though it is probable that their intimacy had commenced, since the Duke's father and mother were friends of the old dean, that intimacy ought not to aggravate any unfavorable inference as to Young's Oxford life. It is less likely that he fell into any exceptional vice than that he differed from the men around him chiefly in his episodes of theological advocacy and rhapsodic solemnity. He probably sowed his wild oats after the coarse fashion of his times, for he has left us sufficient evidence that his moral sense was not delicate; but his companions, who were occupied in sowing their own oats, perhaps took it as a matter of course that he should be a rake, and were only struck with the exceptional circumstance that he was a pious and moralizing rake.

There is some irony in the fact that the two first poetical productions of Young, published in the same year, were his "Epistles to Lord Lansdowne," celebrating the recent creation of peers—Lord Lansdowne's creation in particular; and the "Last Day." Other poets besides Young found the device for obtaining a Tory majority by turning twelve insignificant commoners into insignificant lords, an irresistible stimulus to verse; but no other poet showed so versatile an enthusiasm—so nearly equal an ardor for the honor of the new baron and the honor of the Deity. But the twofold nature of the sycophant and the psalmist is not more strikingly shown in the contrasted themes of the two poems than in the transitions from bombast about monarchs to bombast about the resurrection, in the "Last Day" itself. The dedication of the poem to Queen Anne, Young afterward suppressed, for he was always ashamed of having flattered a dead patron. In this dedication, Croft tells us, "he gives her Majesty praise indeed for her victories, but says that the author is more pleased to see her rise from this lower world, soaring above the clouds, passing the first and second heavens, and leaving the fixed stars behind her; nor will he lose her there, he says, but keep her still in view through the boundless spaces on the other side of creation, in her journey toward eternal bliss, till he behold the heaven of heavens open, and angels receiving and conveying her still onward from the stretch of his imagination, which tires in her pursuit, and falls back again to earth."

The self-criticism which prompted the suppression of the dedication did not, however, lead him to improve either the rhyme or the reason of the unfortunate couplet—

"When other Bourbons reign in other lands,
And, if men's sins forbid not, other Annes."

In the "Epistle to Lord Lansdowne" Young indicates his taste for the drama; and there is evidence that his tragedy of "Busiris" was "in the theatre" as early as this very year, 1713, though it was not brought on the stage till nearly six years later; so that Young was now very decidedly bent on authorship, for which his degree of B.C.L., taken in this year, was doubtless a magical equipment. Another poem, "The Force of Religion; or, Vanquished Love," founded on the execution of Lady Jane Grey and her husband, quickly followed, showing fertility in feeble and tasteless verse; and on the Queen's death, in 1714, Young lost no time in making a poetical lament for a departed patron a vehicle for extravagant laudation of the new monarch. No further literary production of his appeared until 1716, when a Latin oration, which he delivered on the foundation of the Codrington Library at All Souls, gave him a new opportunity for displaying his alacrity in inflated panegyric.

In 1717 it is probable that Young accompanied the Duke of Wharton to Ireland, though so slender are the materials for his biography that the chief basis for this supposition is a passage in his "Conjectures on Original Composition," written when he was nearly eighty, in which he intimates that he had once been in that country. But there are many facts surviving to indicate that for the next eight or nine years Young was a sort of *attaché* of Wharton's. In 1719, according to legal records, the Duke granted him an annuity, in consideration of his having relinquished the office of tutor to Lord Burleigh, with a life annuity of £100 a year, on his Grace's assurances that he would provide for him in a much more ample manner. And again, from the same evidence, it appears that in 1721 Young received from Wharton a bond for £600, in compensation of expenses incurred in standing for Parliament at the Duke's desire, and as an earnest of greater services which his Grace had promised him on his refraining from the spiritual and temporal advantages of taking orders, with a certainty of two livings in the gift of his college. It is clear, therefore, that lay advancement, as long as there was any chance of it, had more attractions for Young than clerical preferment; and that at this time he accepted the Duke of Wharton as the pilot of his career.

A more creditable relation of Young's was his friendship with Tickell, with whom he was in the habit of interchanging criticisms, and to whom in 1719—the same year, let us note, in which he took his doctor's degree—he addressed his "Lines on the Death of Addison." Close upon these followed his "Paraphrase of part of the Book of Job," with a dedication to Parker, recently made Lord Chancellor, showing that the possession of Wharton's patronage did not prevent Young from fishing in other waters. He knew nothing of Parker, but that did not prevent him from magnifying the new Chancellor's merits; on the other hand, he *did* know Wharton, but this again did not prevent him from prefixing to his tragedy, "The Revenge," which appeared in 1721, a dedication attributing to the Duke all virtues, as well as all accomplishments. In the concluding sentence of this dedication, Young naïvely indicates that a considerable ingredient in his gratitude was a lively sense of anticipated favors. "My present fortune is his bounty, and my future his care; which I will venture to say will always be remembered to his honor; since he, I know, intended his generosity as an encouragement to merit, through his very pardonable partiality to one who bears him so sincere a duty and respect, I happen to receive the benefit of it." Young was economical with his ideas and images; he was rarely satisfied with using a clever thing once, and this bit of ingenious humility was afterward made to do duty in the "Instalment," a poem addressed to Walpole:

> "Be this thy partial smile, from censure free,
> 'Twas meant for merit, though it fell on me."

It was probably "The Revenge" that Young was writing when, as we learn from Spence's anecdotes, the Duke of Wharton gave him a skull with a candle fixed in it, as the most appropriate lamp by which to write tragedy. According to Young's dedication, the Duke was "accessory" to the scenes of this tragedy in a more important way, "not only by suggesting the most beautiful incident in them, but by making all possible provision for the success of the whole." A statement which is credible, not indeed on the ground of Young's dedicatory assertion, but from the known ability of the Duke, who, as Pope tells us, possessed

> "each gift of Nature and of Art,
> And wanted nothing but an honest heart."

The year 1722 seems to have been the period of a visit to Mr. Dodington, of Eastbury, in Dorsetshire — the "pure Dorsetian downs" celebrated by Thomson—in which Young made the acquaintance of Voltaire; for in the subsequent dedication of his "Sea Piece" to "Mr. Voltaire," he recalls their meeting on "Dorset Downs;" and it was in this year that Christopher Pitt, a gentleman-poet of those days, addressed an

"Epistle to Dr. Edward Young, at Eastbury, in Dorsetshire," which has at least the merit of this biographical couplet:

> "While with your Dodington retired you sit,
> Charm'd with his flowing Burgundy and wit."

Dodington, apparently, was charmed in his turn, for he told Dr. Wharton that Young was "far superior to the French poet in the variety and novelty of his *bon-mots* and repartees." Unfortunately, the only specimen of Young's wit on this occasion that has been preserved to us is the epigram represented as an extempore retort (spoken aside, surely) to Voltaire's criticism of Milton's episode of sin and death:

> "Thou art so witty, profligate, and thin,
> At once, we think thee Milton, Death, and Sin;"—

an epigram which, in the absence of "flowing Burgundy," does not strike us as remarkably brilliant. Let us give Young the benefit of the doubt thrown on the genuineness of this epigram by his own poetical dedication, in which he represents himself as having "soothed" Voltaire's "rage" against Milton "with gentle rhymes;" though in other respects that dedication is anything but favorable to a high estimate of Young's wit. Other evidence apart, we should not be eager for the after-dinner conversation of the man who wrote:

> "Thine is the Drama, how renown'd!
> Thine Epic's loftier trump to sound;—
> *But let Arion's sea-strung harp be mine;*
> *But where's his dolphin? Know'st thou where?*
> *May that be found in thee, Voltaire!*"

The "Satires" appeared in 1725 and 1726, each, of course, with its laudatory dedication and its compliments insinuated among the rhymes. The seventh and last is dedicated to Sir Robert Walpole, is very short, and contains nothing in particular except lunatic flattery of George the First and his prime minister, attributing that royal hog's late escape from a storm at sea to the miraculous influence of his grand and virtuous soul—for George, he says, rivals the angels :

"George, who in foes can soft affections raise,
And charm envenom'd satire into praise.
Nor human rage alone his pow'r perceives,
But the mad winds and the tumultuous waves,
Ev'n storms (Death's fiercest ministers !) forbear,
And in their own wild empire learn to spare.
Thus, Nature's self, supporting Man's decree,
Styles Britain's sovereign, sovereign of the sea."

As for Walpole, what *he* felt at this tremendous crisis

"No powers of language, but his own, can tell,
His own, which Nature and the Graces form,
At will, to raise, or hush, the civil storm."

It is a coincidence worth noticing, that this seventh Satire was published in 1726, and that the warrant of George the First, granting Young a pension of £200 a year from Lady-day, 1725, is dated May 3d, 1726. The gratitude exhibited in this Satire may have been chiefly prospective, but the "Instalment," a poem inspired by the thrilling event of Walpole's installation as Knight of the Garter, was clearly written with the double ardor of a man who has got a pension and hopes for something more. His emotion about Walpole is precisely at the same pitch as his subsequent emotion about the Second Advent. In the "Instalment" he says :

"With invocations some their hearts inflame ;
I need no muse, a Walpole is my theme."

And of God coming to judgment, he says, in the "Night Thoughts :"

"I find my inspiration is my theme ;
The grandeur of my subject is my muse."

Nothing can be feebler than this "Instalment," except in the strength of impudence with which the writer professes to scorn the prostitution of fair fame, the "profanation of celestial fire."

Herbert Croft tells us that Young made more than three thousand pounds by his "Satires"—a surprising statement, taken in connection with the reasonable doubt he throws on the story related in Spence's "Anecdotes," that the Duke of Wharton gave Young £2000 for this work. Young, however, seems to have been tolerably fortunate in the pecuniary results of his publications; and, with his literary profits, his annuity from Wharton, his fellowship, and his pension, not to mention other bounties which may be inferred from the high merits he discovers in many men of wealth and position, we may fairly suppose that he now laid the foundation of the considerable fortune he left at his death.

It is probable that the Duke of Wharton's final departure for the Continent and disgrace at Court in 1726, and the consequent cessation of Young's reliance on his patronage, tended not only to heighten the temperature of his poetical enthusiasm for Sir Robert Walpole, but also to turn his thoughts toward the Church again, as the second-best means of rising in the world. On the accession of George the Second, Young found the same transcendent merits in him as in his predecessor, and celebrated them in a style of poetry previously unattempted by him—the Pindaric ode, a poetic form which helped him to surpass himself in furious bombast. "Ocean, an Ode: concluding with a Wish," was the title of this piece. He afterward pruned it, and cut off, among other things, the concluding Wish, expressing the yearning for humble retirement, which, of course, had prompted him to the effusion; but we may judge of the rejected stanzas by the quality of those he has allowed to remain. For example, calling on Britain's dead mariners to rise and meet their "country's full-blown glory" in the person of the new King, he says:

"What powerful charm
Can Death disarm?
Your long, your iron slumbers break?
By Jove, by Fame,
By George's name,
Awake! awake! awake! awake!"

Soon after this notable production, which was written with the ripe folly of forty-seven, Young took orders, and was presently appointed chaplain to the King. "The Brothers," his third and last tragedy, which was already in rehearsal, he now withdrew from the stage, and sought reputation in a way more accordant with the decorum of his new profession, by turning prose writer. But after publishing "A True Estimate of Human Life," with a dedication to the Queen, as one of the "most shining representatives" of God on earth, and a sermon, entitled "An Apology for Princes; or, the Reverence due to Government," preached before the House of Commons, his Pindaric ambition again seized him, and he matched his former ode by another, called "Imperium Pelagi, a Naval Lyric; written in imitation of Pindar's spirit, occasioned by his Majesty's return from Hanover, 1729, and the succeeding Peace." Since he afterward suppressed this second ode, we must suppose that it was rather worse than the first. Next came his two "Epistles to Pope, concerning the Authors of the Age," remarkable for nothing but the audacity of affectation with which the most servile of poets professes to despise servility.

In 1730 Young was presented by his college with the rectory of Welwyn, in Hertfordshire, and, in the following year, when he was just fifty, he married Lady Elizabeth Lee, a widow with two children, who seems to have been in favor with Queen Caroline, and who probably had an income—two attractions which doubtless enhanced the power of her other charms. Pastoral duties and domesticity probably cured Young of some bad habits; but, unhappily, they did not cure him either of flattery or of fustian. Three more odes followed, quite as bad as those of his bachelorhood, except that in the third he announced the wise resolution of never writing another. It must have been about this time, since Young was now "turned of fifty," that he wrote the letter to Mrs. Howard (afterward Lady Suffolk), George the Second's mistress, which proves that he used other engines, besides Pindaric ones, in "besieging Court favor." The letter is too characteristic to be ommitted:

"Monday Morning.

"MADAM: I know his Majesty's goodness to his servants, and his love of justice in general, so well, that I am confident, if his Majesty knew my case, I should not have any cause to despair of his gracious favor to me.

"Abilities.	Want.	
Good Manners.	Sufferings	for his
Service.	and	Majesty.
Age.	Zeal	

These, madam, are the proper points of consideration in the person that humbly hopes his Majesty's favor.

"As to *Abilities*, all I can presume to say is, I have done the best I could to improve them.

"As to *Good manners*, I desire no favor, if any just objection lies against them.

"As for *Service*, I have been near seven years in his Majesty's and never omitted any duty in it, which few can say.

"As for *Age*, I am turned of fifty.

"As for *Want*, I have no manner of preferment.

"As for *Sufferings*, I have lost £300 per ann. by being in his Majesty's service; as I have shown in a *Representation* which his Majesty has been so good as to read and consider.

"As for *Zeal*, I have written nothing without showing my duty to their Majesties, and some pieces are dedicated to them.

"This, madam, is the short and true state of my case. They that make their court to the ministers, and not their Majesties, succeed better. If my case deserves some consideration, and you can serve me in it, I humbly hope and believe you will: I shall, therefore, trouble you no farther; but beg leave to subscribe myself, with truest respect and gratitude,

"Yours, etc., EDWARD YOUNG.

"P.S. I have some hope that my Lord Townshend is my friend; if therefore soon, and before he leaves the court, you had an opportunity of mentioning me, with that favor you have been so good to show, I think it would not fail of success; and, if not, I shall owe you more than any."—"Suffolk Letters," vol. i. p. 285.

Young's wife died in 1741, leaving him one son, born in 1733. That he had attached himself strongly to her two daughters by her former marriage, there is better evidence in the report, mentioned by Mrs. Montagu, of his practical kindness and liberality to the younger, than in his lamentations over the elder as the "Narcissa" of the "Night Thoughts." "Narcissa" had died in 1735, shortly after marriage to Mr. Temple, the son of Lord Palmerston; and Mr. Temple himself, after a second marriage, died in 1740, a year before Lady Elizabeth Young. These, then, are the three deaths supposed to have inspired "The Complaint," which forms the three first books of the "Night Thoughts:"

"Insatiate archer, could not one suffice?
Thy shaft flew thrice: and thrice my peace was slain:
And thrice, ere thrice yon moon had fill'd her horn."

Since we find Young departing from the truth of dates, in order to heighten the effect of his calamity, or at least of his climax, we need not be surprised that he allowed his imagination great freedom in other matters besides chronology, and that the character of "Philander" can, by no process, be made to fit Mr. Temple. The supposition that the much-lectured "Lorenzo" of the "Night Thoughts" was Young's own son is hardly rendered more absurd by the fact that the poem was written when that son was a boy, than by the obvious artificiality of the characters Young introduces as targets for his arguments and rebukes. Among all the trivial efforts of conjectured criticism, there can hardly be one more futile than the attempts to discover the original of those pitiable lay-figures, the "Lorenzos" and "Altamonts" of Young's didactic prose and poetry. His muse never stood face to face with a genuine living human being; she would have been as much startled by such an encounter as a necromancer whose incantations and blue fire had actually conjured up a demon.

The "Night Thoughts" appeared between 1741 and 1745. Although he declares in them that he has chosen God for his "patron" henceforth, this is not at all to the prejudice of some half dozen lords, duchesses, and right honorables who have the privilege of sharing finely-turned compliments with their co-patron. The line which closed the Second Night in the earlier editions—

"Wits spare not Heaven, O Wilmington!—nor thee"—

is an intense specimen of that perilous juxtaposition of ideas by which Young, in his incessant search after point and novelty, unconsciously converts his compliments into sarcasms; and his apostrophe to the moon as more likely to be favorable to his song if he calls her "fair Portland of the skies," is worthy even of his Pindaric ravings. His ostentatious renunciation of worldly schemes, and especially of his twenty-years' siege of Court favor, are in the tone of one who retains some hope in the midst of his querulousness.

He descended from the astronomical rhapsodies of his "Ninth Night," published in 1745, to more terrestrial strains in his "Reflections on the Public Situation of the Kingdom," dedicated to the Duke of Newcastle; but in this critical year we get a glimpse of him through a more prosaic and less refracting medium. He spent a part of the year at Tunbridge Wells; and Mrs. Montagu, who was there too, gives a very lively picture of the "divine Doctor" in her letters to the Duchess of Portland, on whom Young had bestowed the superlative bombast to which we have recently alluded. We shall borrow the quotations from Dr. Doran, in spite of their length, because, to our mind, they present the most agreeable portrait we possess of Young:

"I have great joy in Dr. Young, whom I disturbed in a reverie. At first he started, then bowed, then fell back into a surprise; then began a speech, relapsed into his astonishment two or three times, forgot what he had been saying; began a new subject, and so went on. I told him your grace desired he would write longer letters; to which he cried 'Ha!' most emphatically, and I leave you to interpret what it meant. He has made a friendship with one person here, whom I believe you would not imagine to have been made for his bosom friend. You would, perhaps, suppose it was a bishop or dean, a prebend, a pious preacher, a clergyman of exemplary life, or, if a layman, of most virtuous conversation, one that had paraphrased St. Matthew, or wrote comments on St. Paul. . . . You would not guess that this associate of the doctor's was—old Cibber! Certainly, in their religious, moral, and civil character, there is no relation; but in their dramatic capacity there is some.—Mrs. Montagu was not aware that Cibber, whom Young had named not disparagingly in his Satires, was the brother of his old school-fellow; but to return to our hero. 'The waters,' says Mrs. Montagu, 'have raised his spirits to a fine pitch, as your grace will imagine, when I tell you how sublime an answer he made to a very vulgar question. I asked him how long he stayed at the Wells; he said, 'As long as my rival stayed;—as long as the sun did.' Among the visitors at the Wells were Lady Sunderland (wife of Sir Robert Sutton), and her sister, Mrs. Tichborne. 'He did an admirable thing to Lady Sunderland: on her mentioning Sir Robert Sutton, he asked her where Sir Robert's lady was; on which we all laughed very heartily, and I brought him off, half ashamed, to my lodgings, where, during breakfast, he assured me he had asked after Lady Sunderland, because he had a great honor for her; and that, having a respect for her sister, he designed to have inquired after her, if we had not put it out of his head by laughing at him. You must know, Mrs. Tichborne sat next to Lady Sunderland. It would have been admirable to have had him finish his compliment in that manner.' . . . 'His expressions all bear the stamp of novelty, and his thoughts of sterling sense. He practises a kind of philosophical abstinence. . . . He carried Mrs. Rolt and myself to Tunbridge, five miles from hence, where we were to see some fine old ruins. First rode the doctor on a tall steed, decently caparisoned in dark gray; next, ambled Mrs. Rolt on a hackney horse; . . . then followed your humble servant on a milk-white palfrey. I rode on in safety, and at leisure to observe the company, especially the two figures that brought up the rear. The first was my servant, valiantly armed with two uncharged pistols; the last was the doctor's man, whose uncombed hair so resembled the mane of the horse he rode, one could not help imagining they were of kin, and wishing, for the honor of the family, that they had had one comb betwixt them. On his head was a velvet cap, much resembling a black saucepan, and on his side hung a little basket. At last we arrived at the King's Head, where the loyalty of the doctor induced him to alight; and then, knight-errant-like, he took his damsels from off their palfreys, and courteously handed us into the inn.' . . . The party returned to the Wells; and 'the silver Cynthia held up her lamp in the heavens' the while. 'The night silenced all but our divine doctor, who sometimes uttered things fit to be spoken in a season when all nature seems to be hushed and hearkening. I followed, gathering wisdom as I went, till I found, by my horse's stumbling, that I was in a bad road, and that the blind was leading the blind. So I placed my servant between the doctor and myself; which he not perceiving, went on in a most philosophical strain, to the great admiration of my poor clown of a servant, who, not being wrought up to any pitch of enthusiasm, nor making any answer to all the fine things he heard, the doctor, wondering I was dumb, and grieving I was so stupid, looked round and declared his surprise.'"

Young's oddity and absence of mind are gathered from other sources besides these stories of Mrs. Montagu's, and gave rise to the report that he was the original of Fielding's "Parson Adams;" but this Croft denies, and mentions another Young, who really sat for the portrait, and who, we imagine, had both more Greek and more genuine simplicity than the poet. His love of chatting with Colley Cibber was an indication that the old predilection for the stage survived, in spite of his emphatic contempt for "all joys but joys that never can expire;" and the production of "The Brothers," at Drury Lane in 1753, after a suppression of fifteen years, was perhaps not entirely due to the expressed desire to give the proceeds to the Society for the Propagation of the Gospel. The author's profits were not more then £400—in those days a disappointing sum; and Young, as we learn from his friend Richardson, did not make this the limit of his donation, but gave a thousand guineas to the Society. "I had some talk with him," says Richardson, in one of his letters, "about this great action. 'I always,' said he, 'intended to do something handsome for the Society. Had I deferred it to my demise, I should have given away my son's money. All the world are inclined to pleasure ; could I have given myself a greater by disposing of the sum to a different use, I should have done it.'" Surely he took his old friend Richardson for "Lorenzo !"

His next work was "The Centaur not Fabulous ; in Six Letters to a Friend, on the Life in Vogue," which reads very much like the most objurgatory parts of the "Night Thoughts" reduced to prose. It is preceded by a preface which, though addressed to a lady, is in its denunciations of vice as grossly indecent and almost as flippant as the epilogues written by "friends," which he allowed to be reprinted after his tragedies in the latest edition of his works. We like much better than "The Centaur," "Conjectures on Original Composition," written in 1759, for the sake, he says, of communicating to the world the well-known anecdote about Addison's deathbed, and with the exception of his poem on Resignation, the last thing he ever published.

The estrangement from his son, which must have embittered the later years of his life, appears to have begun not many years after the mother's death. On the marriage of her second daughter, who had previously presided over Young's household, a Mrs. Hallows, understood to be a woman of discreet age, and the daughter (a widow) of a clergyman who was an old friend of Young's, became housekeeper at Welwyn. Opinions about ladies are apt to differ. "Mrs. Hallows was a woman of piety, improved by reading," says one witness. "She was a very coarse woman," says Dr. Johnson ; and we shall presently find some indirect evidence that her temper was perhaps not quite so much improved as her piety. Servants, it seems, were not fond of remaining long in the house with her ; a satirical curate, named Kidgell, hints at "drops of juniper" taken as a cordial (but perhaps he was spiteful, and a teetotaller) ; and Young's son is said to have told his father that "an old man should not resign himself to the management of anybody." The result was, that the son was banished from home for the rest of his father's life-time, though Young seems never to have thought of disinheriting him.

Our latest glimpses of the aged poet are derived from certain letters of Mr. Jones, his curate—letters preserved in the British Museum, and happily made accessible to common mortals in Nichols's "Anecdotes." Mr. Jones was a man of some literary activity and ambition—a collector of interesting documents, and one of those concerned in the "Free and Candid Disquisitions," the design of which was "to point out such things in our ecclesiastical establishment as want to be reviewed and amended." On these and kindred subjects he corresponded with Dr. Birch, occasionally troubling him with queries and manuscripts. We have a respect for Mr. Jones. Unlike any person who ever troubled *us* with queries or manuscripts, he mitigates the infliction by such gifts as "a fat pullet," wishing he "had anything better to send; but this depauperizing vicarage (of Alconbury) too often checks the freedom and forwardness of my mind." Another day comes a "pound canister of tea," another, a "young fatted goose." Clearly, Mr. Jones was entirely unlike your literary correspondents of the present day; he forwarded manuscripts, but he had "bowels," and forwarded poultry too. His first letter from Welwyn is dated June, 1759, not quite six years before Young's death. In June, 1762, he expresses a wish to go to London "this summer. But," he continues:

"My time and pains are almost continually taken up here, and . . . I have been (I now find) a considerable loser, upon the whole, by continuing here so long. The consideration of this, and the inconveniences I sustained, and do still experience, from my late illness, obliged me at last to acquaint the Doctor (Young) with my case, and to assure him that I plainly perceived the duty and confinement here to be too much for me; for which reason I must (I said) beg to be at liberty to resign my charge at Michaelmas. I began to give him these notices in February, when I was very ill; and now I perceive, by what he told me the other day, that he is in some difficulty: for which reason he is at last (he says) resolved to advertise, *and even (which is much wondered at) to raise the salary considerably higher*. (What he allowed my predecessors was 20*l*. per annum; and now he proposes 50*l*., as he tells me.) I never asked him to raise it for me, though I well knew it was not equal to the duty; nor did I say a word about myself when he lately suggested to me his intentions upon this subject."

In a postscript to this letter he says:

"I may mention to you farther, as a friend that may be trusted, that in all likelihood the poor old gentleman will not find it a very easy matter, unless by dint of money, *and force upon himself*, to procure a man that he can like for his next curate, *nor one that will stay with him so long as I have done*. Then, his great age will recur to people's thoughts; and if he has any foibles, either in temper or conduct, they will be sure not to be forgotten on this occasion by those who know him; and those who do not will probably be on their guard. On these and the like considerations, it is by no means an eligible office to be seeking out for a curate for him, as he has several times wished me to do; and would, if he knew that I am now writing to you, wish your assistance also. But my best friends here, *who well foresee the probable consequences*, and wish me well, earnestly dissuade me from complying: and I will decline the office with as much decency as I can: but high salary will, I suppose, fetch in somebody or other, soon."

In the following July he writes:

"The old gentleman here (I may venture to tell you freely) seems to me to be in a pretty odd way of late—moping, dejected, self-willed, and as if surrounded with some perplexing circumstances. Though I visit him pretty frequently for short intervals, I say very little to his affairs, not choosing to be a party concerned, especially in cases of so critical and tender a nature. There is much mystery in almost all his temporal affairs, as well as in many of his speculative theories. Whoever lives in this neighborhood to see his exit will probably see and hear some very strange things. Time will show;—I am afraid, not greatly to his credit. There is thought to be *an irremovable obstruction to his happiness within his walls, as well as another without them*; but the former is the more powerful, and like to continue so. He has this day been trying anew to engage me to stay with him. No lucrative views can tempt me to sacrifice my liberty or my health, to such measures as are proposed here. *Nor do I like to have to do with persons whose word and honor cannot be depended on.* So much for this very odd and unhappy topic."

In August Mr. Jones's tone is slightly modified. Earnest entreaties, not lucrative considerations, have induced him to cheer the Doctor's dejected heart by remaining at Welwyn some time longer. The Doctor is, "in various respects, a very unhappy man," and few know so much of these respects as Mr. Jones. In September he recurs to the subject:

"My ancient gentleman here is still full of trouble, which moves my concern, though it moves only the secret laughter of many, and some untoward surmises in disfavor of him and his household. The loss of a very large sum of money (about 200*l.*) is talked of; whereof this vill and neighborhood is full. Some disbelieve; others says, '*It is no wonder, where about eighteen or more servants are sometimes taken and dismissed in the course of a year.*' The gentleman himself is allowed by all to be far more harmless and easy in his family than some one else who hath too much the lead in it. This, among others, was one reason for my late motion to quit."

No other mention of Young's affairs occurs until April 2d, 1765, when he says that Dr. Young is very ill, attended by two physicians.

"Having mentioned this young gentleman (Dr. Young's son), I would acquaint you next, that he came hither this morning, having been sent for, as I am told, by the direction of Mrs. Hallows. Indeed, she intimated to me as much herself. And if this be so, I must say, that it is one of the most prudent acts she ever did, or could have done in such a case as this; as it may prove a means of preventing much confusion after the death of the Doctor. I have had some little discourse with the son: he seems much affected, and I believe really is so. He earnestly wishes his father might be pleased to ask after him; for you must know he has not yet done this, nor is, in my opinion, like to do it. And it has been said farther, that upon a late application made to him on the behalf of his son, he desired that no more might be said to him about it. How true this may be I cannot as yet be certain; all I shall say is, it seems not improbable . . . I heartily wish the ancient man's heart may prove tender toward his son; *though, knowing him so well, I can scarce hope to hear such desirable news.*"

Eleven days later he writes :

"I have now the pleasure to acquaint you, that the late Dr. Young, though he had for many years kept his son at a distance from him, yet has now at last left him all his possessions, after the payment of certain legacies ; so that the young gentleman (who bears a fair character, and behaves well, as far as I can hear or see) will, I hope, soon enjoy and make a prudent use of a handsome fortune. The father, on his deathbed, and since my return from London, was applied to in the tenderest manner, by one of his physicians, and by another person, to admit the son into his presence, to make submission, intreat forgiveness, and obtain his blessing. As to an interview with his son, he intimated that he chose to decline it, as his spirits were then low and his nerves weak. With regard to the next particular, he said, '*I heartily forgive him;*' and upon mention of this last, he gently lifted up his hand, and letting it gently fall, pronounced these words, '*God bless him!*' . . . I know it will give you pleasure to be farther informed that he was pleased to make respectful mention of me in his will ; expressing his satisfaction in my care of his parish, *bequeathing to me a handsome legacy*, and appointing me to be one of his executors."

So far Mr. Jones, in his confidential correspondence with a "friend, who may be trusted." In a letter communicated apparently by him to the *Gentleman's Magazine*, seven years later, namely, in 1782, on the appearance of Croft's biography of Young, we find him speaking of "the ancient gentleman" in a tone of reverential eulogy, quite at variance with the free comments we have just quoted. But the Rev. John Jones was probably of opinion, with Mrs. Montagu, whose contemporary and retrospective letters are also set in a different key, that "the interests of religion were connected with the character of a man so distinguished for piety as Dr. Young." At all events, a subsequent quasi-official statement weighs nothing as evidence against contemporary, spontaneous, and confidential hints.

To Mrs. Hallows, Young left a legacy of £1000, with the request that she would destroy all his manuscripts. This final request, from some unknown cause, was not complied with, and among the papers he left behind him was the following letter from Archbishop Secker, which probably marks the date of his latest effort after preferment:

"DEANERY OF ST. PAUL'S, July 8, 1758.

"GOOD DR. YOUNG: I have long wondered that more suitable notice of your great merit hath not been taken by persons in power. But how to remedy the omission I see not. No encouragement hath ever been given me to mention things of this nature to his Majesty. And therefore, in all likelihood, the only consequence of doing it would be weakening the little influence which else I may possibly have on some other occasions. *Your fortune and your reputation set you above the need of advancement; and your sentiments above that concern for it, on your own account*, which, on that of the public, is sincerely felt by

"Your loving Brother,

"THO. CANT."

The loving brother's irony is severe!

Perhaps the least questionable testimony to the better side of Young's character is that of Bishop Hildesley, who, as the vicar of a parish near Welwyn, had been Young's neighbor for upward of twenty years. The affection of the clergy for each other, we have observed, is, like that of the fair sex, not at all of a blind and infatuated kind; and we may therefore the rather believe them when they give each other any extra-official praise. Bishop Hildesley, then writing of Young to Richardson, says:

"The impertinence of my frequent visits to him was amply rewarded; forasmuch as, I can truly say, he never received me but with agreeable open complacency; and I never left him but with profitable pleasure and improvement. He was one or other, the most modest, the most patient of contradiction, and the most informing and entertaining I ever conversed with—at least, of any man who had so just pretensions to pertinacity and reserve."

Mr. Langton, however, who was also a frequent visitor of Young's, informed Boswell—

"That there was an air of benevolence in his manner; but that he could obtain from him less information than he had hoped to receive from one who had lived so much in intercourse with the brightest men of what had been called the Augustan age of England; and that he showed a degree of eager curiosity concerning the common occurrences that were then passing, which appeared somewhat remarkable in a man of such intellectual stores, of such an advanced age, and who had retired from life with declared disappointment in his expectations."

The same substance, we know, will exhibit different qualities under different tests; and, after all, imperfect reports of individual impressions, whether immediate or traditional, are a very frail basis on which to build our opinion of a man. One's character may be very indifferently mirrored in the mind of the most intimate neighbor; it all depends on the quality of that gentleman's reflecting surface.

But, discarding any inferences from such uncertain evidence, the outline of Young's character is too distinctly traceable in the well-attested facts of his life, and yet more in the self-betrayal that runs through all his works, for us to fear that our general estimate of him may be false. For, while no poet seems less easy and spontaneous than Young, no poet discloses himself more completely. Men's minds have no hiding-place out of themselves—their affectations do but betray another phase of their nature. And if, in the present view of Young, we seem to be more intent on laying bare unfavorable facts than on shrouding them in "charitable speeches," it is not because we have any irreverential pleasure in turning men's characters "the seamy side without," but because we see no great advantage in considering a man as he was *not*. Young's biographers and critics have usually set out from the position that he was a great religious teacher, and that his poetry is morally sublime; and they have toned down his failings into harmony with their conception of the divine and the poet. For our own part, we set out from precisely the opposite conviction—namely, that the religious and moral spirit of Young's poetry is low and false, and we think it of some importance to show that the "Night Thoughts" are the reflex of the mind in which the higher human sympathies were inactive. This judgment is entirely opposed to our youthful predilections and enthusiasm. The sweet garden-breath of early enjoyment lingers about many a page of the "Night Thoughts," and even of the "Last Day," giving an extrinsic charm to passages of stilted rhetoric and false sentiment; but the sober and repeated reading of maturer years has convinced us that it would hardly be possible to find a more typical instance than Young's poetry, of the mistake which substitutes interested obedience for sympathetic emotion, and baptizes egoism as religion.

Pope said of Young, that he had "much of a sublime genius without common-sense." The deficiency Pope meant to indicate was, we imagine, moral rather than intellectual: it was the want of that fine sense of what is fitting in speech and action, which is often eminently possessed by men and women whose intellect is of a very common order, but who have the sincerity and dignity which can never coexist with the selfish preoccupations of vanity or interest. This was the "common-sense" in which Young was conspicuously deficient; and it was partly owing to this deficiency that his genius, waiting to be determined by the highest prize, fluttered uncertainly from effort to effort, until, when he was more than sixty, it suddenly spread its broad wing, and soared so as to arrest the gaze of other generations besides his own. For he had no versatility of faculty to mislead him. The "Night Thoughts" only differ from his previous works in the degree and not in the kind of power they manifest. Whether he writes prose or poetry, rhyme or blank verse, dramas, satires, odes, or meditations, we see everywhere the same Young—the same narrow circle of thoughts, the same love of abstractions, the same telescopic view of human things, the same appetency toward antithetic apothegm and rhapsodic climax. The passages that arrest us in his tragedies are those in which he anticipates some fine passage in the "Night Thoughts," and where his characters are only transparent shadows through which we see the bewigged *embonpoint* of the didactic poet, excogitating epigrams or ecstatic soliloquies by the light of a candle fixed in a skull. Thus, in "The Revenge," "Alonzo," in the conflict of jealousy and love that at once urges and forbids him to murder his wife, says:

> "This vast and solid earth, that blazing sun,
> Those skies, through which it rolls, must all have end.
> What then is man? The smallest part of nothing.
> Day buries day; month, month; and year the year!
> Our life is but a chain of many deaths.
> Can then Death's self be feared? Our life much rather:
> *Life is the desert, life the solitude;*
> Death joins us to the great majority;
> 'Tis to be born to Plato and to Cæsar;
> 'Tis to be great forever;
> 'Tis pleasure, 'tis ambition, then, to die."

His prose writings all read like the "Night Thoughts," either diluted into prose or not yet crystallized into poetry. For example, in his "Thoughts for Age," he says:

> "Though we stand on its awful brink, such our leaden bias to the world, we turn our faces the wrong way; we are still looking on our old acquaintance, *Time;* though now so wasted and reduced, that we can see little more of him than his wings and his scythe: our age enlarges his wings to our imagination; and our fear of death, his scythe; as Time himself grows less. His consumption is deep; his annihilation is at hand."

This is a dilution of the magnificent image—

> "Time in advance behind him hides his wings,
> And seems to creep decrepit with his age.
> Behold him when past by! What then is seen
> But his proud pinions, swifter than the winds?"

Again:

> "A requesting Omnipotence? What can stun and confound thy reason more? What more can ravish and exalt thy heart? It cannot but ravish and exalt; it cannot but gloriously disturb and perplex thee, to take in all *that* suggests. Thou child of the dust! Thou speck of misery and sin! How abject thy weakness! how great is thy power! Thou crawler on earth, and possible (I was about to say) controller of the skies! Weigh, and weigh well, the wondrous truths I have in view: which cannot be weighed too much; which

the more they are weighed, amaze the more; which to have supposed, before they were revealed, would have been as great madness, and to have presumed on as great sin, as it is now madness and sin not to believe."

Even in his Pindaric odes, in which he made the most violent efforts against nature, he is still neither more nor less than the Young of the "Last Day," emptied and swept of his genius, and possessed by seven demons of fustian and bad rhyme. Even here his "Ercles' Vein" alternates with his moral platitudes, and we have the perpetual text of the "Night Thoughts:"

"Gold pleasure buys;
But pleasure dies,
For soon the gross fruition cloys;
Though raptures court,
The sense is short;
But virtue kindles living joys;—

"Joys felt alone!
Joys asked of none!
Which Time's and fortune's arrows miss:
Joys that subsist,
Though fates resist,
An unprecarious, endless bliss!

"Unhappy they!
And falsely gay!
Who bask forever in success;
A constant feast
Quite palls the taste,
And long enjoyment is distress."

In the "Last Day," again, which is the earliest thing he wrote, we have an anticipation of all his greatest faults and merits. Conspicuous among the faults is that attempt to exalt our conceptions of Deity by vulgar images and comparisons, which is so offensive in the later "Night Thoughts." In a burst of prayer and homage to God, called forth by the contemplation of Christ coming to judgment, he asks, Who brings the change of the seasons? and answers:

"Not the great Ottoman, or Greater Czar;
Not Europe's arbitress of peace and war!

Conceive the soul in its most solemn moments, assuring God that it doesn't place his power below that of Louis Napoleon or Queen Victoria!

But in the midst of uneasy rhymes, inappropriate imagery, vaulting sublimity that o'erleaps itself, and vulgar emotions, we have in this poem an occasional flash of genius, a touch of simple grandeur, which promises as much as Young ever achieved. Describing the on-coming of the dissolution of all things, he says:

"No sun in radiant glory shines on high;
No light but from the terrors of the sky."

And again, speaking of great armies:

"Whose rear lay wrapt in night, while breaking dawn
Rous'd the broad front, and call'd the battle on."

And this wail of the lost souls is fine:

"And this for sin?
Could I offend if I had never been?
But still increas'd the senseless, happy mass,
Flow'd in the stream, *or shiver'd in the grass?*
Father of mercies! Why from silent earth
Didst thou awake and curse me into birth?
Tear me from quiet, ravish me from night,
And make a thankless present of thy light?
Push into being a reverse of Thee,
And *animate a clod with misery?*"

But it is seldom in Young's rhymed poems that the effect of a felicitous thought or image is not counteracted by our sense of the constraint he suffered from the necessities of rhyme—that "Gothic demon," as he afterward called it, "which, modern poetry tasting, became mortal." In relation to his own power, no one will question the truth of this dictum, that "blank verse is verse unfallen, uncurst; verse reclaimed, reinthroned in the true language of the gods; who never thundered nor suffered their Homer to thunder in rhyme." His want of mastery in rhyme is especially a drawback on the effects of his Satires; for epigrams and witticisms are peculiarly susceptible to the intrusion of a superfluous word, or to an inversion which implies constraint. Here, even more than elsewhere, the art that conceals art is an absolute requisite, and to have a witticism presented to us in limping or cumbrous rhythm is as counteractive to any electrifying effect as to see the tentative grimaces by which a comedian prepares a grotesque countenance. We discern the process, instead of being startled by the result.

This is one reason why the Satires, read *seriatim*, have a flatness to us, which, when we afterward read picked passages, we are inclined to disbelieve in, and to attribute to some deficiency in our own mood. But there are deeper reasons for that dissatisfaction. Young is not a satirist of a high order. His satire has neither the terrible vigor, the lacerating energy of genuine indignation, nor the humor which owns loving fellowship with the poor human nature it laughs at; nor yet the personal bitterness which, as in Pope's characters of Sporus and Atticus, insures those living touches by virtue of which the individual and particular in Art becomes the universal and immortal. Young could never describe a real, complex human being; but what he *could* do with eminent success was to describe, with neat and finished point, obvious *types*, of manners rather than of character—to write cold and clever epigrams on personified vices and absurdities. There is no more emotion in his satire than if he were turning witty verses on a waxen image of Cupid or a lady's glove. He has none of these felicitious epithets, none of those pregnant lines, by which Pope's Satires have enriched the ordinary speech of educated men. Young's wit will be found in almost every instance to consist in that antithetic combination of ideas which, of all the forms of wit, is most within reach of a clever effort. In his gravest arguments, as well as in his lightest satire, one might imagine that he had set himself to work out the problem, how much antithesis might be got out of a given subject. And there he completely succeeds. His neatest portraits are all wrought on this plan. "Narcissus," for example, who

"Omits no duty; nor can Envy say
He miss'd, these many years, the Church or Play:

He makes no noise in Parliament, 'tis true ;
But pays his debts, and visit when 'tis due ;
His character and gloves are ever clean,
And then he can out-bow the bowing Dean ;
A smile eternal on his lip he wears,
Which equally the wise and worthless shares.
In gay fatigues, this most undaunted chief,
Patient of idleness beyond belief,
Most charitably lends the town his face
For ornament in every public place ;
As sure as cards he to th' assembly comes,
And is the furniture of drawing-rooms :
When Ombre calls, his hand and heart are free,
And, joined to two, he fails not—to make three ;
Narcissus is the glory of his race ;
For who does nothing with a better grace ?
To deck my list by nature were designed
Such shining expletives of human kind,
Who want, while through blank life they dream along,
Sense to be right and passion to be wrong."

It is but seldom that we find a touch of that easy slyness which gives an additional zest to surprise ; but here is an instance :

" See Tityrus, with merriment possest,
Is burst with laughter ere he hears the jest,
What need he stay, for when the joke is o'er,
His *teeth* will be no whiter than before."

Like Pope, whom he imitated, he sets out with a psychological mistake as the basis of his satire, attributing all forms of folly to one passion—the love of fame, or vanity—a much grosser mistake, indeed, than Pope's, exaggeration of the extent to which the "ruling passion" determines conduct in the individual. Not that Young is consistent in his mistake. He sometimes implies no more than what is the truth—that the love of fame is the cause, not of all follies, but of many.

Young's satires on women are superior to Pope's, which is only saying that they are superior to Pope's greatest failure. We can more frequently pick out a couplet as successful than an entire sketch. Of the too emphatic "Syrena" he says :

" Her judgment just, her sentence is too strong ;
Because she's right, she's ever in the wrong."

Of the diplomatic "Julia :"

> " For her own breakfast she'll project a scheme,
> Nor take her tea without a stratagem."

Of "Lyce," the old painted coquette :

> " In vain the cock has summoned sprites away ;
> She walks at noon and blasts the bloom of day."

Of the nymph, who, "gratis, clears religious mysteries :"

> " 'Tis hard, too, she who makes no use but chat
> Of her religion, should be barr'd in that."

The description of the literary *belle*, "Daphne," well prefaces that of "Stella," admired by Johnson :

> " With legs toss'd high, on her sophee she sits,
> Vouchsafing audience to contending wits :
> Of each performance she's the final test ;
> One act read o'er, she prophecies the rest ;
> And then, pronouncing with decisive air,
> Fully convinces all the town—*she's fair.*
> Had lonely Daphne Hecatessa's face,
> How would her elegance of taste decrease !
> Some ladies' judgment in their features lies,
> And all their genius sparkles in their eyes.
> But hold, she cries, lampooner ! have a care ;
> Must I want common sense because I'm fair ?
> O no ; see Stella : her eyes shine as bright
> As if her tongue was never in the right ;
> And yet what real learning, judgment, fire !
> She seems inspir'd, and can herself inspire.
> How then (if malice ruled not all the fair)
> *Could Daphne publish, and could she forbear ?*"

After all, when we have gone through Young's seven Satires, we seem to have made but an indifferent meal. They are a sort of fricassee, with some little solid meat in them, and yet the flavor is not always piquant. It is curious to find him, when he pauses a moment from his satiric sketching, recurring to his old platitudes :

> " Can gold calm passion, or make reason shine ?
> Can we dig peace or wisdom from the mine ?
> Wisdom to gold prefer ;"—

platitudes which he seems inevitably to fall into, for the same reason that some men are constantly asserting their contempt for criticism—because he felt the opposite so keenly.

The outburst of genius in the earlier books of the "Night Thoughts" is the more remarkable, that in the interval between them and the Satires he had produced nothing but his Pindaric odes, in which he fell far below the level of his previous works. Two sources of this sudden strength were the freedom of blank verse and the presence of a genuine emotion. Most persons, in speaking of the "Night Thoughts," have in their minds only the two or three first Nights, the majority of readers rarely getting beyond these, unless, as Wilson says, they "have but few books, are poor, and live in the country." And in these earlier Nights there is enough genuine sublimity and genuine sadness to bribe us into too favorable a judgment of them as a whole. Young had only a very few things to say or sing—such as that life is vain, that death is imminent, that man is immortal, that virtue is wisdom, that friendship is sweet, and that the source of virtue is the contemplation of death and immortality—and even in his two first Nights he had said almost all he had to say in his finest manner. Through these first outpourings of "complaint" we feel that the poet is really sad, that the bird is singing over a rifled nest; and we bear with his morbid picture of the world and of life, as the Job-like lament of a man whom "the hand of God hath touched." Death has carried away his best-beloved, and that "silent land" whither they are gone has more reality for the desolate one than this world which is empty of their love:

> "This is the desert, this the solitude;
> How populous, how vital is the grave!"

Joy died with the loved one:

> "The disenchanted earth
> Lost all her lustre. Where her glitt'ring towers?
> Her golden mountains, where? All darken'd down
> To naked waste; a dreary vale of tears:
> *The great magician's dead!*"

Under the pang of parting, it seems to the bereaved man as if love were only a nerve to suffer with, and he sickens at the thought of every joy of which he must one day say—"*it was.*" In its unreasoning anguish, the soul rushes to the idea of perpetuity as the one element of bliss:

> "O ye blest scenes of permanent delight!—
> Could ye, so rich in rapture, fear an end,—
> That ghastly thought would drink up all your joy,
> And quite unparadise the realms of light."

In a man under the immediate pressure of a great sorrow, we tolerate morbid exaggerations; we are prepared to see him turn away a weary eye from sunlight and flowers and sweet human faces, as if this rich and glorious life had no significance but as a preliminary of death; we do not criticise his views, we compassionate his feelings. And so it is with Young in these earlier Nights. There is already some artificiality even in his grief, and feeling often slides into rhetoric, but through it all we are thrilled with the unmistakable cry of pain, which makes us tolerant of egoism and hyperbole:

> "In every varied posture, place, and hour,
> How widow'd every thought of every joy!
> Thought, busy thought! too busy for my peace!
> Through the dark postern of time long elapsed
> Led softly, by the stillness of the night,—
> Led like a murderer (and such it proves!)
> Strays (wretched rover!) o'er the pleasing past,—
> In quest of wretchedness, perversely strays;
> And finds all desert now; and meets the ghosts
> Of my departed joys."

But when he becomes didactic, rather then complaining—when he ceases to sing his sorrows, and begins to insist on his opinions—when that distaste for life which we pity as a transient feeling is thrust upon us as a theory, we become perfectly cool and critical, and are not in the least inclined to be indulgent to false views and selfish sentiments.

Seeing that we are about to be severe on Young's failings and failures, we ought, if a reviewer's space were elastic, to dwell also on his merits—on the startling vigor of his imagery—on the occasional grandeur of his thought—on the piquant force of that grave satire into which his meditations continually run. But, since our "limits" are rigorous, we must content ourselves with the less agreeable half of the critic's duty; and we may the rather do so, because it would be difficult to say anything new of Young, in the way of admiration, while we think there are many salutary lessons remaining to be drawn from his faults.

One of the most striking characteristics of Young is his *radical insincerity as a poetic artist.* This, added to the thin and artificial texture of his wit, is the true explanation of the paradox—that a poet who is often inopportunely witty has the opposite vice of bombastic absurdity. The source of all grandiloquence is the want of taking for a criterion the true qualities of the object described or the emotion expressed. The grandiloquent man is never bent on saying what he feels or what he sees, but on producing a certain effect on his audience ; hence he may float away into utter inanity without meeting any criterion to arrest him. Here lies the distinction between grandiloquence and genuine fancy or bold imaginativeness. The fantastic or the boldly imaginative poet may be as sincere as the most realistic : he is true to his own sensibilities or inward vision, and in his wildest flights he never breaks loose from his criterion—the truth of his own mental state. Now, this disruption of language from genuine thought and feeling is what we are constantly detecting in Young ; and his insincerity is the more likely to betray him into absurdity, because he habitually treats of abstractions, and not of concrete objects or specific emotions. He descants perpetually on virtue, religion, "the good man," life, death, immortality, eternity—subjects which are apt to give a factitious grandeur to empty wordiness. When a poet floats in the empyrean, and only takes a bird's-eye view of the earth, some people accept the mere fact of his soaring for sublimity, and mistake his dim vision of earth for proximity to heaven. Thus :

> "His hand the good man fixes on the skies,
> And bids earth roll, nor feels her idle whirl,"

may, perhaps, pass for sublime with some readers. But pause a moment to realize the image, and the monstrous absurdity of a man's grasping the skies, and hanging habitually suspended there, while he contemptuously bids the earth roll, warns you that no genuine feeling could have suggested so unnatural a conception.

Again,

> "See the man immortal: him, I mean,
> Who lives as such; whose heart, full bent on Heaven,
> Leans all that way, his bias to the stars."

This is worse than the previous example: for you can at least form some imperfect conception of a man hanging from the skies, though the position strikes you as uncomfortable and of no particular use; but you are utterly unable to imagine how his heart can lean toward the stars. Examples of such vicious imagery, resulting from insincerity, may be found, perhaps, in almost every page of the "Night Thoughts." But simple assertions or aspirations, undisguised by imagery, are often equally false. No writer whose rhetoric was checked by the slightest truthful intentions could have said—

> "An eye of awe and wonder let me roll,
> And roll forever."

Abstracting the more poetical associations with the eye, this is hardly less absurd than if he had wished to stand forever with his mouth open.

Again:

> "Far beneath
> A soul immortal is a mortal joy."

Happily for human nature, we are sure no man really believes that. Which of us has the impiety not to feel that our souls are only too narrow for the joy of looking into the trusting eyes of our children, of reposing on the love of a husband or a wife—nay, of listening to the divine voice of music, or watching the calm brightness of autumnal afternoons? But Young could utter this falsity without detecting it, because, when he spoke of "mortal joys," he rarely had in his mind any object to which he could attach sacredness. He was thinking of bishoprics, and benefices, of smiling monarchs, patronizing prime ministers, and a "much indebted muse."

Of anything between these and eternal bliss he was but rarely and moderately conscious. Often, indeed, he sinks very much below even the bishopric, and seems to have no notion of earthly pleasure but such as breathes gaslight and the fumes of wine. His picture of life is precisely such as you would expect from a man who has risen from his bed at two o'clock in the afternoon with a headache and a dim remembrance that he has added to his "debts of honor:"

"What wretched repetition cloys us here!
What periodic potions for the sick,
Distemper'd bodies, and distemper'd minds?"

And then he flies off to his usual antithesis:

"In an eternity what scenes shall strike!
Adventures thicken, novelties surprise!"

"Earth" means lords and levees, duchesses and Dalilahs, South-Sea dreams, and illegal percentage; and the only things distinctly preferable to these are eternity and the stars. Deprive Young of this antithesis, and more than half his eloquence would be shrivelled up. Place him on a breezy common, where the furze is in its golden bloom, where children are playing, and horses are standing in the sunshine with fondling necks, and he would have nothing to say. Here are neither depths of guilt nor heights of glory; and we doubt whether in such a scene he would be able to pay his usual compliment to the Creator:

"Where'er I turn, what claim on all applause!"

It is true that he sometimes—not often—speaks of virtue as capable of sweetening life, as well as of taking the sting from death and winning heaven; and, lest we should be guilty of any unfairness to him, we will quote the two passages which convey this sentiment the most explicitly. In the one he gives "Lorenzo" this excellent recipe for obtaining cheerfulness;

"Go, fix some weighty truth;
Chain down some passion; do some generous good;
Teach Ignorance to see, or Grief to smile;

Correct thy friend; befriend thy greatest foe;
Or, with warm heart, and confidence divine,
Spring up, and lay strong hold on Him who made thee."

The other passage is vague, but beautiful, and its music has murmured in our minds for many years:

"The cuckoo seasons sing
The same dull note to such as nothing prize
But what those seasons from the teeming earth
To doting sense indulge. But nobler minds,
Which relish fruit unripened by the sun,
Make their days various; various as the dyes
On the dove's neck, which wanton in his rays.
On minds of dove-like innocence possess'd,
On lighten'd minds that bask in Virtue's beams,
Nothing hangs tedious, nothing old revolves
In that for which they long, for which they live.
Their glorious efforts, winged with heavenly hopes,
Each rising morning sees still higher rise;
Each bounteous dawn its novelty presents
To worth maturing, new strength, lustre, fame;
While Nature's circle, like a chariot wheel,
Rolling beneath their elevated aims,
Makes their fair prospect fairer every hour;
Advancing virtue in a line to bliss."

Even here, where he is in his most amiable mood, you see at what a telescopic distance he stands from mother Earth and simple human joys—"Nature's circle rolls beneath." Indeed, we remember no mind in poetic literature that seems to have absorbed less of the beauty and the healthy breath of the common landscape than Young's. His images, often grand and finely presented—witness that sublimely sudden leap of thought,

"Embryos we must be till we burst the shell,
Yon ambient azure shell, and spring to life"—

lie almost entirely within that circle of observation which would be familiar to a man who lived in town, hung about the theatres, read the newspaper, and went home often by moon and starlight.

There is no natural object nearer than the moon that seems to have any strong attraction for him, and even to the moon he chiefly appeals for patronage, and "pays his court" to her. It is reckoned among the many deficiencies of "Lorenzo" that he "never asked the moon one question"—an omission which Young thinks eminently unbecoming a rational being. He describes nothing so well as a comet, and is tempted to linger with fond detail over nothing more familiar than the day of judgment and an imaginary journey among the stars. Once on Saturn's ring he feels at home, and his language becomes quite easy:

> "What behold I now?
> A wilderness of wonders burning round,
> Where larger suns inhabit higher spheres;
> Perhaps *the villas of descending gods!*"

It is like a sudden relief from a strained posture when, in the "Night Thoughts," we come on any allusion that carries us to the lanes, woods, or fields. Such allusions are amazingly rare, and we could almost count them on a single hand. That we may do him no injustice, we will quote the three best:

> "Like *blossom'd trees o'erturned by vernal storm,*
> Lovely in death the beauteous ruin lay.
>
> * * * * *
>
> "In the same brook none ever bathed him twice:
> To the same life none ever twice awoke.
> We call the brook the same—the same we think
> Our life, though still more rapid in its flow;
> Nor mark the much irrevocably lapsed
> And mingled with the sea."
>
> * * * * *
>
> "The crown of manhood is a winter joy;
> An evergreen that stands the northern blast,
> And blossoms in the rigor of our fate."

The adherence to abstractions, or to the personification of abstractions, is closely allied in Young to the *want of genuine emotion.* He sees virtue sitting on a mount serene, far above the mists and storms of earth; he sees Religion coming down from the skies, with this world in her left hand and the other world in her right; but we never find him dwelling on virtue or religion as it really exists—in the emotions of a man dressed in an ordinary coat, and seated by his fireside of an evening, with his hand resting on the head of his little daughter, in courageous effort for unselfish ends, in the internal triumph of justice and pity over personal resentment, in all the sublime self-renunciation and sweet charities which are found in the details of ordinary life. Now, emotion links itself with particulars, and only in a faint and secondary manner with abstractions. An orator may discourse very eloquently on injustice in general, and leave his audience cold; but let him state a special case of oppression, and every heart will throb. The most untheoretic persons are aware of this relation between true emotion and particular facts, as opposed to general terms, and implicitly recognize it in the repulsion they feel toward any one who professes strong feeling about abstractions—in the interjectional "Humbug!" which immediately rises to their lips. Wherever abstractions appear to excite strong emotion, this occurs in men of active intellect and imagination, in whom the abstract term rapidly and vividly calls up the particulars it represents, these particulars being the true source of the emotion; and such men, if they wished to express their feeling, would be infallibly prompted to the presentation of details. Strong emotion can no more be directed to generalities apart from particulars, than skill in figures can be directed to arithmetic apart from numbers. Generalities are the refuge at once of deficient intellectual activity and deficient feeling.

If we except the passages in "Philander," "Narcissa," and "Lucia," there is hardly a trace of human sympathy, of self-forgetfulness in the joy or sorrow of a fellow-being, throughout this long poem, which professes to treat the various phases of man's destiny. And even in the "Narcissa" Night, Young repels us by the low moral tone of his exaggerated lament. This married step-daughter died at Lyons, and, being a Protestant, was denied burial, so that her friends had to bury her in secret—one of the many miserable results of superstition, but not a fact to throw an educated, still less a Christian man, into a fury of hatred and vengeance, in contemplating it after the lapse of five years. Young, however, takes great pains to simulate a bad feeling:

> Of grief
> And indignation rival bursts I pour'd,
> Half execration mingled with my pray'r;
> Kindled at man, while I his God adored;
> Sore grudg'd the savage land her sacred dust;
> Stamp'd the cursed soil; *and with humanity*
> (Denied Narcissa) *wish'd them all a grave*."

The unlucky bad taste of this last clause makes us hope that it is simply a platitude, and not intended as witticism, until he removes the possibility of this favorable doubt by immediately asking, "Flows my resentment into guilt?"

When, by an afterthought, he attempts something like sympathy, he only betrays more clearly his want of it. Thus, in the first Night, when he turns from his private griefs to depict earth as a hideous abode of misery for all mankind, and asks,

> "What then am I, who sorrow for myself?"

he falls at once into calculating the benefit of sorrowing for others:

> "More generous sorrow, while it sinks, exalts;
> *And conscious virtue mitigates the pang*.
> Nor virtue, more than prudence, bids me give
> Swollen thought a second channel."

This remarkable negation of sympathy is in perfect consistency with Young's theory of ethics:

> "Virtue is a crime,
> A crime of reason, if it costs us pain
> Unpaid."

If there is no immortality for man—

> "Sense! take the rein; blind Passion, drive us on;
> And Ignorance! befriend us on our way. . .
> Yes; give the pulse full empire; live the Brute,
> Since as the brute we die. The sum of man,
> Of godlike man, to revel and to rot."

* * * * *

> "If this life's gain invites him to the deed,
> Why not his country sold, his father slain?"

* * * * *

> "Ambition, avarice, by the wise disdain'd,
> Is perfect wisdom, while mankind are fools,
> And think a turf or tombstone covers all."

* * * * *

"Die for thy country, thou romantic fool!
Seize, seize the plank thyself, and let her sink."
* * * * *
"As in the dying parent dies the child,
Virtue with Immortality expires.
Who tells me he denies his soul immortal,
Whate'er his boast, has told me he's a knave.
His duty 'tis to love himself alone.
Nor care though mankind perish if he smiles."

We can imagine the man who "denies his soul immortal," replying, "It is quite possible that *you* would be a knave, and love yourself alone, if it were not for your belief in immortality; but you are not to force upon me what would result from your own utter want of moral emotion. I am just and honest, not because I expect to live in another world, but because, having felt the pain of injustice and dishonesty toward myself, I have a fellow-feeling with other men, who would suffer the same pain if I were unjust or dishonest toward them. Why should I give my neighbor short weight in this world, because there is not another world in which I should have nothing to weigh out to him? I am honest, because I don't like to inflict evil on others in this life, not because I'm afraid of evil to myself in another. The fact is, I do *not* love myself alone, whatever logical necessity there may be for that in your mind. I have a tender love for my wife, and children, and friends, and through that love I sympathize with like affections in other men. It is a pang to me to witness the sufferings of a fellow-being, and I feel his suffering the more acutely because he is *mortal*—because his life is so short, and I would have it, if possible, filled with happiness and not misery. Through my union and fellowship with the men and women I *have* seen, I feel a like, though a fainter, sympathy with those I have *not* seen; and I am able so to live in imagination with the generations to come, that their good is not alien to me, and is a stimulus to me to labor for ends which may not benefit myself, but will benefit them. It is possible that you may prefer to 'live the brute,' to sell your country, or to slay your father, if you were not afraid of some disagreeable consequences from the criminal laws of another world; but even if I could conceive no motive but my own worldly interest or the gratification of my animal desire, I have not observed that beastliness, treachery, and parricide are the direct way to happiness and comfort on earth. And I should say, that if you feel no motive to common morality but your fear of a criminal bar in heaven, you are decidedly a man for the police on earth to keep their eye upon, since it is matter of world-old experience that fear of distant consequences is a very insufficient barrier against the rush of immediate desire. Fear of consequences is only one form of egoism, which will hardly stand against half a dozen other forms of egoism bearing down upon it. And in opposition to your theory that a belief in immortality is the only source of virtue, I maintain that, so far as moral action is dependent on that belief, so far the emotion which prompts it is not truly moral—is still in the stage of egoism, and has not yet attained the higher development of sympathy. In proportion as a man would care less for the rights and welfare of his fellow, if he did not believe in a future life, in that proportion is he wanting in the genuine feelings of justice and benevolence; as the musician who would care less to play a sonata of Beethoven's finely in solitude than in public, where he was to be paid for it, is wanting in genuine enthusiasm for music."

Thus far might answer the man who "denies himself immortal;" and, allowing for that deficient recognition of the finer and more indirect influences exercised by the idea of immortality which might be expected from one who took up a dogmatic position on such a subject, we think he would have given a sufficient reply to Young and other theological advocates who, like him, pique themselves on the loftiness of their doctrine when they maintain that "virtue with immortality expires." We may admit, indeed, that if the better part of virtue consists, as Young appears to think, in contempt for mortal joys, in "meditation of our own decease," and in "applause" of God in the style of a congratulatory address to Her Majesty—all which has small relation to the well-being of mankind on this earth—the motive to it must be gathered from something that lies quite outside the sphere of human sympathy. But, for certain other elements of virtue, which are of more obvious importance to untheological minds—a delicate sense of our neighbor's rights, an active participation in the joys and sorrows of our fellow-men, a magnanimous acceptance of privation or suffering for ourselves when it is the condition of good to others, in a word, the extension and intensification of our sympathetic nature—we think it of some importance to contend that they have no more direct relation to the belief in a future state than the interchange of gases in the lungs has to the plurality of worlds. Nay, to us it is conceivable that in some minds the deep pathos lying in the thought of human mortality—that we are here for a little while and then vanish away, that this earthly life is all that is given to our loved ones and to our many suffering fellow-men—lies nearer the fountains of moral emotion than the conception of extended existence. And surely it ought to be a welcome fact, if the thought of *mortality*, as well as of immortality, be favorable to virtue. Do writers of sermons and religious novels prefer that men should be vicious in order that there may be a more evident political and social necessity for printed sermons and clerical fictions? Because learned gentlemen are theological, are we to have no more simple honesty and good-will? We can imagine that the proprietors of a patent water-supply have a dread of common springs; but, for our own part, we think there cannot be too great a security against a lack of fresh water or of pure morality. To us it is a matter of unmixed rejoicing that this latter necessary of healthful life is independent of theological ink, and that its evolution is insured in the interaction of human souls as certainly as the evolution of science or of art, with which, indeed, it is but a twin ray, melting into them with undefinable limits.

To return to Young. We can often detect a man's deficiencies in what he admires more clearly than in what he contemns—in the sentiments he presents as laudable rather than in those he decries. And in Young's notion of what is lofty he casts a shadow by which we can measure him without further trouble. For example, in arguing for human immortality, he says:

> "First, what is *true ambition?* The pursuit
> Of glory *nothing less than man can share.*
>
> * * * *
>
> The Visible and Present are for brutes,
> A slender portion, and a narrow bound!
> These Reason, with an energy divine,
> O'erleaps, and claims the Future and Unseen;
> The vast Unseen, the Future fathomless!
> When the great soul buoys up to this high point,
> Leaving gross Nature's sediments below,
> Then, and then only, Adam's offspring quits
> The sage and hero of the fields and woods,
> Asserts his rank, and rises into man."

So, then, if it were certified that, as some benevolent minds have tried to infer, our dumb fellow-creatures would share a future existence, in which it is to be hoped we should neither beat, starve, nor maim them, our ambition for a future life would cease to be "lofty!" This is a notion of loftiness which may pair off with Dr. Whewell's celebrated observation, that Bentham's moral theory is low because it includes justice and mercy to brutes.

But, for a reflection of Young's moral personality on a colossal scale, we must turn to those passages where his rhetoric is at its utmost stretch of inflation—where he addresses the Deity, discourses of the Divine operations, or describes the last judgment. As a compound of vulgar pomp, crawling adulation, and hard selfishness, presented under the guise of piety, there are few things in literature to surpass the Ninth Night, entitled "Consolation," especially in the pages where he describes the last judgment—a subject to which, with naïve self-betrayal, he applies phraseology favored by the exuberant penny-a-liner. Thus, when God descends, and the groans of hell are opposed by "shouts of joy," much as cheers and groans contend at a public meeting where the resolutions are *not* passed unanimously, the poet completes his climax in this way:

"Hence, in one peal of loud, eternal praise,
The *charmed spectators* thunder their applause."

In the same taste he sings:

"Eternity, the various sentence past,
Assigns the sever'd throng distinct abodes,
Sulphureous or ambrosial."

Exquisite delicacy of indication! He is too nice to be specific as to the interior of the "sulphureous" abode; but when once half the human race are shut up there, hear how he enjoys turning the key on them!

"What ensues?
The deed predominant, the deed of deeds!
Which makes a hell of hell, a *heaven of heaven!*
The goddess, with determin'd aspect turns
Her adamantine key's enormous size
Through Destiny's inextricable wards,
Deep driving every bolt on both their fates.
Then, from the crystal battlements of heaven,
Down, down she hurls it through the dark profound,
Ten thousand, thousand fathom; there to rust
And ne'er unlock her resolution more.
The deep resounds; and Hell, through all her glooms,
Returns, in groans, the melancholy roar."

This is one of the blessings for which Dr. Young thanks God "most:"

"For all I bless thee, most, for the severe;
Her death—my own at hand—*the fiery gulf,*
That flaming bound of wrath omnipotent!
It thunders;—but it thunders to preserve;
. . . . . its wholesome dread
Averts the dreaded pain; *its hideous groans*
Join Heaven's sweet Hallelujahs in Thy praise,
Great Source of good alone! How kind in all!
In vengeance kind! Pain, Death, Gehenna, *save*". . .

i.e., save *me*, Dr. Young, who, in return for that favor, promise to give my divine patron the monopoly of that exuberance in laudatory epithet, of which specimens may be seen at any moment in a large number of dedications and odes to kings, queens, prime ministers, and other persons of distinction. *That*, in Young's conception, is what God delights in. His crowning aim in the "drama" of the ages, is to vindicate his own renown. The God of the "Night Thoughts" is simply Young himself "writ large"—a didactic poet, who "lectures" mankind in the antithetic hyperbole of mortal and immortal joys, earth and the stars, hell and heaven; and expects the tribute of inexhaustible "applause." Young has no conception of religion as anything else than egoism turned heavenward; and he does not merely imply this, he insists on it. Religion, he tells us, in argumentative passages too long to quote, is "ambition, pleasure, and the love of gain," directed toward the joys of the future life instead of the present. And his ethics correspond to his religion. He vacillates, indeed, in his ethical theory, and shifts his position in order to suit his immediate purpose in argument; but he never changes his level so as to see beyond the horizon of mere selfishness. Sometimes he insists, as we have seen, that the belief in a future life is the only basis of morality; but elsewhere he tells us—

"In self-applause is virtue's golden prize."

Virtue, with Young, must always squint—must never look straight toward the immediate object of its emotion and effort. Thus, if a man risks perishing in the snow himself rather than forsake a weaker comrade, he must either do this because his hopes and fears are directed to another world, or because he desires to applaud himself afterward! Young, if we may believe him, would despise the action as folly unless it had these motives. Let us hope he was not so bad as he pretended to be! The tides of the divine life in man move under the thickest ice of theory.

Another indication of Young's deficiency in moral, *i.e.*, in sympathetic emotion, is his unintermitting habit of pedagogic moralizing. On its theoretic and perceptive side, morality touches science; on its emotional side, Art. Now, the products of Art are great in proportion as they result from that immediate prompting of innate power which we call Genius, and not from labored obedience to a theory or rule; and the presence of genius or innate prompting is directly opposed to the perpetual consciousness of a rule. The action of faculty is imperious, and excludes the reflection *why* it should act. In the same way, in proportion as morality is emotional, *i.e.*, has affinity with Art, it will exhibit itself in direct sympathetic feeling and action, and not as the recognition of a rule. Love does not say, "I ought to love"—it loves. Pity does not say, "It is right to be pitiful"—it pities. Justice does not say, "I am bound to be just"—it feels justly. It is only where moral emotion is comparatively weak that the contemplation of a rule or theory habitually mingles with its action; and in accordance with this, we think experience, both in literature and life, has shown that the minds which are pre-eminently didactic—which insist on a "lesson," and despise everything that will not convey a moral, are deficient in sympathetic emotion. A certain poet is recorded to have said that he "wished everything of his burned that did not impress some moral; even in love-verses, it might be flung in by the way." What poet was it who took this medicinal view of poetry? Dr. Watts, or James Montgomery, or some other singer of spotless life and ardent piety? Not at all. It was *Waller*. A significant fact in relation to our position, that the predominant didactic tendency proceeds rather from the poet's perception that it is good for other men to be moral, than from any overflow of moral feeling in himself. A man who is perpetually thinking in apothegms, who has an unintermittent flux of admonition, can have little energy left for simple emotion. And this is the case with Young. In his highest flights of contemplation and his most wailing soliloquies he interrupts himself to fling an admonitory parenthesis at "Lorenzo," or to hint that "folly's creed" is the reverse of his own. Before his thoughts can flow, he must fix his eye on an imaginary miscreant, who gives unlimited scope for lecturing, and recriminates just enough to keep the spring of admonition and argument going to the extent of nine books. It is curious to see how this pedagogic habit of mind runs through Young's contemplation of Nature. As the tendency to see our own sadness reflected in the external world has been called by Mr. Ruskin the "pathetic fallacy," so we may call Young's disposition to see a rebuke or a warning in every natural object, the "pedagogic fallacy." To his mind, the heavens are "forever *scolding* as they shine;" and the great function of the stars is to be a "lecture to mankind." The conception of the Deity as a didactic author is not merely an implicit point of view with him; he works it out in elaborate imagery, and at length makes it the occasion of his most extraordinary achievement in the "art of sinking," by exclaiming, *à propos*, we need hardly say, of the nocturnal heavens,

"Divine Instructor! Thy first volume this
For man's perusal! all in CAPITALS!"

It is this pedagogic tendency, this sermonizing attitude of Young's mind, which produces the wearisome monotony of his pauses. After the first two or three nights he is rarely singing, rarely pouring forth any continuous melody inspired by the spontaneous flow of thought or feeling. He is rather occupied with argumentative insistance, with hammering in the proofs of his propositions by disconnected verses, which he puts down at intervals. The perpetual recurrence of the pause at the end of the line throughout long passages makes them as fatiguing to the ear as a monotonous chant, which consists of the endless repetition of one short musical phrase. For example:

"Past hours,
If not by guilt, yet wound us by their flight,
If folly bound our prospect by the grave,
All feeling of futurity be numb'd,
All godlike passion for eternals quench'd,
All relish of realities expired;
Renounced all correspondence with the skies;
Our freedom chain'd; quite wingless our desire;
In sense dark-prison'd all that ought to soar;
Prone to the centre; crawling in the dust;
Dismounted every great and glorious aim;
Enthralled every faculty divine,
Heart-buried in the rubbish of the world."

How different from the easy, graceful melody of Cowper's blank verse! Indeed, it is hardly possible to criticise Young without being reminded at every step of the contrast presented to him by Cowper. And this contrast urges itself upon us the more from the fact that there is, to a certain extent, a parallelism between the "Night Thoughts" and the "Task." In both poems the author achieves his greatest in virtue of the new freedom conferred by blank verse; both poems are professionally didactic, and mingle much satire with their graver meditations; both poems are the productions of men whose estimate of this life was formed by the light of a belief in immortality, and who were intensely attached to Christianity. On some grounds we might have anticipated a more morbid view of things from Cowper than from Young. Cowper's religion was dogmatically the more gloomy, for he was a Calvinist; while Young was a "low" Arminian, believing that Christ died for all, and that the only obstacle to any man's salvation lay in his will, which he could change if he chose. There was real and deep sadness involved in Cowper's personal lot; while Young, apart from his ambitious and greedy discontent, seems to have had no great sorrow.

Yet, see how a lovely, sympathetic nature manifests itself in spite of creed and circumstance! Where is the poem that surpasses the "Task" in the genuine love it breathes, at once toward inanimate and animate existence—in truthfulness of perception and sincerity of presentation—in the calm gladness that springs from a delight in objects for their own sake, without self-reference—in divine sympathy with the lowliest pleasures, with the most short-lived capacity for pain? Here is no railing at the earth's "melancholy map," but the happiest lingering over her simplest scenes with all the fond minuteness of attention that belongs to love; no pompous rhetoric about the inferiority of the "brutes," but a warm plea on their behalf against man's inconsiderateness and cruelty, and a sense of enlarged happiness from their companionship in enjoyment; no vague rant about human misery and human virtue, but that close and vivid presentation of particular sorrows and privations, of particular deeds and misdeeds, which is the direct road to the emotions. How Cowper's exquisite mind falls with the mild warmth of morning sunlight on the commonest objects, at once disclosing every detail, and investing every detail with beauty! No object is too small to prompt his song—not the sooty film on the bars, or the spoutless teapot holding a bit of mignonette that serves to cheer the dingy town-lodging with a "hint that Nature lives;" and yet his song is never trivial, for he is alive to small objects, not because his mind is narrow, but because his glance is clear and his heart is large. Instead of trying to edify us by supercilious allusions to the "brutes" and the "stalls," he interests us in that tragedy of the hen-roost when the thief has wrenched the door,

> "Where Chanticleer amidst his harem sleeps
> *In unsuspecting pomp;*"

in the patient cattle, that on the winter's morning

> "Mourn in corners where the fence
> Screens them, and seem half petrified to sleep
> *In unrecumbent sadness;*"

in the little squirrel, that, surprised by him in his woodland walk,

> "At once, swift as a bird,
> Ascends the neighboring beech; there whisks his brush,
> And perks his ears, and stamps, and cries aloud,
> With all the prettiness of feign'd alarm
> And anger insignificantly fierce."

And then he passes into reflection, not with curt apothegm and snappish reproof, but with that melodious flow of utterance which belongs to thought when it is carried along in a stream of feeling:

> "The heart is hard in nature, and unfit
> For human fellowship, as being void
> Of sympathy, and therefore dead alike
> To love and friendship both, that is not pleased
> With sight of animals enjoying life,
> Nor feels their happiness augment his own."

His large and tender heart embraces the most every-day forms of human life—the carter driving his team through the wintry storm; the cottager's wife who, painfully nursing the embers on her hearth, while her infants "sit cowering o'er the sparks,"

> "Retires, content to quake, so they be warm'd;"

or the villager, with her little ones, going out to pick

> "A cheap but wholesome salad from the brook;"

and he compels our colder natures to follow his in its manifold sympathies, not by exhortations, not by telling us to meditate at midnight, to "indulge" the thought of death, or to ask ourselves how we shall "weather an eternal night," *but by presenting to us the object of his compassion truthfully and lovingly.* And when he handles greater themes, when he takes a wider survey, and considers the men or the deeds which have a direct influence on the welfare of communities and nations, there is the same unselfish warmth of feeling, the same scrupulous truthfulness. He is never vague in his remonstrance or his satire, but puts his finger on some particular vice or folly which excites his indignation or "dissolves his heart in pity," because of some specific injury it does to his fellow-man or to a sacred cause. And when he is asked why he interests himself about the sorrows and wrongs of others, hear what is the reason he gives. Not, like Young, that the movements of the planets show a mutual dependence, and that

> "Thus man his sovereign duty learns in this
> Material picture of benevolence,"

or that—

> "More generous sorrow, while it sinks, exalts,
> And conscious virtue mitigates the pang."

What is Cowper's answer, when he imagines some "sage, erudite, profound," asking him "What's the world to you?"

> "Much. *I was born of woman, and drew milk*
> *As sweet as charity from human breasts.*
> I think, articulate, I laugh and weep,
> And exercise all functions of a man.
> How then should I and any man that lives
> Be strangers to each other?"

Young is astonished that men can make war on each other—that any one can "seize his brother's throat," while

> "The Planets cry, 'Forbear.'"

Cowper weeps because

> "There is no flesh in man's obdurate heart:
> *It does not feel for man.*"

Young applauds God as a monarch with an empire and a court quite superior to the English, or as an author who produces "volumes for man's perusal." Cowper sees his father's love in all the gentle pleasures of the home fireside, in the charms even of the wintry landscape, and thinks—

"Happy who walks with him! whom what he finds
Of flavor or of scent in fruit or flower,
Or what he views of beautiful or grand
In nature, from the broad, majestic oak
To the green blade that twinkles in the sun,
Prompts with remembrance of a present God."

To conclude—for we must arrest ourselves in a contrast that would lead us beyond our bounds:—Young flies for his utmost consolation to the day of judgment, when

"Final Ruin fiercely drives
Her ploughshare o'er creation;"

when earth, stars, and sun are swept aside,

"And now, all dross removed, Heaven's own pure day,
Full on the confines of our ether, flames:
While (dreadful contrast!) far (how far!) beneath,
Hell, bursting, belches forth her blazing seas,
And storms suphureous; her voracious jaws
Expanding wide, and roaring for her prey,"

Dr. Young and similar "ornaments of religion and virtue" passing of course with grateful "applause" into the upper region. Cowper finds his highest inspiration in the Millennium—in the restoration of this our beloved home of earth to perfect holiness and bliss, when the Supreme

"Shall visit earth in mercy; shall descend
Propitious in his chariot paved with love;
And what his storms have blasted and defaced
For man's revolt, shall with a smile repair."

And into what delicious melody his song flows at the thought of that blessedness to be enjoyed by future generations on earth!

"The dwellers in the vales and on the rocks
Shout to each other, and the mountains tops
From distant mountains catch the flying joy;
Till, nation after nation taught the strain,
Earth rolls the rapturous Hosanna round!"

The sum of our comparison is this: In Young we have the type of that deficient human sympathy, that impiety toward the present and the visible, which flies for its motives, its sanctities, and its religion, to the remote, the vague, and the unknown: in Cowper we have the type of that genuine love which cherishes things in proportion to their nearness, and feels its reverence grow in proportion to the intimacy of its knowledge.

VIII.

THE INFLUENCE OF RATIONALISM.*

There is a valuable class of books on great subjects which have something of the character and functions of good popular lecturing. They are not original, not subtle, not of close logical texture, not exquisite either in thought or style; but by virtue of these negatives they are all the more fit to act on the average intelligence. They have enough of organizing purpose in them to make their facts illustrative, and to leave a distinct result in the mind even when most of the facts are forgotten; and they have enough of vagueness and vacillation in their theory to win them ready acceptance from a mixed audience. The vagueness and vacillation are not devices of timidity; they are the honest result of the writer's own mental character, which adapts him to be the instructor and the favorite of "the general reader." For the most part, the general reader of the present day does not exactly know what distance he goes; he only knows that he does not go "too far." Of any remarkable thinker, whose writings have excited controversy, he likes to have it said that "his errors are to be deplored," leaving it not too certain what those errors are; he is fond of what may be called disembodied opinions, that float in vapory phrases above all systems of thought or action; he likes an undefined Christianity which opposes itself to nothing in particular, an undefined education of the people, an undefined amelioration of all things: in fact, he likes sound views—nothing extreme, but something between the excesses of the past and the excesses of the present. This modern type of the general reader may be known in conversation by the cordiality with which he assents to indistinct, blurred statements: say that black is black, he will shake his head and hardly think it; say that black is not so very black, he will reply, "Exactly."

* "History of the Rise and Influence of the Spirit of Rationalism in Europe." By W. E. H. Lecky, M.A. Longman & Co., London.

He has no hesitation, if you wish it, even to get up at a public meeting and express his conviction that at times, and within certain limits, the radii of a circle have a tendency to be equal; but, on the other hand, he would urge that the spirit of geometry may be carried a little too far. His only bigotry is a bigotry against any clearly defined opinion; not in the least based on a scientific scepticism, but belonging to a lack of coherent thought—a spongy texture of mind, that gravitates strongly to nothing. The one thing he is staunch for is, the utmost liberty of private haziness.

But precisely these characteristics of the general reader, rendering him incapable of assimilating ideas unless they are administered in a highly diluted form, make it a matter of rejoicing that there are clever, fair-minded men, who will write books for him—men very much above him in knowledge and ability, but not too remote from him in their habits of thinking, and who can thus prepare for him infusions of history and science that will leave some solidifying deposit, and save him from a fatal softening of the intellectual skeleton. Among such serviceable writers, Mr. Lecky's "History of the Rise and Influence of the Spirit of Rationalism in Europe" entitles him to a high place. He has prepared himself for its production by an unusual amount of well-directed reading; he has chosen his facts and quotations with much judgment; and he gives proof of those important moral qualifications, impartiality, seriousness, and modesty. This praise is chiefly applicable to the long chapter on the history of Magic and Witchcraft, which opens the work, and to the two chapters on the antecedents and history of Persecution, which occur, the one at the end of the first volume, the other at the beginning of the second. In these chapters Mr. Lecky has a narrower and better-traced path before him than in other portions of his work; he is more occupied with presenting a particular class of facts in their historical sequence, and in their relation to certain grand tide-marks of opinion, than with disquisition; and his writing is freer than elsewhere from an apparent confusedness of thought and an exuberance of approximative phrases, which can be serviceable in no other way than as diluents needful for the sort of reader we have just described.

The history of magic and witchcraft has been judiciously chosen by Mr. Lecky as the subject of his first section on the Declining Sense of the Miraculous, because it is strikingly illustrative of a position with the truth of which he is strongly impressed, though he does not always treat of it with desirable clearness and precision, namely, that certain beliefs become obsolete, not in consequence of direct arguments against them, but because of their incongruity with prevalent habits of thought. Here is his statement of the two "classes of influences" by which the mass of men, in what is called civilized society, get their beliefs gradually modified:

"If we ask why it is that the world has rejected what was once so universally and so intensely believed, why a narrative of an old woman who had been seen riding on a broomstick, or who was proved to have transformed herself into a wolf, and to have devoured the flocks of her neighbors, is deemed so entirely incredible, most persons would probably be unable to give a very definite answer to the question. It is not because we have examined the evidence and found it insufficient, for the disbelief always precedes, when it does not prevent, examination. It is rather because the idea of absurdity is so strongly attached to such narratives, that it is difficult even to consider them with gravity. Yet at one time no such improbability was felt, and hundreds of persons have been burnt simply on the two grounds I have mentioned.

"When so complete a change takes place in public opinion, it may be ascribed to one or other of two causes. It may be the result of a controversy which has conclusively settled the question, establishing to the satisfaction of all parties a clear preponderance of argument or fact in favor of one opinion, and making that opinion a truism which is accepted by all enlightened men, even though they have not themselves examined the evidence on which it rests. Thus, if any one in a company of ordinarily educated persons were to deny the motion of the earth, or the circulation of the blood, his statement would be received with derision, though it is probable that some of his audience would be unable to demonstrate the first truth, and that very few of them could give sufficient reasons for the second. They may not themselves be able to defend their position; but they are aware that, at certain known periods of history, controversies on those subjects took place, and that known writers then brought forward some definite arguments or experiments, which were ultimately accepted by the whole learned world as rigid and conclusive demonstrations. It is possible, also, for as complete a change to be effected by what is called the spirit of the age. The general intellectual tendencies pervading the literature of a century profoundly modify the character of the public mind. They form a new tone and habit of thought. They alter the measure of probability. They create new attractions and new antipathies, and they eventually cause as absolute a rejection of certain old opinions as could be produced by the most cogent and definite arguments."

Mr. Lecky proceeds to some questionable views concerning the evidences of witchcraft, which seem to be irreconcilable even with his own remarks later on; but they lead him to the statement, thoroughly made out by his historical survey, that the movement was mainly silent, unargumentative, and insensible; that men came gradually to disbelieve in witchcraft, because they came gradually to look upon it as absurd; and that this new tone of thought appeared, first of all, in those who were least subject to theological influences, and soon spread through the educated laity, and, last of all, took possession of the clergy."

We have rather painful proof that this "second class of influences," with a vast number go hardly deeper than Fashion, and that witchcraft to many of us is absurd only on the same ground that our grandfathers' gigs are absurd. It is felt preposterous to think of spiritual agencies in connection with ragged beldames soaring on broomsticks, in an age when it is known that mediums of communication with the invisible world are usually unctuous personages dressed in excellent broadcloth, who soar above the curtain-poles without any broomstick, and who are not given to unprofitable intrigues. The enlightened imagination rejects the figure of a witch with her profile in dark relief against the moon and her broomstick cutting a constellation. No undiscovered natural laws, no names of "respectable" witnesses, are invoked to make us feel our presumption in questioning the diabolic intimacies of that obsolete old woman, for it is known now that the undiscovered laws, and the witnesses qualified by the payment of income tax, are all in favor of a different conception—the image of a heavy gentleman in boots and black coat-tails foreshortened against the cornice. Yet no less a person than Sir Thomas Browne once wrote that those who denied there were witches, inasmuch as they thereby denied spirits also, were "obliquely and upon consequence a sort, not of infidels, but of atheists." At present, doubtless, in certain circles, unbelievers in heavy gentlemen who float in the air by means of undiscovered laws are also taxed with atheism; illiberal as it is not to admit that mere weakness of understanding may prevent one from seeing how that phenomenon is necessarily involved in the Divine origin of things. With still more remarkable parallelism, Sir Thomas Browne goes on: "Those that, to refute their incredulity, desire to see apparitions, shall questionless never behold any, nor have the power to be so much as witches. The devil hath made them already in a heresy as capital as witchcraft, *and to appear to them were but to convert them.*" It would be difficult to see what has been changed here but the mere drapery of circumstance, if it were not for this prominent difference between our own days and the days of witchcraft, that instead of torturing, drowning, or burning the innocent, we give hospitality and large pay to—the highly distinguished medium. At least we are safely rid of certain horrors; but if the multitude—that "farraginous concurrence of all conditions, tempers, sexes, and ages"—do not roll back even to a superstition that carries cruelty in its train, it is not because they possess a cultivated reason, but because they are pressed upon and held up by what we may call an external reason—the sum of conditions resulting from the laws of material growth, from changes produced by great historical collisions shattering the structures of ages and making new highways for events and ideas, and from the activities of higher minds no longer existing merely as opinions and teaching, but as institutions and organizations with which the interests, the affections, and the habits of the multitude are inextricably interwoven. No undiscovered laws accounting for small phenomena going forward under drawing-room tables are likely to affect the tremendous facts of the increase of population, the rejection of convicts by our colonies, the exhaustion of the soil by cotton plantations, which urge even upon the foolish certain questions, certain claims, certain views concerning the scheme of the world, that can never again be silenced. If right reason is a right representation of the co-existence and sequences of things, here are co-existences and sequences that do not wait to be discovered, but press themselves upon us like bars of iron. No séances at a guinea a head for the sake of being pinched by "Mary Jane" can annihilate railways, steamships, and electric telegraphs, which are demonstrating the interdependence of all human interests, and making self-interest a duct for sympathy. These things are part of the external Reason to which internal silliness has inevitably to accommodate itself.

Three points in the history of magic and witchcraft are well brought out by Mr. Lecky. First, that the cruelties connected with it did not begin until men's minds had ceased to repose implicitly in a sacramental system which made them feel well armed against evil spirits; that is, until the eleventh century, when there came a sort of morning dream of doubt and heresy, bringing on the one side the terror of timid consciences, and on the other the terrorism of authority or zeal bent on checking the rising struggle. In that time of comparative mental repose, says Mr. Lecky,

"All those conceptions of diabolical presence; all that predisposition toward the miraculous, which acted so fearfully upon the imaginations of the fifteenth and sixteenth centuries, existed; but the implicit faith, the boundless and triumphant credulity with which the virtue of ecclesiastical rites was accepted, rendered them comparatively innocuous. If men had been a little less superstitious, the effects of their superstition would have been much more terrible. It was firmly believed that any one who deviated from the strict line of orthodoxy must soon succumb beneath the power of Satan; but as there was no spirit of rebellion or doubt, this persuasion did not produce any extraordinary terrorism."

The Church was disposed to confound heretical opinion with sorcery; false doctrine was especially the devil's work, and it was a ready conclusion that a denier or innovator had held consultation with the father of lies. It is a saying of a zealous Catholic in the sixteenth century, quoted by Maury in his excellent work, "De la Magie"—"*Crescit cum magia hæresis, cum hæresi magia.*" Even those who doubted were terrified at their doubts, for trust is more easily undermined than terror. Fear is earlier born than hope, lays a stronger grasp on man's system than any other passion, and remains master of a larger group of involuntary actions. A chief aspect of man's moral development is the slow subduing of fear by the gradual growth of intelligence, and its suppression as a motive by the presence of impulses less animally selfish; so that in relation to invisible Power, fear at last ceases to exist, save in that interfusion with higher faculties which we call awe.

Secondly, Mr. Lecky shows clearly that dogmatic Protestantism, holding the vivid belief in Satanic agency to be an essential of piety, would have felt it shame to be a whit behind Catholicism in severity against the devil's servants. Luther's sentiment was that he would not suffer a witch to live (he was not much more merciful to Jews); and, in spite of his fondness for children, believing a certain child to have been begotten by the devil, he recommended the parents to throw it into the river. The torch must be turned on the worst errors of heroic minds—not in irreverent ingratitude, but for the sake of measuring our vast and various debt to all the influences which have concurred, in the intervening ages, to make us recognize as detestable errors the honest convictions of men who, in mere individual capacity and moral force, were very much above us. Again, the Scotch Puritans, during the comparatively short period of their ascendency, surpassed all Christians before them in the elaborate ingenuity of the tortures they applied for the discovery of witchcraft and sorcery, and did their utmost to prove that if Scotch Calvinism was the true religion, the chief "note" of the true religion was cruelty. It is hardly an endurable task to read the story of their doings; thoroughly to imagine them as a past reality is already a sort of torture. One detail is enough, and it is a comparatively mild one. It was the regular profession of men called "prickers" to thrust long pins into the body of a suspected witch in order to detect the insensible spot which was the infallible sign of her guilt. On a superficial view one would be in danger of saying that the main difference between the teachers who sanctioned these things and the much-despised ancestors who offered human victims inside a huge wicker idol, was that they arrived at a more elaborate barbarity by a longer series of dependent propositions. We do not share Mr. Buckle's opinion that a Scotch minister's groans were a part of his deliberate plan for keeping the people in a state of terrified subjection; the ministers themselves held the belief they taught, and might well groan over it. What a blessing has a little false logic been to the world! Seeing that men are so slow to question their premises, they must have made each other much more miserable, if pity had not sometimes drawn tender conclusions not warranted by Major and Minor; if there had not been people with an amiable imbecility of reasoning which enabled them at once to cling to hideous beliefs, and to be conscientiously inconsistent with them in their conduct. There is nothing like acute deductive reasoning for keeping a man in the dark: it might be called the *technique* of the intellect, and the concentration of the mind upon it corresponds to that predominance of technical skill in art which ends in degradation of the artist's function, unless new inspiration and invention come to guide it.

And of this there is some good illustration furnished by that third node in the history of witchcraft, the beginning of its end, which is treated in an interesting manner by Mr. Lecky. It is worth noticing, that the most important defences of the belief in witchcraft, against the growing scepticism in the latter part of the sixteenth century and in the seventeenth, were the productions of men who in some departments were among the foremost thinkers of their time. One of them was Jean Bodin, the famous writer on government and jurisprudence, whose "Republic," Hallam thinks, had an important influence in England, and furnished "a store of arguments and examples that were not lost on the thoughtful minds of our countrymen." In some of his views he was original and bold; for example, he anticipated Montesquieu in attempting to appreciate the relations of government and climate. Hallam inclines to the opinion that he was a Jew, and attached Divine authority only to the Old Testament. But this was enough to furnish him with his chief data for the existence of witches and for their capital punishment; and in the account of his "Republic," given by Hallam, there is enough evidence that the sagacity which often enabled him to make fine use of his learning was also often entangled in it, to temper our surprise at finding a writer on political science of whom it could be said that, along with Montesquieu, he was "the most philosophical of those who had read so deeply, the most learned of those who had thought so much," in the van of the forlorn hope to maintain the reality of witchcraft. It should be said that he was equally confident of the unreality of the Copernican hypothesis, on the gound that it was contrary to the tenets of the theologians and philosophers and to common-sense, and therefore subversive of the foundations of every science. Of his work on witchcraft, Mr. Lecky says:

"The 'Démonomanie des Sorciers' is chiefly an appeal to authority, which the author deemed on this subject so unanimous and so conclusive, that it was scarcely possible for any sane man to resist it. He appealed to the popular belief in all countries, in all ages, and in all religions. He cited the opinions of an immense multitude of the greatest writers of pagan antiquity, and of the most illustrious of the Fathers. He showed how the laws of all nations recognized the existence of witchcraft; and he collected hundreds of cases which had been investigated before the tribunals of his own or of other countries. He relates with the most minute and circumstantial detail, and with the most unfaltering confidence, all the proceedings at the witches' Sabbath, the methods which the witches employed in transporting themselves through the air, their transformations, their carnal intercourse with the devil, their various means of injuring their enemies, the signs that lead to their detection, their confessions when condemned, and their demeanor at the stake."

Something must be allowed for a lawyer's affection toward a belief which had furnished so many "cases." Bodin's work had been immediately prompted by the treatise "De Prestigiis Dæmonum," written by John Wier, a German physician, a treatise which is worth notice as an example of a transitional form of opinion for which many analogies may be found in the history both of religion and science. Wier believed in demons, and in possession by demons; but his practice as a physician had convinced him that the so-called witches were patients and victims, that the devil took advantage of their diseased condition to delude them, and that there was no consent of an evil will on the part of the women. He argued that the word in Leviticus translated "witch" meant "poisoner," and besought the princes of Europe to hinder the further spilling of innocent blood. These heresies of Wier threw Bodin into such a state of amazed indignation that if he had been an ancient Jew instead of a modern economical one, he would have rent his garments. "No one had ever heard of pardon being accorded to sorcerers;" and probably the reason why Charles IX. died young was because he had pardoned the sorcerer, Trios Echelles! We must remember that this was in 1581, when the great scientific movement of the Renaissance had hardly begun—when Galileo was a youth of seventeen, and Kepler a boy of ten.

But directly afterward, on the other side, came Montaigne, whose sceptical acuteness could arrive at negatives without any apparatus of method. A certain keen narrowness of nature will secure a man from many absurd beliefs which the larger soul, vibrating to more manifold influences, would have a long struggle to part with. And so we find the charming, chatty Montaigne—in one of the brightest of his essays, "Des Boiteux," where he declares that, from his own observation of witches and sorcerers, he should have recommended them to be treated with curative hellebore—stating in his own way a pregnant doctrine, since taught more gravely. It seems to him much less of a prodigy that men should lie, or that their imaginations should deceive them, than that a human body should be carried through the air on a broomstick, or up a chimney by some unknown spirit. He thinks it a sad business to persuade oneself that the test of truth lies in the multitude of believers—"en une presse où les fols surpassent de tant les sages en nombre." Ordinarily, he has observed, when men have something stated to them as a fact, they are more ready to explain it than to inquire whether it is real: "ils passent par-dessus les propositions, mais ils examinent les conséquences; *ils laissent les choses, et courent aux causes.*" There is a sort of strong and generous ignorance which is as honorable and courageous as science—"ignorance pour laquelle concevoir il n'y a pas moins de science qu'à concevoir la science." And *à propos* of the immense traditional evidence which weighed with such men as Bodin, he says—"As for the proofs and arguments founded on experience and facts, I do not pretend to unravel these. What end of a thread is there to lay hold of? I often cut them as Alexander did his knot. *Après tout, c'est mettre ses conjectures à bien haut prix, que d'en faire cuire un homme tout vif.*"

Writing like this, when it finds eager readers, is a sign that the weather is changing; yet much later, namely, after 1665, when the Royal Society had been founded, our own Glanvil, the author of the "Scepsis Scientifica," a work that was a remarkable advance toward the true definition of the limits of inquiry, and that won him his election as fellow of the society, published an energetic vindication of the belief in witchcraft, of which Mr. Lecky gives the following sketch:

"The 'Sadducismus Triumphatus,' which is probably the ablest book ever published in defence of the superstition, opens with a striking picture of the rapid progress of the scepticism in England. Everywhere, a disbelief in witchcraft was becoming fashionable in the upper classes; but it was a disbelief that arose entirely from a strong sense of its antecedent improbability. All who were opposed to the orthodox faith united in discrediting witchcraft. They laughed at it, as palpably absurd, as involving the most grotesque and ludicrous conceptions, as so essentially incredible that it would be a waste of time to examine it. This spirit had arisen since the Restoration, although the laws were still in force, and although little or no direct reasoning had been brought to bear upon the subject. In order to combat it, Glanvil proceeded to examine the general question of the credibility of the miraculous. He saw that the reason why witchcraft was ridiculed was, because it was a phase of the miraculous and the work of the devil; that the scepticism was chiefly due to those who disbelieved in miracles and the devil; and that the instances of witchcraft or possession in the Bible were invariably placed on a level with those that were tried in the law courts of England. That the evidence of the belief was overwhelming, he firmly believed; and this, indeed, was scarcely disputed; but, until the sense of *à priori* improbability was removed, no possible accumulation of facts would cause men to believe it. To that task he accordingly addressed himself. Anticipating the idea and almost the words of modern controversialists, he urged that there was such a thing as a credulity of unbelief; and that those who believed so strange a concurrence of delusions, as was necessary on the supposition of the unreality of witchcraft, were far more credulous than those who accepted the belief. He made his very scepticism his principal weapon; and, analyzing with much acuteness the *à priori* objections, he showed that they rested upon an unwarrantable confidence in our knowledge of the laws of the spirit world; that they implied the existence of some strict analogy between the faculties of men and of spirits; and that, as such analogy most probably did not exist, no reasoning based on the supposition could dispense men from examining the evidence. He concluded with a large collection of cases, the evidence of which was, as he thought, incontestible."

We have quoted this sketch because Glanvil's argument against the *à priori* objection of absurdity is fatiguingly urged in relation to other alleged marvels which, to busy people seriously occupied with the difficulties of affairs, of science, or of art, seem as little worthy of examination as aëronautic broomsticks. And also because we here see Glanvil, in combating an incredulity that does not happen to be his own, wielding that very argument of traditional evidence which he had made the subject of vigorous attack in his "Scepsis Scientifica." But perhaps large minds have been peculiarly liable to this fluctuation concerning the sphere of tradition, because, while they have attacked its misapplications, they have been the more solicited by the vague sense that tradition is really the basis of our best life. Our sentiments may be called organized traditions; and a large part of our actions gather all their justification, all their attraction and aroma, from the memory of the life lived, of the actions done, before we were born. In the absence of any profound research into psychological functions or into the mysteries of inheritance, in the absence of any comprehensive view of man's historical development and the dependence of one age on another, a mind at all rich in sensibilities must always have had an indefinite uneasiness in an undistinguishing attack on the coercive influence of tradition. And this may be the apology for the apparent inconsistency of Glanvil's acute criticism on the one side, and his indignation at the "looser gentry," who laughed at the evidences for witchcraft on the other. We have already taken up too much space with this subject of witchcraft, else we should be tempted to dwell on Sir Thomas Browne, who far surpassed Glanvil in magnificent incongruity of opinion, and whose works are the most remarkable combination existing, of witty sarcasm against ancient nonsense and modern obsequiousness, with indications of a capacious credulity. After all, we may be sharing what seems to us the hardness of these men, who sat in their studies and argued at their ease about a belief that would be reckoned to have caused more misery and bloodshed than any other superstition, if there had been no such thing as persecution on the ground of religious opinion.

On this subject of Persecution, Mr. Lecky writes his best: with clearness of conception, with calm justice, bent on appreciating the necessary tendency of ideas, and with an appropriateness of illustration that could be supplied only by extensive and intelligent reading. Persecution, he shows, is not in any sense peculiar to the Catholic Church; it is a direct sequence of the doctrines that salvation is to be had only within the Church, and that erroneous belief is damnatory—doctrines held as fully by Protestant sects as by the Catholics; and in proportion to its power, Protestantism has been as persecuting as Catholicism. He maintains, in opposition to the favorite modern notion of persecution defeating its own object, that the Church, holding the dogma of exclusive salvation, was perfectly consequent, and really achieved its end of spreading one belief and quenching another, by calling in the aid of the civil arm. Who will say that governments, by their power over institutions and patronage, as well as over punishment, have not power also over the interests and inclinations of men, and over most of those external conditions into which subjects are born, and which make them adopt the prevalent belief as a second nature? Hence, to a sincere believer in the doctrine of exclusive salvation, governments had it in their power to save men from perdition; and wherever the clergy were at the elbow of the civil arm, no matter whether they were Catholic or Protestant, persecution was the result. "Compel them to come in" was a rule that seemed sanctioned by mercy, and the horrible sufferings it led men to inflict seemed small to minds accustomed to contemplate, as a perpetual source of motive, the eternal unmitigated miseries of a hell that was the inevitable destination of a majority among mankind.

It is a significant fact, noted by Mr. Lecky, that the only two leaders of the Reformation who advocated tolerance were Zuinglius and Socinus, both of them disbelievers in exclusive salvation. And in corroboration of other evidence that the chief triumphs of the Reformation were due to coercion, he commends to the special attention of his readers the following quotation from a work attributed without question to the famous Protestant theologian, Jurieu, who had himself been hindered, as a Protestant, from exercising his professional functions in France, and was settled as pastor at Rotterdam. It should be remembered that Jurieu's labors fell in the latter part of the seventeenth century and in the beginning of the eighteenth, and that he was the contemporary of Bayle, with whom he was in bitter controversial hostility. He wrote, then, at a time when there was warm debate on the question of Toleration; and it was his great object to vindicate himself and his French fellow-Protestants from all laxity on this point.

"Peut on nier que le panganisme est tombé dans le monde par l'autorité des empereurs Romains? On peut assurer sans temerité que le paganisme seroit encore debout, et que les trois quarts de l'Europe seroient encore payens si Constantin et ses successeurs n'avaient employé leur autorité pour l'abolir. Mais, je vous prie, de quelles voies Dieu s'est il servi dans ces derniers siècles pour rétablir la veritable religion dans l'Occident? *Les rois de Suède, ceux de Danemarck, ceux d'Angleterre, les magistrats souverains de Suisse, des Païs Bas, des villes livres d'Allemagne, les princes électeurs, et autres princes souverains de l'empire, n'ont ils pas emploié leur autorité pour abbattre le Papisme?*"

Indeed, wherever the tremendous alternative of everlasting torments is believed in—believed in so that it becomes a motive determining the life—not only persecution, but every other form of severity and gloom are the legitimate consequences. There is much ready declamation in these days against the spirit of asceticism and against zeal for doctrinal conversion; but surely the macerated form of a Saint Francis, the fierce denunciations of a Saint Dominic, the groans and prayerful wrestlings of the Puritan who seasoned his bread with tears and made all pleasurable sensation sin, are more in keeping with the contemplation of unending anguish as the destiny of a vast multitude whose nature we share, than the rubicund cheerfulness of some modern divines, who profess to unite a smiling liberalism with a well-bred and tacit but unshaken confidence in the reality of the bottomless pit. But, in fact, as Mr. Lecky maintains, that awful image, with its group of associated dogmas concerning the inherited curse, and the damnation of unbaptized infants, of heathens, and of heretics, has passed away from what he is fond of calling "the realizations" of Christendom. These things are no longer the objects of practical belief. They may be mourned for in encyclical letters; bishops may regret them; doctors of divinity may sign testimonials to the excellent character of these decayed beliefs; but for the mass of Christians they are no more influential than unrepealed but forgotten statutes. And with these dogmas has melted away the strong basis for the defence of persecution. No man now writes eager vindications of himself and his colleagues from the suspicion of adhering to the principle of toleration. And this momentous change, it is Mr. Lecky's object to show, is due to that concurrence of conditions which he has chosen to call "the advance of the Spirit of Rationalism."

In other parts of his work, where he attempts to trace the action of the same conditions on the acceptance of miracles and on other chief phases of our historical development, Mr. Lecky has laid himself open to considerable criticism. The chapters on the "Miracles of the Church," the æsthetic, scientific, and moral development of Rationalism, the Secularization of Politics, and the Industrial History of Rationalism, embrace a wide range of diligently gathered facts; but they are nowhere illuminated by a sufficiently clear conception and statement of the agencies at work, or the mode of their action, in the gradual modification of opinion and of life. The writer frequently impresses us as being in a state of hesitation concerning his own standing-point, which may form a desirable stage in private meditation but not in published exposition. Certain epochs in theoretic conception, certain considerations, which should be fundamental to his survey, are introduced quite incidentally in a sentence or two, or in a note which seems to be an afterthought. Great writers and their ideas are touched upon too slightly and with too little discrimination, and important theories are sometimes characterized with a rashness which conscientious revision will correct. There is a fatiguing use of vague or shifting phrases, such as "modern civilization," "spirit of the age," "tone of thought," intellectual type of the age," bias of the imagination," "habits of religious thought," unbalanced by any precise definition; and the spirit of rationalism is sometimes treated of as if it lay outside the specific mental activities of which it is a generalized expression. Mr. Curdle's famous definition of the dramatic unities as "a sort of a general oneness," is not totally false; but such luminousness as it has could only be perceived by those who already knew what the unities were. Mr. Lecky has the advantage of being strongly impressed with the great part played by the emotions in the formation of opinion, and with the high complexity of the causes at work in social evolution; but he frequently writes as if he had never yet distinguished between the complexity of the conditions that produce prevalent states of mind and the inability of particular minds to give distinct reasons for the preferences or persuasions produced by those states. In brief, he does not discriminate, or does not help his reader to discriminate, between objective complexity and subjective confusion. But the most muddle-headed gentleman who represents the spirit of the age by observing, as he settles his collar, that the development theory is quite "the thing" is a result of definite processes, if we could only trace them. "Mental attitudes," and "predispositions," however vague in consciousness, have not vague causes, any more than the "blind motions of the spring" in plants and animals.

The word "Rationalism" has the misfortune, shared by most words in this gray world, of being somewhat equivocal. This evil may be nearly overcome by careful preliminary definition; but Mr. Lecky does not supply this, and the original specific application of the word to a particular phase of biblical interpretation seems to have clung about his use of it with a misleading effect. Through some parts of his book he appears to regard the grand characteristic of modern thought and civilization, compared with ancient, as a radiation in the first instance from a change in religious conceptions. The supremely important fact, that the gradual reduction of all phenomena within the sphere of established law, which carries as a consequence the rejection of the miraculous, has its determining current in the development of physical science, seems to have engaged comparatively little of his attention; at least, he gives it no prominence. The great conception of universal regular sequence, without partiality and without caprice—the conception which is the most potent force at work in the modification of our faith, and of the practical form given to our sentiments—could only grow out of that patient watching of external fact, and that silencing of preconceived notions, which are urged upon the mind by the problems of physical science.

There is not room here to explain and justify the impressions of dissatisfaction which have been briefly indicated, but a serious writer like Mr. Lecky will not find such suggestions altogether useless. The objections, even the misunderstandings, of a reader who is not careless or ill-disposed, may serve to stimulate an author's vigilance over his thoughts as well as his style. It would be gratifying to see some future proof that Mr. Lecky has acquired juster views than are implied in the assertion that philosophers of the sensational school "can never rise to the conception of the disinterested;" and that he has freed himself from all temptation to that mingled laxity of statement and ill-pitched elevation of tone which are painfully present in the closing pages of his second volume.

IX.

THE GRAMMAR OF ORNAMENT.*

The inventor of movable types, says the venerable Teufelsdröckh, was disbanding hired armies, cashiering most kings and senates, and creating a whole new democratic world. Has any one yet said what great things are being done by the men who are trying to banish ugliness from our streets and our homes, and to make both the outside and inside of our dwellings worthy of a world where there are forests and flower-tressed meadows, and the plumage of birds; where the insects carry lessons of color on their wings, and even the surface of a stagnant pool will show us the wonders of iridescence and the most delicate forms of leafage? They, too, are modifying opinions, for they are modifying men's moods and habits, which are the mothers of opinions, having quite as much to do with their formation as the responsible father—Reason. Think of certain hideous manufacturing towns where the piety is chiefly a belief in copious perdition, and the pleasure is chiefly gin. The dingy surface of wall pierced by the ugliest windows, the staring shop-fronts, paper-hangings, carpets, brass and gilt mouldings, and advertising placards, have an effect akin to that of malaria; it is easy to understand that with such surroundings there is more belief in cruelty than in beneficence, and that the best earthly bliss attainable is the dulling of the external senses. For it is a fatal mistake to suppose that ugliness which is taken for beauty will answer all the purposes of beauty; the subtle relation between all kinds of truth and fitness in our life forbids that bad taste should ever be harmless to our moral sensibility or our intellectual discernment; and—more than that—as it is probable that fine musical harmonies have a sanative influence over our bodily organization, it is also probable

* "The Grammar of Ornament." By Owen Jones, Architect. Illustrated by Examples from various Styles of Ornament. One hundred and twelve plates. Day & Son, London.

that just coloring and lovely combinations of lines may be necessary to the complete well-being of our systems apart from any conscious delight in them. A savage may indulge in discordant chuckles and shrieks and gutturals, and think that they please the gods, but it does not follow that his frame would not be favorably wrought upon by the vibrations of a grand church organ. One sees a person capable of choosing the worst style of wall-paper become suddenly afflicted by its ugliness under an attack of illness. And if an evil state of blood and lymph usually goes along with an evil state of mind, who shall say that the ugliness of our streets, the falsity of our ornamentation, the vulgarity of our upholstery, have not something to do with those bad tempers which breed false conclusions?

On several grounds it is possible to make a more speedy and extensive application of artistic reform to our interior decoration than to our external architecture. One of these grounds is that most of our ugly buildings must stand; we cannot afford to pull them down. But every year we are decorating interiors afresh, and people of modest means may benefit by the introduction of beautiful designs into stucco ornaments, paper-hangings, draperies, and carpets. Fine taste in the decoration of interiors is a benefit that spreads from the palace to the clerk's house with one parlor.

All honor, then, to the architect who has zealously vindicated the claim of internal ornamentation to be a part of the architect's function, and has labored to rescue that form of art which is most closely connected with the sanctities and pleasures of our hearths from the hands of uncultured tradesmen. All the nation ought at present to know that this effort is peculiarly associated with the name of Mr. Owen Jones; and those who are most disposed to dispute with the architect about his coloring must at least recognize the high artistic principle which has directed his attention to colored ornamentation as a proper branch of architecture. One monument of his effort in this way is his "Grammar of Ornament," of which a new and cheaper edition has just been issued. The one point in which it differs from the original and more expensive edition, viz., the reduction in the size of the pages (the amount of matter and number of plates are unaltered), is really an advantage; it is now a very manageable folio, and when the reader is in a lounging mood may be held easily on the knees. It is a magnificent book; and those who know no more of it than the title should be told that they will find in it a pictorial history of ornamental design, from its rudimentary condition as seen in the productions of savage tribes, through all the other great types of art—the Egyptian, Assyrian, ancient Persian, Greek, Roman, Byzantine, Arabian, Moresque, Mohammedan-Persian, Indian, Celtic, Mediæval, Renaissance, Elizabethan, and Italian. The letter-press consists, first, of an introductory statement of fundamental principles of ornamentation—principles, says the author, which will be found to have been obeyed more or less instinctively by all nations in proportion as their art has been a genuine product of the national genius; and, secondly, of brief historical essays, some of them contributed by other eminent artists, presenting a commentary on each characteristic series of illustrations, with the useful appendage of bibliographical lists.

The title "Grammar of Ornament" is so far appropriate that it indicates what Mr. Owen Jones is most anxious to be understood concerning the object of his work, namely, that it is intended to illustrate historically the application of principles, and not to present a collection of models for mere copyists. The plates correspond to examples in syntax, not to be repeated parrot-like, but to be studied as embodiments of syntactical principles. There is a logic of form which cannot be departed from in ornamental design without a corresponding remoteness from perfection; unmeaning, irrelevant lines are as bad as irrelevant words or clauses, that tend no whither. And as a suggestion toward the origination of fresh ornamental design, the work concludes with some beautiful drawings of leaves and flowers from nature, that the student, tracing in them the simple laws of form which underlie an immense variety in beauty, may the better discern the method by which the same laws were applied in the finest decorative work of the past, and may have all the clearer prospect of the unexhausted possibilities of freshness which lie before him, if, refraining from mere imitation, he will seek only such likeness to existing forms of ornamental art as arises from following like principles of combination.

X.

ADDRESS TO WORKING MEN, BY FELIX HOLT.

Fellow-Workmen: I am not going to take up your time by complimenting you. It has been the fashion to compliment kings and other authorities when they have come into power, and to tell them that, under their wise and beneficent rule, happiness would certainly overflow the land. But the end has not always corresponded to that beginning. If it were true that we who work for wages had more of the wisdom and virtue necessary to the right use of power than has been shown by the aristocratic and mercantile classes, we should not glory much in that fact, or consider that it carried with it any near approach to infallibility.

In my opinion, there has been too much complimenting of that sort; and whenever a speaker, whether he is one of ourselves or not, wastes our time in boasting or flattery, I say, let us hiss him. If we have the beginning of wisdom, which is, to know a little truth about ourselves, we know that as a body we are neither very wise nor very virtuous. And to prove this, I will not point specially to our own habits and doings, but to the general state of the country. Any nation that had within it a majority of men—and we are the majority—possessed of much wisdom and virtue, would not tolerate the bad practices, the commercial lying and swindling, the poisonous adulteration of goods, the retail cheating, and the political bribery which are carried on boldly in the midst of us. A majority has the power of creating a public opinion. We could groan and hiss before we had the franchise: if we had groaned and hissed in the right place, if we had discerned better between good and evil, if the multitude of us artisans, and factory hands, and miners, and laborers of all sorts, had been skilful, faithful, well-judging, industrious, sober—and I don't see how there can be wisdom and virtue anywhere without these qualities—we should have made an audience that would have shamed the other classes out of their share in the national vices. We should have had better members of Parliament, better religious teachers, honester tradesmen, fewer foolish demagogues, less impudence in infamous and brutal men; and we should not have had among us the abomination of men calling themselves religious while living in splendor on ill-gotten gains. I say, it is not possible for any society in which there is a very large body of wise and virtuous men to be as vicious as our society is—to have as low a standard of right and wrong, to have so much belief in falsehood, or to have so degrading, barbarous a notion of what pleasure is, or of what justly raises a man above his fellows. Therefore, let us have done with this nonsense about our being much better than the rest of our countrymen, or the pretence that that was a reason why we ought to have such an extension of the franchise as has been given to us. The reason for our having the franchise, as I want presently to show, lies somewhere else than in our personal good qualities, and does not in the least lie in any high betting chance that a delegate is a better man than a duke, or that a Sheffield grinder is a better man than any one of the firm he works for.

However, we have got our franchise now. We have been sarcastically called in the House of Commons the future masters of the country; and if that sarcasm contains any truth, it seems to me that the first thing we had better think of is, our heavy responsibility; that is to say, the terrible risk we run of working mischief and missing good, as others have done before us. Suppose certain men, discontented with the irrigation of a country which depended for all its prosperity on the right direction being given to the waters of a great river, had got the management of the irrigation before they were quite sure how exactly it could be altered for the better, or whether they could command the necessary agency for such an alteration. Those men would have a difficult and dangerous business on their hands; and the more sense, feeling, and knowledge they had, the more they would be likely to tremble rather than to triumph. Our situation is not altogether unlike theirs. For general prosperity and well-being is a vast crop, that like the corn in Egypt can be come at, not at all by hurried snatching, but only by a well-judged patient process; and whether our political power will be any good to us now we have got it, must depend entirely on the means and materials—the knowledge, ability, and honesty we have at command. These three things are the only conditions on which we can get any lasting benefit, as every clever workman among us knows: he knows that for an article to be worth much there must be a good invention or plan to go upon, there must be a well-prepared material, and there must be skilful and honest work in carrying out the plan. And by this test we may try those who want to be our leaders. Have they anything to offer us besides indignant talk? When they tell us we ought to have this, that, or the other thing, can they explain to us any reasonable, fair, safe way of getting it? Can they argue in favor of a particular change by showing us pretty closely how the change is likely to work? I don't want to decry a just indignation; on the contrary, I should like it to be more thorough and general. A wise man, more than two thousand years ago, when he was asked what would most tend to lessen injustice in the world, said, "If every bystander felt as indignant at a wrong as if he himself were the sufferer." Let us cherish such indignation. But the long-growing evils of a great nation are a tangled business, asking for a good deal more than indignation in order to be got rid of. Indignation is a fine war-horse, but the war-horse must be ridden by a man: it must be ridden by rationality, skill, courage, armed with the right weapons, and taking definite aim.

We have reason to be discontented with many things, and, looking back either through the history of England to much earlier generations or to the legislation and administrations of later times, we are justified in saying that many of the evils under which our country now suffers are the consequences of folly, ignorance, neglect, or self-seeking in those who, at different times have wielded the powers of rank, office, and money. But the more bitterly we feel this, the more loudly we utter it, the stronger is the obligation we lay on ourselves to beware, lest we also, by a too hasty wresting of measures which seem to promise an immediate partial relief, make a worse time of it for our own generation, and leave a bad inheritance to our children. The deepest curse of wrong-doing, whether of the foolish or wicked sort, is that its effects are difficult to be undone. I suppose there is hardly anything more to be shuddered at than that part of the history of disease which shows how, when a man injures his constitution by a life of vicious excess, his children and grandchildren inherit diseased bodies and minds, and how the effects of that unhappy inheritance continue to spread beyond our calculation. This is only one example of the law by which human lives are linked together; another example of what we complain of when we point to our pauperism, to the brutal ignorance of multitudes among our fellow countrymen, to the weight of taxation laid on us by blamable wars, to the wasteful channels made for the public money, to the expense and trouble of getting justice, and call these the effects of bad rule. This is the law that we all bear the yoke of, the law of no man's making, and which no man can undo. Everybody now sees an example of it in the case of Ireland. We who are living now are sufferers by the wrong-doing of those who lived before us; we are the sufferers by each other's wrong-doing; and the children who come after us are and will be sufferers from the same causes. Will any man say he doesn't care for that law—it is nothing to him—what he wants is to better himself? With what face then will he complain of any injury? If he says that in politics or in any sort of social action he will not care to know what are likely to be the consequences to others besides himself, he is defending the very worst doings that have brought about his discontent. He might as well say that there is no better rule needful for men than that each should tug and drive for what will please him, without caring how that tugging will act on the fine wide-spread network of society in which he is fast meshed. If any man taught that as a doctrine, we should know him for a fool. But there are men who act upon it; every scoundrel, for example, whether he is a rich religious scoundrel who lies and cheats on a large scale, and will perhaps come and ask you to send him to Parliament, or a poor pocket-picking scoundrel, who will steal your loose pence while you are listening round the platform. None of us are so ignorant as not to know that a society, a nation is held together by just the opposite doctrine and action—by the dependence of men on each other and the sense they have of a common interest in preventing injury. And we working men are, I think, of all classes the last that can afford to forget this; for if we did we should be much like sailors cutting away the timbers of our own ship to warm our grog with. For what else is the meaning of our trades-unions? What else is the meaning of every flag we carry, every procession we make, every crowd we collect for the sake of making some protest on behalf of our body as receivers of wages, if not this: that it is our interest to stand by each other, and that this being the common interest, no one of us will try to make a good bargain for himself without considering what will be good for his fellows? And every member of a union believes that the wider he can spread his union, the stronger and surer will be the effect of it. So I think I shall be borne out in saying that a working man who can put two and two together, or take three from four and see what will be the remainder, can understand that a society, to be well off, must be made up chiefly of men who consider the general good as well as their own.

Well, but taking the world as it is—and this is one way we must take it when we want to find out how it can be improved —no society is made up of a single class: society stands before us like that wonderful piece of life, the human body, with all its various parts depending on one another, and with a terrible liability to get wrong because of that delicate dependence. We all know how many diseases the human body is apt to suffer from, and how difficult it is even for the doctors to find out exactly where the seat or beginning of the disorder is. That is because the body is made up of so many various parts, all related to each other, or likely all to feel the effect if any one of them goes wrong. It is somewhat the same with our old nations or societies. No society ever stood long in the world without getting to be composed of different classes. Now, it is all pretence to say that there is no such thing as class interest. It is clear that if any particular number of men get a particular benefit from any existing institution, they are likely to band together, in order to keep up that benefit and increase it, until it is perceived to be unfair and injurious to another large number, who get knowledge and strength enough to set up a resistance. And this, again, has been part of the history of every great society since history began. But the simple reason for this being, that any large body of men is likely to have more of stupidity, narrowness, and greed than of farsightedness and generosity, it is plain that the number who resist unfairness and injury are in danger of becoming injurious in their turn. And in this way a justifiable resistance has become a damaging convulsion, making everything worse instead of better. This has been seen so often that we ought to profit a little by the experience. So long as there is selfishness in men; so long as they have not found out for themselves institutions which express and carry into practice the truth, that the highest interest of mankind must at last be a common and not a divided interest; so long as the gradual operation of steady causes has not made that truth a part of every man's knowledge and feeling, just as we now not only know that it is good for our health to be cleanly, but feel that cleanliness is only another word for comfort, which is the under-side or lining of all pleasure; so long, I say as men wink at their own knowingness, or hold their heads high because they have got an advantage over their fellows; so long class interest will be in danger of making itself felt injuriously.

No set of men will get any sort of power without being in danger of wanting more than their right share. But, on the other hand, it is just as certain that no set of men will get angry at having less than their right share, and set up a claim on that ground, without falling into just the same danger of exacting too much, and exacting it in wrong ways. It's human nature we have got to work with all round, and nothing else. That seems like saying something very commonplace—nay, obvious; as if one should say that where there are hands there are mouths. Yet, to hear a good deal of the speechifying and to see a good deal of the action that go forward, one might suppose it was forgotten.

But I come back to this: that, in our old society, there are old institutions, and among them the various distinctions and inherited advantages of classes, which have shaped themselves along with all the wonderful slow-growing system of things made up of our laws, our commerce, and our stores of all sorts, whether in material objects, such as buildings and machinery, or in knowledge, such as scientific thought and professional skill. Just as in that case I spoke of before, the irrigation of a country, which must absolutely have its water distributed or it will bear no crop; there are the old channels, the old banks, and the old pumps, which must be used as they are until new and better have been prepared, or the structure of the old has been gradually altered. But it would be fool's work to batter down a pump only because a better might be made, when you had no machinery ready for a new one: it would be wicked work, if villages lost their crops by it. Now the only safe way by which society can be steadily improved and our worst evils reduced, is not by any attempt to do away directly with the actually existing class distinctions and advantages, as if everybody could have the same sort of work, or lead the same sort of life (which none of my hearers are stupid enough to suppose), but by the turning of class interests into class functions or duties. What I mean is, that each class should be urged by the surrounding conditions to perform its particular work under the strong pressure of responsibility to the nation at large; that our public affairs should be got into a state in which there should be no impunity for foolish or faithless conduct. In this way the public judgment would sift out incapability and dishonesty from posts of high charge, and even personal ambition would necessarily become of a worthier sort, since the desires of the most selfish men must be a good deal shaped by the opinions of those around them; and for one person to put on a cap and bells, or to go about dishonest or paltry ways of getting rich that he may spend a vast sum of money in having more finery than his neighbors, he must be pretty sure of a crowd who will applaud him. Now, changes can only be good in proportion as they help to bring about this sort of result: in proportion as they put knowledge in the place of ignorance, and fellow-feeling in the place of selfishness. In the course of that substitution class distinctions must inevitably change their character, and represent the varying duties of men, not their varying interests. But this end will not come by impatience. "Day will not break the sooner because we get up before the twilight." Still less will it come by mere undoing, or change merely as change. And moreover, if we believed that it would be unconditionally hastened by our getting the franchise, we should be what I call superstitious men, believing in magic, or the production of a result by hocus-pocus. Our getting the franchise will greatly hasten that good end in proportion only as every one of us has the knowledge, the foresight, the conscience, that will make him well-judging and scrupulous in the use of it. The nature of things in this world has been determined for us beforehand, and in such a way that no ship can be expected to sail well on a difficult voyage, and reach the right port, unless it is well manned: the nature of the winds and the waves, of the timbers, the sails, and the cordage, will not accommodate itself to drunken, mutinous sailors.

You will not suspect me of wanting to preach any cant to you, or of joining in the pretence that everything is in a fine way, and need not be made better. What I am striving to keep in our minds is the care, the precaution, with which we should go about making things better, so that the public order may not be destroyed, so that no fatal shock may be given to this society of ours, this living body in which our lives are bound up. After the Reform Bill of 1832 I was in an election riot, which showed me clearly, on a small scale, what public disorder must always be; and I have never forgotten that the riot was brought about chiefly by the agency of dishonest men who professed to be on the people's side. Now, the danger hanging over change is great, just in proportion as it tends to produce such disorder by giving any large number of ignorant men, whose notions of what is good are of a low and brutal sort, the belief that they have got power into their hands, and may do pretty much as they like. If any one can look round us and say that he sees no signs of any such danger now, and that our national condition is running along like a clear broadening stream, safe not to get choked with mud, I call him a cheerful man : perhaps he does his own gardening, and seldom takes exercise far away from home. To us who have no gardens, and often walk abroad, it is plain that we can never get into a bit of a crowd but we must rub clothes with a set of roughs, who have the worst vices of the worst rich—who are gamblers, sots, libertines, knaves, or else mere sensual simpletons and victims. They are the ugly crop that has sprung up while the stewards have been sleeping; they are the multiplying brood begotten by parents who have been left without all teaching save that of a too craving body, without all well-being save the fading delusions of drugged beer and gin. They are the hideous margin of society, at one edge drawing toward it the undesigning ignorant poor, at the other darkening imperceptibly into the lowest criminal class. Here is one of the evils which cannot be got rid of quickly, and against which any of us who have got sense, decency, and instruction have need to watch. That these degraded fellow-men could really get the mastery in a persistent disobedience to the laws and in a struggle to subvert order, I do not believe; but wretched calamities must come from the very beginning of such a struggle, and the continuance of it would be a civil war, in which the inspiration on both sides might soon cease to be even a false notion of good, and might become the direct savage impulse of ferocity. We have all to see to it that we do not help to rouse what I may call the savage beast in the breasts of our generation—that we do not help to poison the nation's blood, and make richer provision for bestiality to come. We know well enough that oppressors have sinned in this way—that oppression has notoriously made men mad; and we are determined to resist oppression. But let us, if possible, show that we can keep sane in our resistance, and shape our means more and more reasonably toward the least harmful, and therefore the speediest, attainment of our end. Let us, I say, show that our spirits are too strong to be driven mad, but can keep that sober determination which alone gives mastery over the adaptation of means. And a first guarantee of this sanity will be to act as if we understood that the fundamental duty of a government is to preserve order, to enforce obedience of the laws. It has been held hitherto that a man can be depended on as a guardian of order only when he has much money and comfort to lose. But a better state of things would be, that men who had little money and not much comfort should still be guardians of order, because they had sense to see that disorder would do no good, and had a heart of justice, pity, and fortitude, to keep them from making more misery only because they felt some misery themselves. There are thousands of artisans who have already shown this fine spirit, and have endured much with patient heroism. If such a spirit spread, and penetrated us all, we should soon become the masters of the country in the best sense and to the best ends. For, the public order being preserved, there can be no government in future that will not be determined by our insistance on our fair and practicable demands. It is only by disorder that our demands will be choked, that we shall find ourselves lost among a brutal rabble, with all the intelligence of the country opposed to us, and see government in the shape of guns that will sweep us down in the ignoble martyrdom of fools.

It has been a too common notion that to insist much on the preservation of order is the part of a selfish aristocracy and a selfish commercial class, because among these, in the nature of things, have been found the opponents of change. I am a Radical; and, what is more, I am not a Radical with a title, or a French cook, or even an entrance into fine society. I expect great changes, and I desire them. But I don't expect them to come in a hurry, by mere inconsiderate sweeping. A Hercules with a big besom is a fine thing for a filthy stable, but not for weeding a seed-bed, where his besom would soon make a barren floor.

That is old-fashioned talk, some one may say. We know all that.

Yes, when things are put in an extreme way, most people think they know them; but, after all, they are comparatively few who see the small degrees by which those extremes are arrived at, or have the resolution and self-control to resist the little impulses by which they creep on surely toward a fatal end. Does anybody set out meaning to ruin himself, or to drink himself to death, or to waste his life so that he becomes a despicable old man, a superannuated nuisance, like a fly in winter. Yet there are plenty, of whose lot this is the pitiable story. Well now, supposing us all to have the best intentions, we working men, as a body, run some risk of bringing evil on the nation in that unconscious manner—half hurrying, half pushed in a jostling march toward an end we are not thinking of. For just as there are many things which we know better and feel much more strongly than the richer, softer-handed classes can know or feel them; so there are many things—many precious benefits—which we, by the very fact of our privations, our lack of leisure and instruction, are not so likely to be aware of and take into our account. Those precious benefits form a chief part of what I may call the common estate of society: a wealth over and above buildings, machinery, produce, shipping, and so on, though closely connected with these; a wealth of a more delicate kind, that we may more unconsciously bring into danger, doing harm and not knowing that we do it. I mean that treasure of knowledge, science, poetry, refinement of thought, feeling, and manners, great memories and the interpretation of great records, which is carried on from the minds of one generation to the minds of another. This is something distinct from the indulgences of luxury and the pursuit of vain finery; and one of the hardships in the lot of working men is that they have been for the most part shut out from sharing in this treasure. It can make a man's life very great, very full of delight, though he has no smart furniture and no horses: it also yields a great deal of discovery that corrects error, and of invention that lessens bodily pain, and must at least make life easier for all.

Now the security of this treasure demands, not only the preservation of order, but a certain patience on our part with many institutions and facts of various kinds, especially touching the accumulation of wealth, which from the light we stand in, we are more likely to discern the evil than the good of. It is constantly the task of practical wisdom not to say, "This is good, and I will have it," but to say, "This is the less of two unavoidable evils, and I will bear it." And this treasure of knowledge, which consists in the fine activity, the exalted vision of many minds, is bound up at present with conditions which have much evil in them. Just as in the case of material wealth and its distribution we are obliged to take the selfishness and weaknesses of human nature into account, and however we insist that men might act better, are forced, unless we are fanatical simpletons, to consider how they are likely to act; so in this matter of the wealth that is carried in men's minds, we have to reflect that the too absolute predominance of a class whose wants have been of a common sort, who are chiefly struggling to get better and more food, clothing, shelter, and bodily recreation, may lead to hasty measures for the sake of having things more fairly shared, which, even if they did not fail of their object, would at last debase the life of the nation. Do anything which will throw the classes who hold the treasures of knowledge—nay, I may say, the treasure of refined needs—into the background, cause them to withdraw from public affairs, stop too suddenly any of the sources by which their leisure and ease are furnished, rob them of the chances by which they may be influential and pre-eminent, and you do something as short-sighted as the acts of France and Spain when in jealousy and wrath, not altogether unprovoked, they drove from among them races and classes that held the traditions of handicraft and agriculture. You injure your own inheritance and the inheritance of your children. You may truly say that this which I call the common estate of society has been anything but common to you; but the same may be said, by many of us, of the sunlight and the air, of the sky and the fields, of parks and holiday games. Nevertheless that these blessings exist makes life worthier to us, and urges us the more to energetic, likely means of getting our share in them; and I say, let us watch carefully, lest we do anything to lessen this treasure which is held in the minds of men, while we exert ourselves, first of all, and to the very utmost, that we and our children may share in all its benefits. Yes; exert ourselves to the utmost, to break the yoke of ignorance. If we demand more leisure, more ease in our lives, let us show that we don't deserve the reproach of wanting to shirk that industry which, in some form or other, every man, whether rich or poor, should feel himself as much bound to as he is bound to decency. Let us show that we want to have some time and strength left to us, that we may use it, not for brutal indulgence, but for the rational exercise of the faculties which make us men. Without this no political measures can benefit us. No political institution will alter the nature of Ignorance, or hinder it from producing vice and misery. Let Ignorance start how it will, it must run the same round of low appetites, poverty, slavery, and superstition. Some of us know this well—nay, I will say, feel it; for knowledge of this kind cuts deep; and to us it is one of the most painful facts belonging to our condition that there are numbers of our fellow-workmen who are so far from feeling in the same way, that they never use the imperfect opportunities already offered them for giving their children some schooling, but turn their little ones of tender age into bread-winners, often at cruel tasks, exposed to the horrible infection of childish vice. Of course, the causes of these hideous things go a long way back. Parents' misery has made parents' wickedness. But we, who are still blessed with the hearts of fathers and the consciences of men—we who have some knowledge of the curse entailed on broods of creatures in human shape, whose enfeebled bodies and dull perverted minds are mere centres of uneasiness in whom even appetite is feeble and joy impossible—I say we are bound to use all the means at our command to help in putting a stop to this horror. Here, it seems to me, is a way in which we may use extended co-operation among us to the most momentous of all purposes, and make conditions of enrolment that would strengthen all educational measures. It is true enough that there is a low sense of parental duties in the nation at large, and that numbers who have no excuse in bodily hardship seem to think it a light thing to beget children, to bring human beings with all their tremendous possibilities into this difficult world, and then take little heed how they are disciplined and furnished for the perilous journey they are sent on without any asking of their own. This is a sin shared in more or less by all classes; but there are sins which, like taxation, fall the heaviest on the poorest, and none have such galling reasons as we working men to try and rouse to the utmost the feeling of responsibility in fathers and mothers. We have been urged into co-operation by the pressure of common demands. In war men need each other more; and where a given point has to be defended, fighters inevitably find themselves shoulder to shoulder. So fellowship grows, so grow the rules of fellowship, which gradually shape themselves to thoroughness as the idea of a common good becomes more complete. We feel a right to say, If you will be one of us, you must make such and such a contribution—you must renounce such and such a separate advantage—you must set your face against such and such an infringement. If we have any false ideas about our common good, our rules will be wrong, and we shall be co-operating to damage each other. But, now, here is a part of our good, without which everything else we strive for will be worthless—I mean the rescue of our children. Let us demand from the members of our unions that they fulfil their duty as parents in this definite matter, which rules can reach. Let us demand that they send their children to school, so as not to go on recklessly, breeding a moral pestilence among us, just as strictly as we demand that they pay their contributions to a common fund, understood to be for a common benefit. While we watch our public men, let us watch one another as to this duty, which is also public, and more momentous even than obedience to sanitary regulations. While we resolutely declare against the wickedness in high places, let us set ourselves also against the wickedness in low places, not quarrelling which came first, or which is the worse of the two—not trying to settle the miserable precedence of plague or famine, but insisting unflinchingly on remedies once ascertained, and summoning those who hold the treasure of knowledge to remember that they hold it in trust, and that with them lies the task of searching for new remedies, and finding the right methods of applying them.

To find right remedies and right methods. Here is the great function of knowledge: here the life of one man may make a fresh era straight away, in which a sort of suffering that has existed shall exist no more. For the thousands of years down to the middle of the sixteenth century that human limbs had been hacked and amputated, nobody knew how to stop the bleeding except by searing the ends of the vessels with red-hot iron. But then came a man named Ambrose Paré, and said, "Tie up the arteries!" That was a fine word to utter. It contained the statement of a method—a plan by which a particular evil was forever assuaged. Let us try to discern the men whose words carry that sort of kernel, and choose such men to be our guides and representatives—not choose platform swaggerers, who bring us nothing but the ocean to make our broth with.

To get the chief power into the hands of the wisest, which means to get our life regulated according to the truest principles mankind is in possession of, is a problem as old as the very notion of wisdom. The solution comes slowly, because men collectively can only be made to embrace principles, and to act on them, by the slow stupendous teaching of the world's events. Men will go on planting potatoes, and nothing else but potatoes, till a potato disease comes and forces them to find out the advantage of a varied crop. Selfishness, stupidity, sloth, persist in trying to adapt the world to their desires, till a time comes when the world manifests itself as too decidedly inconvenient to them. Wisdom stands outside of man and urges itself upon him, like the marks of the changing seasons, before it finds a home within him, directs his actions, and from the precious effects of obedience begets a corresponding love.

But while still outside of us, wisdom often looks terrible, and wears strange forms, wrapped in the changing conditions of a struggling world. It wears now the form of wants and just demands in a great multitude of British men: wants and demands urged into existence by the forces of a maturing world. And it is in virtue of this—in virtue of this presence of wisdom on our side as a mighty fact, physical and moral, which must enter into and shape the thoughts and actions of mankind—that we working men have obtained the suffrage. Not because we are an excellent multitude, but because we are a needy multitude.

But now, for our own part, we have seriously to consider this outside wisdom which lies in the supreme unalterable nature of things, and watch to give it a home within us and obey it. If the claims of the unendowed multitude of working men hold within them principles which must shape the future, it is not less true that the endowed classes, in their inheritance from the past, hold the precious material without which no worthy, noble future can be moulded. Many of the highest uses of life are in their keeping; and if privilege has often been abused, it has also been the nurse of excellence. Here again we have to submit ourselves to the great law of inheritance. If we quarrel with the way in which the labors and earnings of the past have been preserved and handed down, we are just as bigoted, just as narrow, just as wanting in that religion which keeps an open ear and an obedient mind to the teachings of fact, as we accuse those of being, who quarrel with the new truths and new needs which are disclosed in the present. The deeper insight we get into the causes of human trouble, and the ways by which men are made better and happier, the less we shall be inclined to the unprofitable spirit and practice of reproaching classes as such in a wholesale fashion. Not all the evils of our condition are such as we can justly blame others for; and, I repeat, many of them are such as no changes of institutions can quickly remedy. To discern between the evils that energy can remove and the evils that patience must bear, makes the difference between manliness and childishness, between good sense and folly. And more than that, without such discernment, seeing that we have grave duties toward our own body and the country at large, we can hardly escape acts of fatal rashness and injustice.

I am addressing a mixed assembly of workmen, and some of you may be as well or better fitted than I am to take up this office. But they will not think it amiss in me that I have tried to bring together the considerations most likely to be of service to us in preparing ourselves for the use of our new opportunities. I have avoided touching on special questions. The best help toward judging well on these is to approach them in the right temper without vain expectation, and with a resolution which is mixed with temperance.

Printed in the United States
137065LV00003B/82/A